EVANGELICAL
ETHICS

EVANGELICAL ETHICS

ISSUES FACING THE CHURCH TODAY

SECOND EDITION

JOHN JEFFERSON DAVIS

PUBLISHING

P.O. BOX 817 • PHILLIPSBURG • NEW JERSEY 08865

Printed in the United States of America

Library of Congress Cataloging-in-Publication Data

Davis, John Jefferson.
    Evangelical ethics : issues facing the church today / John Jefferson Davis. — 2nd ed.
      p.   cm.
    Includes bibliographical references and indexes.
    ISBN 0-87552-223-8
    1. Christian ethics—Presbyterian authors. 2. Civilization, Modern—20th century. 3. Evangelicalism. I. Title.
BJ1251.D28 1993
241'.0404—dc20   93-2513

To

Robin, Nathaniel, Elizabeth,
Susannah, Hilary, and Elliot

Contents

Preface

Should Christian parents attempt to select the gender of their children prior to conception? Is in vitro fertilization morally acceptable? Do modern nuclear weapons make traditional just-war arguments obsolete? When, if ever, is it morally appropriate to "pull the plug" on a dying patient? These are only a few of the complex and agonizing issues that face the Christian in the latter part of the twentieth century.

This book reflects both my involvement in classroom teaching and my practical engagement in life-related issues through the pro-life movement. I wish to give a special word of thanks to Dr. Joseph M. Stanton, my colleague in Massachusetts Citizens for Life, who has supplied much helpful information in the area of medical ethics, and also to my students and colleagues at Gordon-Conwell Seminary, who have helped me along the way with their questions and observations. I also wish to thank my wife, Robin, for her patient proofreading.

I have attempted to relate biblical principles to current information from the disciplines of law and medicine. In this second edition I have updated much of the statistical information presented in the earlier work. I realize that much of the discussion relating to nuclear war and U.S.-Soviet relations in chapter 10 has been superseded by the events of recent years in the former Soviet Union. Nevertheless, it seemed worthwhile to retain this material in the second edition because of the historical lessons that can be drawn from this information and its possible implications for foreign policy in the future.

I also wish to express my heartfelt thanks to my research assistant, Martin Dotterweich, who prepared the Scripture, author, and subject indices, and to Dianne Newhall, who helped with proofreading.

It is my hope that this book will both challenge and inform the student, the pastor, and the alert layperson as they seek to relate the Christian faith to the pressing ethical issues of the modern world.

JOHN JEFFERSON DAVIS
S. HAMILTON, MASSACHUSETTS

CHAPTER 1

Dimensions of Decision Making

"In some of this research," noted Dr. Robert Foote of Cornell, "I am reminded of a story where the pilot came on and said, 'This is your captain speaking. We are flying at an altitude of 35,000 feet and the speed of 700 miles an hour. We have some good news and some bad news. The bad news is that we are lost. The good news is that we are making excellent time.'"

This story, told by Professor Foote in testimony on in vitro fertilization before the federal Ethics Advisory Board, expresses in a humorous way the very serious dilemma facing modern man in the closing decades of the twentieth century. Technologically we are making "excellent time"; morally we at times appear to be lost.

Developments in modern medical technology have been outstripping our ability to understand adequately their long-range ethical ramifications. Does in vitro fertilization represent a welcome solution to the problem of infertility, or does it raise the specter of the further dehumanization of marriage and human sexuality? If the technology is available to parents for the pre-conception selection of the gender of their children, is it morally legitimate to use such methods? Under what conditions, if any, could sterilization be a legitimate contraceptive choice for the Christian?

Evangelical Christians are challenged to formulate their positions on what are literally matters of life and death. Is it ever morally justifiable to abort an unborn child because of anticipated birth defects? Under what conditions can artificial life-support systems be discontinued in cases of terminal illness? In today's society, can capital punishment be applied in a truly nondiscriminatory way? Could a Christian ever be legitimately involved in a violent revolution? Do modern nuclear weapons make the traditional arguments for a just war obsolete? These are some of the pressing issues that will be examined in this volume in the light of Scripture, human reason, and the empirical data of medicine, law, and the social sciences.

CASES AND ISSUES

The focus in this work is on specific issues and cases that are likely to confront the pastor and Christian lay person today, rather than on a general discussion of moral virtues and dispositions[1] or the history of Christian ethics.[2] Although the latter considerations are important for a comprehensive Christian ethical stance, they are outside the immediate scope of this book.

Since the time of the Reformation, the subject of moral *casuistry* (the study of specific "cases") has become less fashionable in Protestant circles. That in part represents an understandable reaction to abuses associated with practices of the medieval church, such as penance, priestly confession, the subtleties of scholastic theology and canon law, and the later excesses of Jesuitical speculation.

As the noted evangelical church historian Geoffrey Bromiley has observed, however, the principle of casuistry should not be thrown out with the abuse. "The commands of God have to be worked out in the stuff of daily life. . . . some guidance must be offered even if in the last resort the Christian must form his own judgment and bear responsibility for his own act."[3]

Although Christ condemned the casuistry of the scribes and Pharisees, which perverted the law of God through human speculation, he in no way minimized the role of specific obedience to the commandments of God, but made such specific obedience a test of the genuineness of the disciple's love (John 14:21). Though obedience to the law of God can never be the basis for earning one's salvation, nevertheless the clear teaching of the apostle Paul is that the law in and of itself is holy, just, and good (Rom. 7:12). Genuine Christian love motivates the believer to fulfill the requirements of the moral law (cf. Rom. 13:10).

John Calvin taught that the moral law plays a positive role in the believer's life. The law is the instrument for learning more thoroughly the nature of God's will and becoming confirmed in the understanding of it.[4]

In the post-Reformation period, notable English Puritan pastors and theologians recognized the need to provide believers with moral guidance in specific cases of conscience. The works of William Perkins (*Decisions of Certain Cases* [Latin, 1603]), William Ames (*De Conscientia* [Amsterdam, 1630]), and Richard Baxter (*Christian Directory* [1673]) are prime examples.[5] Given the highly complex and rapidly changing conditions of life in the twentieth century, it is both appropriate and necessary to recover the best elements in this tradition of Protestant pastoral and moral theology.

BIBLICAL AUTHORITY

The teachings of Scripture are the final court of appeal for ethics. Human reason, church tradition, and the natural and social sciences may aid moral reflection, but divine revelation, found in the canonical Scriptures of the Old and New Testaments, constitutes the "bottom line" of the decision making process.[6] Informed ethical reflection will carefully weigh the various words of men, both past and present, but the Word of God must cast the deciding vote. Evangelicals believe that the canonical Scriptures are the very Word of God, the only infallible and inerrant rule of faith and practice, and consequently are the highest authority for both doctrine and morals.

The Bible functions normatively in evangelical ethics through its specific commands and precepts, general principles, various precedents, and overall world view. Many of the specific commandments of Scripture (e.g., "Do not commit adultery") are directly translatable into our present context.[7] General biblical principles, such as the sacredness of human life made in God's image (Gen. 1:26, 28), have crucial implications for modern ethical issues not addressed explicitly in Scripture, such as in vitro fertilization and genetic engineering. Old Testament practices such as tithing, while not specifically commanded in the New Testament, can function as a precedent as the people of God seek to fulfill their stewardship obligations in the present age. By teaching foundational truths concerning the nature of God, man, good, and evil, and the meaning and destiny of human life, the Bible provides a basic *world view* within which the various data of the human sciences can be understood.[8] It has been said that "good facts make good ethics," but these "facts" must be seen within the proper framework if their true ethical significance is to be understood.

The understanding of Christian morals being advocated here exemplifies the *prescriptive* and *deontological* (Greek: *deon*, that which is obligatory) tradition in the history of ethics.[9] According to this school of thought, Christian ethics is to be not merely descriptive of human behavior, but prescriptive in the sense of discerning the will of God in concrete situations, and the specific duties that follow from it. Evangelical ethics is concerned not with personal preferences and feelings, but with obligations that command the conscience.

There has been a widespread tendency in modern biblical scholarship to minimize the prescriptive element in New Testament ethics in favor of generalized appeals to Christian "faith" and "love" apart from the specifics of law. As Rudolf Schnackenburg has pointed out, however, "Jesus was not concerned only with interior dispositions, but wanted his demands to be interpreted as real commandments that are to be converted into action."[10] W. D. Davies has noted that in the mind of the Apostle Paul, the exalted Lord was never divorced from Jesus the rabbi, and the Holy Spirit was never divorced from the historic teachings of Jesus.[11] Likewise in I John there is constant appeal to the commandments of the Lord, and frequent echoes of them.[12] The love of God shed abroad in the heart of the believer is indeed the dynamic motivation of Christian behavior, but this love demonstrates itself in harmony with, and not apart from, the specific commands and precepts of Holy Scripture.

EMPIRICAL AND DELIBERATIVE ELEMENTS

Harmon Smith and Louis Hodges have written that there are two poles between which all Christian decision making must be done: "the reality of God on the one hand and the concrete, contingent situation of the actor on the other."[13] Biblical authority represents the "revelational-normative" dimension of Christian ethics; human reason, applying the biblical norms to the concrete situation in light of the specific data at hand, represents the "empirical-deliberative" dimension. Good principles and good facts are both necessary for sound decision making.

In the classic language of the Westminster Confession of Faith, the "whole counsel of God, concerning all things necessary for his own glory, man's salvation, faith, and life, is either expressly set down in

Scripture, *or by good and necessary consequence may be deduced from Scripture . . .* " (I,6; emphasis added).[14] In this formulation human reason has a legitimate role in extending the general principles of Scripture to analogous circumstances not explicitly addressed in the canonical texts.

Cocaine abuse, for example, while not explicitly addressed in the Bible, is certainly inconsistent with the teaching that the body is the temple of the Holy Spirit and is not to be abused (I Cor. 6:19, 20). The principles of medical ethics that the physician is to "do no harm" and is always to treat the patient as an end and never as a means only[15]— so crucial in the treatment of comatose or incompetent subjects—are essentially applications of the spirit of the Golden Rule to the new challenges of modern medicine. This use of reason in evangelical ethics is similar to the deliberations of a civil judge, who, being faced with entirely new circumstances in a pending case, attempts to apply existing law in the light of precedents and all the relevant data in order to serve the cause of justice.

While human reason plays an essential role in evangelical ethics, that role is not an autonomous one, independent of the authority of Scripture. Human reason, being impaired by sin, is not to serve as a separate norm as over against Scripture, but rather as the servant of divine revelation in the application of biblical truth.[16] Information from the social sciences, for example, may be relevant to discussions of homosexuality, but the evangelical ethicist will, in the words of J. Robertson McQuilken, maintain "a jealous commitment to the Bible first and last as the originating and controlling source of ideas about man and his relationships."[17] The Christian ethicist will seek all the facts relevant to the matter at hand, but will recognize the need to interpret those facts with a mind renewed by the Holy Spirit, and within a framework of meaning controlled by the teachings of Holy Scripture.[18]

CASES OF CONFLICTING OBLIGATION

In a sinful world, believers may occasionally find themselves confronted with conflicting ethical obligations. In the early church Peter and the other apostles faced conflicting demands for obedience, from the governing authorities and from God (Acts 5:27-29). After Rahab the harlot received the Israelite spies, she was met with a choice between telling the truth or preserving life (Josh. 2). Corrie Ten Boom, when hiding

Jews in her home during the Second World War and queried by the Nazi authorities, "Are there any Jews in this house?" faced a dilemma similar to Rahab's.

Some ethicists have distinguished between *prima facie* ("on first appearance") duties and *actual* duties.[19] *Prima facie* duties are duties, *other things being equal.* *Actual* duties are duties, *all things considered.*[20] Is such a distinction biblical? In a sinful world, is it always possible to find a course of action that is thoroughly pleasing to God, or is it sometimes necessary to choose between the lesser of two sins? Are there general principles from Scripture that can furnish guidelines for resolving cases of conflicting obligations? These and related issues will be addressed in the analysis that follows.

One unsuccessful answer to the problem of conflicting moral obligations is known as "situation ethics." In this approach there can be no real conflict between two or more absolutes, because presumably there is only one absolute: "love." In each and every situation, one's moral obligation is to take the most "loving" course of action, even if that should mean discarding traditional ethical standards.

Joseph Fletcher, the leading proponent of this school of thought, has little use for codes and rules. "Christian situation ethics," he says, "reduces law from a statutory system of rules to the love canon alone."[21] Universal rules and principles are treated as love's servants and subordinates, "to be quickly kicked out of the house if they forget their place and try to take over."[22]

This "situational" and incipiently antinomian perspective was not entirely new with Fletcher, but had been anticipated by earlier trends in neoorthodox theology. Emil Brunner, for example, in the widely read *The Divine Imperative,* had written that "we are united to our neighbor by the Command of love, which excludes all legalistic rules and every attempt to stereotype human relationships."[23] A protest against legalism in the Christian life can easily become a rejection of the binding moral authority of the specific precepts of God's written Word.

The fundamental difficulty with the "situational" approach, of course, is the absence of a definite criterion for what constitutes a "loving" course of action in any given situation. Harmon Smith asks, "How does a person know that he is doing (or has done) the loving thing in the situation?"[24] The question is very much to the point. Apart from the abiding norms of divine revelation, the moral agent is left to the vagaries of personal preference and the constantly changing "spirit of the age" to discern the "loving" thing.

The Bible clearly indicates that human beings, who possess sinful and fallen natures, cannot be left to their own devices to discern the will of God; the ability to rationalize selfish desires in the name of high-sounding principles is all too real. Paul Lehmann, for example, attempts to legitimize extramarital sex by appealing to the "fulfillment of human wholeness" and "free obedience to what God is doing in the world."[25]

James Gustafson relates a conversation with a student at a liberal seminary during the late sixties—a conversation that illustrates how "situationism" can lead to the trivialization of serious moral principle. "I get up in the morning and look out the window," the student said, "to see what God is doing in the world. I read the *New York Times* to find out where he is doing these things today. Then I get with it."[26]

Evidently it did not occur to the student that reading (and obeying) the Bible had anything to do with discerning "what God was doing in the world." The serious reader of Scripture is confronted by the statement of Jesus that *authentic* love for God is demonstrated by keeping his commandments (John 14:21). The Bible points the moral agent away from the short-term rationalizations of personal preference toward the long-term perspective of eternity—the perspective that alone provides the proper framework for evaluating man's true and lasting interests.

The view advocated in this work regarding conflicting moral obligations could be termed "contextual absolutism."[27] According to this perspective, there are many moral absolutes, not just one absolute of "love," as in situation ethics. Examples of moral absolutes are provided by the Decalogue: idolatry, murder, blasphemy, adultery, stealing, and so forth are always morally wrong.[28]

Contextual absolutism holds that in each and every ethical situation, no matter how extreme, there is a course of action that is morally right and free of sin. God promises that in every situation of temptation or testing there will be a way of escape so that the believer will be able to endure it (I Cor. 10:13). This position differs from the "lesser-of-two-evils" position, which holds that in some circumstances any course of action open to the believer will be sinful to some degree.

In some cases the right course of action may require suffering or even martyrdom. Jesus Christ, who is presented as the believer's moral ideal in the New Testament, did not commit any sin, but always obeyed the Father's will, even to the point of suffering and death (cf. I Pet. 2:21, 22). Daniel and his friends were willing to be martyred rather than compromise their convictions by committing an act of idolatry (Dan. 3:17, 18).

Following the course of action that is well pleasing to God may not always be easy in a sinful and fallen world, but such obedient and even heroic options can, by the grace of God, be found and followed even in the most extreme conditions. Such unswerving commitment to discerning and obeying the will of God—including a willingness to pay the "cost of discipleship"—is much needed in the twentieth-century American church, where believers are all too often tempted by the comforts and compromises of the surrounding culture.

The term "*contextual* absolutism" contains the implicit reminder that the moral absolutes of Scripture need to be understood and applied within their proper context. Some normal or *prima facie* duties may not be actual duties when all things are taken into consideration. As Charles Hodge, the famous conservative theologian of the previous century, has noted, occasionally a higher obligation suspends a lower one.[29] Several examples may help to make this point clear.

There are a number of illustrations in Scripture of the principle that obedience to God takes precedence over the normal obligation (Rom. 13:1) to obey the government. The Hebrew midwives refused to obey the command of Pharaoh to kill the male Hebrew infants, and God blessed them for their courage (Exod. 1:15-17). In the early church the apostles refused to obey the orders of the Jewish authorities to refrain from preaching the gospel, replying, "We must obey God rather than men" (Acts 5:29). Daniel and his friends were willing to suffer martyrdom rather than obey Nebuchadnezzar's command to worship the idol (Dan. 3:17, 18). When the laws of God conflict with the laws of men, human laws must yield to the higher authority of God.

The Bible endorses the principle that human life is of far greater value than physical property or possessions. One human life or soul is more valuable in God's sight than the entire physical world (cf. Matt. 16:26: "What does it profit a man if he gains the whole world and forfeits his life?"). A fireman who breaks down the door of a burning home in order to save a child's life is not guilty of breaking the eighth commandment's prohibition of stealing, which normally applies to the willful destruction of another's property. In such an emergency, any reasonable person, if asked, would give permission for the destruction of property in order to save a life. One can suppose that an implied consent justifies the fireman's action.

Cases involving possible conflicts between telling the truth and saving lives are more difficult to analyze. When Rahab the harlot (Josh. 2:1-7), for example, spoke falsehood to protect the Israelite spies, was she choosing the "lesser of two evils," or a course of action acceptable to God?

Charles Hodge has pointed out that in such cases one's *definition* of a lie is crucial. Not every act of deception is the moral equivalent of a lie; a lie involves "an intention to deceive when we are expected and bound to speak the truth."[30] In certain contexts full disclosure is not expected. In football, for example, a quarterback is not expected to reveal his plays to the opposing linemen; he intentionally tries to deceive the defense when he fakes to the fullback but passes to the wide receiver. In warfare, opposing generals do not expect their counterparts to willingly reveal their battle plans; deception by camouflage and other means is the "name of the game."

It could be argued that Rahab, living in the context of war (the invasion of Canaan), and having shifted her allegiance from the king of Jericho to the God of Israel as her true King, had no obligation to make full disclosure to the soldiers. Her higher duty to protect the lives of the servants of God suspended the *prima facie* duty to tell the truth, and her course of action was acceptable to God. In the New Testament, Rahab is cited as an example of faith for receiving the spies and sending them out in a different way (James 2:25). Nowhere in Scripture is Rahab condemned for her action. On this construction Rahab fulfilled the moral absolute that applied in this wartime context, namely, to save the lives of God's people; and her actions, rather than being the lesser of two evils, were actually good.[31]

CHRISTIAN ETHICS AND LAW IN A PLURALISTIC SOCIETY

For the Christian the Bible is the inspired and infallible Word of God, the final authority for faith and practice. The believer lives, however, in a pluralistic society, which does not officially recognize the authority of the Scriptures. To what extent should Christians attempt to have their moral convictions reflected in American law and public policy? Would such attempts constitute an inappropriate effort to "impose" alien moral standards on unbelievers or those of other faiths? Is "legislating morality" an inherently unworkable concept?

Such questions are far from academic. Contemporary issues such as abortion, pornography, "gay rights," state-sponsored lotteries—to name a few—make such questions urgent ones for the Christian community. Historically, the Judeo-Christian values derived from the Bible have formed the basis for civil law in Western civilization.[32] Since the Second World War, however, that basis has increasingly been contested and even repudiated by secular humanists. The following analysis is an attempt to outline some basic guidelines for evangelical action in this complex area of biblical values and public policy in a pluralistic society.

In our American context discussions of "legislating morality" inevitably involve the concept of the "separation of church and state" derived from the First Amendment. The amendment does not actually contain the words "separation of church and state," but declares that "Congress shall make no law respecting an establishment of religion, or prohibiting the free exercise thereof."[33] In recent years the federal courts have taken this to mean a virtual separation of Christian *values* from government rather than the separation of church and state as *institutions*, but that is, as we shall see, an understanding quite foreign to the intention of the framers of the Constitution and Bill of Rights.

An examination of American legal and constitutional documents before and after the enactment of the First Amendment in 1792 makes it clear that the framers never intended to exclude Christian values from law and public policy.[34] Maryland's state constitution, enacted in 1776, specified as a test of office holders a "declaration of belief in the Christian religion."[35] Article 38 of the state constitution of South Carolina, formulated in 1778, was even more specific, stating that "the Christian Protestant religion shall be deemed the established religion of this state."[36] The founding fathers saw no conflict between such practices of the states and the First Amendment. The Establishment Clause was intended to prevent the U.S. Congress from establishing any one *denomination* as the preferred American church, but the amendment left the *states* free to do so if they wished. The state of Massachusetts, for example, continued to have an established state church until 1832, a generation after the adoption of the First Amendment.

U.S. Supreme Court decisions prior to 1947 reflected this historically correct understanding of the framers' intention.[37] Justice Joseph Story, in a unanimous decision, *Vidal v. Girard's Executors* (1843), could state that "the Christian religion is part of the common law." The Court clearly understood that the First Amendment was intended to rule out preferential treatment for any single Christian denomination, rather than excluding Christian influence as such.

In an 1890 decision, *Church of Latter-Day Saints v. U.S.*, the Court held that the Mormon practice of polygamy was illegal, being "contrary to the spirit of Christianity." In *Church of Holy Trinity v. U.S.*, the Court could say that "this is a Christian nation." As late as 1931, in the case of *United States v. Macintosh*, the Court could state that "we are a Christian people, according to one another the equal right of religious freedom, and acknowledging with reverence the duty of obedience to the will of God." It was only as recently as 1947, in the case of *Everson v. Board of Education*, that the concept of "a wall of separation between church and state" began to take on a perverse life of its own and a meaning quite foreign to the intention of the founding fathers.

If the First Amendment, then, is no barrier to Christian attempts to influence public policy, are there biblical principles that can furnish guidelines for such action? How much Christian morality should be legislated? Is there common moral ground between the believer and the unbeliever? These are only a few of the many questions that naturally arise in this difficult but timely area.

The biblical teachings concerning the *image of God* and *general revelation* are certainly germane to such discussions. All men and women are in fact created in the image and likeness of God (Gen. 1:26-28) and, whether they acknowledge the fact or not, live in the moral universe created by God and have an inborn awareness of God's moral requirements. God reveals his moral will for mankind not only in the special revelation given in the Bible, but also in the general revelation of nature and conscience (Rom. 1:18-32; 2:14, 15).[38] The Apostle Paul clearly teaches that the unbeliever, entirely apart from the Bible, has not only an awareness that God exists, but also an awareness of the fundamental demands of God's moral law. One does not have to be a Christian to be intuitively aware that murder, stealing, adultery, and disrespect for parents, for example, are contrary to the divine will. Even though this moral awareness is distorted and suppressed by a sinful human nature (Rom. 1:18), it is nevertheless still present and can provide a point of contact in the discussion of public policy issues with moral dimensions.

History also teaches that God calls nations to account for the violation of the basic moral principles revealed in creation and conscience. God sent judgment upon the generation of the flood (Gen. 6) and upon Sodom and Gomorrah (Gen. 18). Amos denounced the war atrocities committed by one pagan nation against another (Amos 2:1). Jonah was sent to announce God's judgment against the pagan city of Nineveh (Jonah). Not having the written revelation of God was no excuse; they were sinning against the light of nature and the moral law engraved upon the heart (cf. Rom. 1:18-32; 2:14, 15).

The moral wisdom of God's general revelation has been confirmed in history by the studies of anthropologists. Based on his extensive studies of both ancient and modern civilizations, the British anthropologist J. D. Unwin concluded that the whole of human history does not provide a single example of a society that achieved and consistently maintained a high level of culture without adopting heterosexual monogamy as the standard for marriage and family life.[39] Societies that adopted more permissive sexual practices entered into periods of decline in art, science, religion, and military power. The "track record of history" has confirmed the wisdom of the moral standards revealed not only to believers, in Scripture, but to all peoples, through general revelation.

On the basis of the foregoing considerations, the following general principle may be stated: Where Scripture indicates that unbelievers can have moral awareness on a given issue through *general revelation,* then it may be appropriate for Christians to press for legislation in that area.[40] For example, laws prohibiting the killing of innocent human life and forbidding homosexuality as a way of life are consistent with the basic moral intuitions of believers and unbelievers alike, according to Romans 1:18-32 and 2:14, 15. In such cases the unbeliever *ought* to know better, even though in some instances the unbeliever will deny in very vocal terms the voice of conscience. Other behavioral standards, such as attendance at Christian worship, are not mandates of general revelation, but presuppose special revelation and a personal faith commitment, and hence are not appropriate subjects for civil legislation.[41]

Christians seeking to influence law and public policy must be sensitive not only to basic biblical and theological principles, but to practical considerations as well. Would the proposed law be enforceable? If not, the actual effect of legislation might be to undercut respect for the rule of law and the credibility of Christian political action. The unsuccessful attempt to outlaw the production and sale of alcoholic beverages during Prohibition is an example.[42] The enforceability of a given law presupposes a significant degree of *community consensus* regarding its justice and wisdom. At times, however, a prophetic minority may be called to *create* a consensus on a given issue where none exists, as did the abolitionists in the nineteenth century. In certain controversial areas where matters of fundamental justice are at stake, legal change may come first, and community consensus later, as with the civil rights movement in the sixties. The historical examples illustrate the variety and complexity of the circumstances that confront Christians who work for change in the public arena.

One might also consider the criterion known as the "clear and present danger." That is to say, at any given time there may be a whole spectrum of moral issues in society that could be the focus of efforts to change the laws. Given limited time and energy, however, an individual or a church will need to focus on issues that have special urgency or crucial implications for the body politic. Both state-run lotteries and abortion, for example, are public policy issues with moral dimensions. But abortion is literally a matter of life and death, while lotteries are not, and hence the former concern deserves a higher place in the list of priorities for social action, other considerations being equal.

Christians seeking to influence public policy will recognize both the value and limitations of civil law as an instrument of social change. The believer will not (or should not) have *utopian* expectations of what laws can accomplish; only the gospel of Jesus Christ and the Holy Spirit can produce radical transformations in the human heart. At the same time, law not only restrains violent behavior, but serves as an educator. As Lynn Buzzard has observed, "Law not only expresses what is, but is a summons to what ought to be."[43] Civil laws that are consistent with the teachings of Scripture point society to a higher standard of righteousness, which is fulfilled only in Jesus Christ. Such laws remain a worthy object of Christian concern and social action.

CHAPTER 2

Contraception

In recent years, "a Berlin Wall separating parents from their children" has been erected by government agencies and by private agencies sponsored by the government, stated former Secretary of Health and Human Services Richard Schweiker.[1] The secretary's remarks were sparked by the continuing controversy concerning the right of parents to be notified when their minor children receive contraceptive devices from family planning clinics funded by the federal government. In the spring of 1983 Planned Parenthood and the American Civil Liberties Union brought a suit against the Department of Health and Human Services to block the implementation of federal rules requiring parental notification when teenage minors are given prescription contraceptives. Manhattan Federal Judge Henry F. Werker granted a temporary injunction blocking implementation of the rule. The controversy over parental notification has aroused within the Christian community a new concern over contraception reminiscent of the flurry of attention created in the 1960s by Pope Paul VI's encyclical *Humanae Vitae* and the general introduction of the birth control pill.

The question of the use of artificial means of contraception raises profound moral questions. At the personal level, the meaning of human sexuality and love and the very purpose of marriage are at stake. What should a parent tell a teenage son or daughter in today's permissive society, where contraceptive devices are so readily available?

At the global level, does world population growth make the widespread use of contraceptive devices a moral imperative? Should the U.S. government actively promote their use among the peoples of the de-

15

veloping nations? Are programs of voluntary and even involuntary sterilization—such as those implemented in India and China—legitimate extensions of such moral concerns?

In facing such questions at the personal, societal, and global levels, the Christian must seek new wisdom from the Scriptures, medical science, and the study of history. Such a study will indicate that evangelicals need to take a closer look at many of the features of both the ethics and the practice of artificial contraception, which have largely been taken for granted since the 1960s.

FROM ANCIENT TIMES TO PRESENT

Evidence for the use of artificial means of contraception reaches far back into the records of human history. Egyptian papyri dating from 1900-1100 B.C. show that Egyptian physicians offered prescriptions for the prevention of pregnancy.[2] One document states that pregnancy may be prevented by a mixture containing acacia tips, bitter cucumber, dates, and honey, placed in the uterus. Another papyrus recommends that pregnancy may be prevented by placing crocodile dung on moistened fibers in the opening of the uterus. These prescriptions, though crude and unhygienic by modern standards, show that the ancient Egyptians made conscious attempts to limit fertility by artificial means.

Recommendations concerning contraception are found in various writings from the Greco-Roman world. A potion containing a distillate of copper is discussed in *The Nature of Women* 93, a fifth-century B.C. writing from the Hippocratic school of medicine. Aristotle believed that conception could be prevented by the application of cedar oil, ointment of lead, or frankincense and olive oil on the part of the body "where the seed falls" (*History of Animals* 7.3, 583a). Ancient medical writers such as Pliny and Dioscorides were familiar with a variety of contraceptive drinks and with salves and ointments to be applied to the male genitals in order to act as spermicides. Soranus of Ephesus, a second-century A.D. Greek gynecologist, believed that conception was unlikely to occur during menstruation or just before its onset.

During Old Testament history, there is only one explicit reference in the Jewish Scriptures to contraception. In Genesis 38:8-10 there is the account of Onan, who deliberately spilled his seed rather than beget children for his brother's widow, as required by the custom of levirate marriage (Deut. 25:5). This is the earliest known explicit reference from the ancient world to the practice of coitus interruptus.

While references to contraception are almost nonexistent in the canonical Old Testament, further discussion is found in various tractates of the *Babylonian Talmud*. Yebamoth 34b and Niddah 13a mention coitus interruptus. Vaginal suppositories are mentioned in Yebamoth 35a and Niddah 32, contraceptive potions made from roots in Shabbath 11a-11b and Yebamoth 8.4. Given the very positive regard for large families that characterized Jewish culture, the relative infrequency of references to contraception in the earliest sources is not surprising.[3] During the period of early medieval European history, the Celtic and Germanic peoples of Western Europe were familiar with various herbal potions which were thought to inhibit conception. Eighth-century legislation of Theodolphus, bishop of Orleans, included a condemnation of coitus interruptus, which indicates that this technique was both known and practiced at the time. During the twelfth century the *Canon of Medicine* of the Arabian philosopher and physician Avicenna was translated into Latin, with its discussions of various spermicides, vaginal suppositories, potions, and abortifacients. Avicenna's *Canon* dominated the field for some five hundred years; it was considered the standard medical textbook until the middle of the seventeenth century.

Chaucer's *Canterbury Tales* appears to give evidence of contraceptive practices. In "The Parson's Tale," lines 570-80, the Sin of Wrath is said to include "drynkynge veneouse herbes thurgh which she may not conceive."

The modern period brought the introduction of new contraceptive devices. The condom appeared during the middle of the seventeenth century, but it was neither cheaply nor efficiently produced and initially did not win wide acceptance. Use of the condom became more widespread after the invention of vulcanized rubber in the nineteenth century.

In the United States the first public advocacy of contraception began in 1830 with the publication of Robert Dale Owens' *Moral Physiology: or a Brief and Plain Treatise on the Population Question*. This was followed in 1832 by the publication of *The Fruits of Philosophy* by Charles Knowlton, an eccentric Yankee physician and freethinker.[4] American law and public opinion remained unfavorable to contraception for most of the nineteenth century. The federal Comstock law of 1873 made illegal the mailing or importation of contraceptives, and most American states forbade both their sale and advertisement.

In the year 1880 Wilhelm Mensinger developed the diaphragm. By 1935 over 200 different types of artificial contraceptive devices were in use in Western nations. In 1936 the courts overturned the earlier Comstock law. These changing practices reflected not only the proliferation in the number of contraceptive devices and increasing medical knowledge of the human reproductive system, but also changing social attitudes promoted by Margaret Sanger and other leaders of the American Birth Control League.

The introduction of the birth control pill in the late 1950s proved to be an event of major proportions both in medicine and in social practice. In 1965 the U.S. Supreme Court in *Griswold v. Connecticut* declared unconstitutional Connecticut's nineteenth-century law prohibiting the use of contraceptives. In *Eisenstadt v. Baird* (1972) the Court went even further, voiding a Massachusetts law prohibiting the sale of contraceptive devices to the unmarried. By 1970 contraception was being funded domestically through the Family Planning Services and Population Research Act and, soon after, at the international level by the Foreign Assistance Act of 1971. In little less than a century the practice of contraception had moved from a position of illegality to one of official sponsorship by the federal government.

MODERN METHODS OF CONTRACEPTION

"THE PILL"

Each day some fifty to sixty million women around the world swallow "the pill" in order to avoid pregnancy.[5] Since its commercial introduction in 1960, the oral contraceptive pill in its various forms has become the world's most widely prescribed drug and one of the most intensively studied substances in medical history.

One of the prime developers of the pill, Dr. John Rock, an American physician, discovered that progestin synthesized from the wild Mexican yam could be used as a contraceptive.[6] The original product, "Enovid," contained 150 micrograms of estrogen and 9.85 milligrams of a progestational agent. "That was much too high," noted Dr. Celso-Ramon Garcia, one of Dr. Rock's associates.[7] Pills commonly in use today have lower doses, usually one-tenth the strength of the original version.

Dr. Rock's earlier research in the area of human fertility focused on the isolation of a fertilized human egg. Charity patients who were scheduled for hysterectomies had their operations delayed for as much as seven months in order to accommodate the researchers' schedules. During the first six months the women's menstrual cycles were studied in order to determine the time of their fertile periods, and during the last month they were encouraged to have intercourse during the fertile period. When each woman reached the estimated time of ovulation, she was hurried into surgery, to have her uterus and Fallopian tubes removed, and then rushed into the laboratory for the "egg hunt."[8] One of the first human tests of the birth control pill was performed with 20 Puerto Rican female medical students, who were not informed that the pill they were given was a contraceptive drug.[9]

Around 1975, numbers of reports on adverse side effects stemming from use of the pill began to appear in the medical literature and the popular press. Increased incidence of phlebitis, heart attacks, and strokes was reported by various researchers, causing many American women to seek other methods of birth control.

According to a study published in 1977, data from 13,358 women showed that oral contraceptive use is associated with a slight but statistically significant rise in blood pressure, indicating that caution should be used in prescribing these drugs for women who are already predisposed to cardiovascular disease or stroke.[10]

A 1981 study directed by Dr. Dennis Slone of the Boston University Medical School concluded that women who are longtime users of the pill may face double or triple the risk of heart attacks as long as nine years after they stop taking the pill.[11] The risks did not appear to be especially significant among younger women, however, and the greatest risks were found for women in the 40-to 49-year age range.

The most comprehensive review to date of the side effects of the pill has been conducted by the Population Information Program of the Johns Hopkins University and published under the title "Oral Contraceptives in the 1980's." The study concluded that significant risks were essentially limited to women over 35, and especially to those in this age group who smoke.[12] The study also reported the rather surprising result that the pill actually has beneficial side effects as well. The evidence appears to indicate that users of the pill have a lower incidence of pelvic inflammatory diseases, receive some protection against cancers of the ovaries and uterus, and are less likely to develop rheumatoid arthritis.[13]

The pill would thus appear to have no serious risks for healthy women under 35 who are nonsmokers, although it is always possible that further long-range studies might disclose as yet unknown risks. The pill would also appear to be the most effective means of artificial birth control. One national survey of married women showed a failure rate of 2 percent for oral contraceptives, versus a 4.2 percent failure rate for the IUD, and rates of at least 10 percent for other methods including condoms, foams, jellies, the diaphragm, and rhythm.[14]

There is a form of the birth control pill, commonly known as the "mini-pill," which contains only a small dose of progesterone, rather than the usual combination of estrogen and progesterone. It is taken daily, 30 days per month, rather than on the 21-7 day cycle for the combination pill. There is controversy in medical circles concerning the exact nature of its contraceptive action. There appears to be some evidence, however, that the "mini-pill" does allow for breakthrough ovulation and hence raises the very real possibility of the fertilization of the ovum. Should such fertilization occur, pregnancy would be prevented by an anti-implantation action. In such a case the mini-pill would act as an abortifacient device.[15]

THE IUD

The intrauterine device (IUD) is another widely used contraceptive measure. It is estimated that some 2.5 to 3 million American women use this form of birth control.[16] The use of such devices has tended to level off, however, since the high incidence of infections and other complications led the A. H. Robins firm to remove the Dalkon Shield from the market in June of 1974.[17]

The earliest IUDs, such as the Grafenberg rings and the Birnberg bows, were metallic devices. These IUDs fell into disfavor because of the difficulty of insertion, the frequent need for removal because of cramping and bleeding, and serious complications such as perforation of the uterus and infections.[18]

Later IUDs were made from inert plastic. Between 1962 and 1968 the Lippes Loop was the most commonly used intrauterine device.[19] Plastic devices such as the Lippes Loop and the Saf-T-Coil avoided some of the undesirable side effects of the earlier metallic devices.

In 1969 copper IUDs were introduced, with copper wires or filaments being added to the inert plastic devices. It was discovered that the contraceptive effect was directly proportional to the surface area of the copper used.[20]

The year 1976 saw the appearance of medicated IUDs. Devices such as the Progestasert and the Alza have small amounts of progesterone in the plastic stems, and the gradual release of this drug is thought to reduce the bleeding and cramping experienced by some users of IUDs.[21]

It is generally agreed that the IUD is one of the most effective means of artificial contraception. The combined pregnancy rate for all IUDs is six per 100 woman-years of use.[22]

For many years the exact nature of the contraceptive action of the IUD was not known. It is now well established, however, that the primary action of these devices is to produce an inflammation of the uterine wall, which prevents the implantation of a fertilized ovum. According to Dr. Thomas W. Hilgers of the Mayo Graduate School of Medicine in Rochester, Minnesota, "It is evident that the IUD exerts its birth-preventative effects primarily through the destruction, at a uterine level, of the preimplantation blastocyst." Consequently, "the primary action of the IUD must be classed as an abortifacient," according to Dr. Hilgers.[23]

Significant medical complications continue to attend the use of even the newest forms of the IUD. Recent studies indicate that users of these devices are three to five times more likely than nonusers to develop pelvic inflammatory disease.[24] Such pelvic inflammations can cause permanent sterility. "Infertility following IUD use is an important potential risk," notes Dr. Robert A. Hatcher. Thus, states Hatcher, "I find myself searching more diligently for alternatives and leaning away from the use of IUDs in women who hope to bear children later."[25]

Accidental pregnancies in women using IUDs have an unusual risk of being ectopic ("tubal") or resulting in a septic (infected) abortion.[26] The spontaneous abortion rates for users of IUDs is approximately three times that for pregnancies not complicated by such devices.[27] If a woman becomes pregnant with an IUD in place, the chances are more than one in twenty that the pregnancy will be ectopic.[28]

THE CONDOM

The condom remains one of the most popular methods of contraception after the pill, according to studies by the National Center for Health Statistics. Its use declined somewhat during the period 1973-76, although this trend appears to be reversing itself in response to concern over the epidemic of sexually transmitted diseases in the United States.[29]

The condom, possibly mentioned as early as the sixteenth century by Gabriel Fallopius, the Italian anatomist who discovered the Fallopian tubes, did not come into common use until the nineteenth century.[30]

When consistently used, the condom can be an effective contraceptive device, having a pregnancy rate as low as three per 100 woman-years.[31] It has the advantages of simplicity, low cost, and partial protection against venereal diseases. Its disadvantages include psychological distraction, dulling of sensation, and occasional breakage or leaking.[32] There are no known health hazards associated with its use.

THE DIAPHRAGM

Another commonly used contraceptive device is known as the diaphragm, a molded cap, usually of thin rubber, fitted over the uterine cervix in order to function as a barrier to sperm. In 1974 it was estimated that some 4.6 percent of American women were using this method; by 1979 the figure had increased to 12.6 percent, the increase possibly reflecting concern over adverse side effects of the pill.[33] While the diaphragm has the apparent advantage of lacking some of the undesirable side effects of other methods, its failure rate is said to vary from 2 percent to 20 percent.[34] Some physicians do not take the necessary care in fitting the device, and occasionally the diaphragm can slip out of adjustment during use.

SPERMICIDES

Devices such as condoms and diaphragms are frequently used in conjunction with foams, creams, suppositories, and jellies, which contain spermicidal chemicals. Until recently there was little or no concern about possible harmful side effects of these chemicals. A new study, however, conducted under the auspices of Dr. Herschel Jick and the Boston Collaborative Drug Surveillance Program, raised the possibility of a link between the use of such vaginal spermicides and a higher than normal incidence of birth defects. Researchers studied the children born to a group of 4,772 women in Seattle, Washington during an 18-month period. The incidence of severe birth defects, including Down's syndrome, malignant brain tumors, and limb deformities, was twice the rate of those born to nonusers.[35] While the total rate of serious defects was low—2.2 percent for babies of spermicide users versus 1 percent for nonusers— the results were still a matter for concern. Animal experiments have shown that the spermicidal chemicals can be rapidly absorbed through the vaginal wall into the bloodstream and then carried to the ovaries and uterus. Dr. Jick noted, "It would be prudent to give up spermicides at least two months before getting pregnant, and to stop using them immediately if you suspect you might have already conceived."[36]

In April of 1983 the Food and Drug Administration approved a new nonprescription sponge contraceptive device for women. The soft polyurethane sponge, which contains the spermicidal chemical nonoxynol-9, does not require fitting by a physician.[37] The new device is said to have an effectiveness comparable to other vaginal contraceptives such as the diaphragm, i.e., approximately 85 percent. Given recent concern about the possible link between spermicides and birth defects, as well as the problem of toxic shock syndrome associated with the use of tampons, it remains to be seen whether the new sponge contraceptive will become widely used by American women.

STERILIZATION

Increasingly today, both in the United States and around the world, couples are turning to various forms of sterilization as a form of birth control. Unlike other forms of contraception, techniques such as tubal ligation and vasectomy involve surgical alterations of the human body that are in most instances permanent. Sterilization thus raises new issues for a Christian view of contraception both at the medical and moral level.

According to a study by the World Health Organization in Geneva, female sterilization is the most widespread form of birth control, accounting for 26 percent of all contraceptive usage in the world. This is followed by male sterilization at 19 percent, and oral contraceptives at 15 percent.[38] China, which instituted in 1979 and 1980 an emphasis on the one-child family, accounts for almost half the world's surgical sterilizations.[39]

Other Third World nations such as India, South Korea, and Thailand have also experienced dramatic increases in the number of sterilizations. As infant mortality rates have fallen, the pressure to have very large families as a form of "social insurance" has diminished somewhat. At the same time, coercive government policies such as those enforced for a time in India under the administration of Indira Ghandi have produced significant backlashes. The Indian government was using penalties such as denial of ration cards and automobile licenses in order to pressure peasants to participate in the family planning programs.[40]

In the United States, there has been a dramatic increase in voluntary sterilizations, which increased from three million in 1971 to at least 13 million by 1981.[41]That is remarkable inasmuch as the first vasectomy clinic in the United States was opened in 1969.[42]

According to a report from Princeton University's Office of Population Research, by 1977 6.8 million American couples had chosen elective sterilization of one partner, while another 1.1 million had been sterilized for medical reasons. This compared with a figure of 7.1 million married couples in which the wife was taking oral contraceptives. Thus by 1977 sterilization had surpassed the pill as the most popular form of contraception, both in the United States and in the world as a whole.[43] This unprecedented social phenomenon took place with remarkably little discussion in the Christian community, especially among evangelical Protestants. Evidently for many Christians, as well as for those of no religious faith, such practices were increasingly being considered "personal matters" to which even the church had no prerogative to speak.

Tubal Ligation. Female sterilization involves the procedure of tubal ligation, commonly known as "tying the [Fallopian] tubes." Tubal ligation was first performed on women during the nineteenth century and gained some popularity during the 1930s.[44] By 1975, some 600,000 women each year in this country were having their tubes tied, up from 192,000 in 1970.[45]

The major surgical techniques used in female sterilization include *laparotomy, mini-laparotomy, and laparoscopy.* Laparotomy is the oldest technique and involves an incision in the abdominal wall for the purpose of cutting or closing the Fallopian tubes. This procedure is often done after a delivery or other surgery, thus making a separate hospital visit unnecessary. When done as a separate procedure, laparotomy can involve a hospital recovery period of three to seven days.[46]

The "mini-laparotomy" is a newer and simplified version of the laparotomy. It involves a small incision and the use of a probe to rotate the uterus and push it into a position that allows the Fallopian tubes to be brought out through the incision where the surgeon can then tie them.[47]

The technique known as laparoscopy allows the surgeon to view the abdominal cavity through a laparoscope, a slender tube containing a fiber optics system. The laparoscope is inserted through a small incision below the navel, and the surgeon then seals off the Fallopian tubes by means of electric cautery or plastic or metal clips. This procedure can be done in as little as fifteen minutes under local anesthesia, and it does not require hospitalization. The tiny incision below the navel is then covered with a small strip bandage, giving rise to the terms "Band-aid surgery" or "belly button surgery."[48]

As with all forms of surgery, there are risks of medical complications. All techniques of tubal ligation involve some small risk of hemorrhage and infection, and a failure rate of 1-3 percent, depending on the technique used and the skill and experience of the physician.[49]

Techniques that use electrical devices to cauterize the Fallopian tubes have resulted in three deaths and over 100 cases of serious bowel burn, according to reports from the U.S. Center for Disease Control.[50] The report questions the continued use of such electrical techniques.

Some women have reported various adverse side effects subsequent to tubal ligations. British gynecologists in the small English community of Winchester were surprised to find in 1973 that after almost 1,000 women had undergone voluntary sterilizations in 1972 and 1973, "many patients returned to the hospital, complaining of menstrual abnormality, especially menorrhagia [profuse menstrual flow]."[51] Thirty-nine percent of the women who had undergone laparotomies suffered from heavier than normal menstrual losses, and these same women were also more likely to suffer pain at the time of menstruation.[52] The causes of these irregularities were not clear, but at least one investigator suggested that the sterilization procedure, by disturbing the normal blood circulation between the uterus and the ovaries, might have contributed to the menstrual disturbances suffered by the women.

Some women have unrealistic expectations of what benefits might result from a sterilization procedure. Women who believe that tubal ligation will solve pre-existing marital or sexual difficulties are usually disappointed. Women with serious mental or emotional disturbances have become more depressed or disturbed after such surgery, feeling that they have lost their femininity in the process. Those who undergo such procedures because of pressures from their husbands may develop serious emotional problems afterward.[53]

Although tubal ligation is generally considered an irreversible operation, approximately 1 percent of women who have had such procedures seek to have them surgically reversed each year. Desire for a reversal may result from a changed attitude toward childbearing, or from a marital change such as divorce or death of the husband, or from the death of a child.

Reversals are more feasible since the development of micro-surgery techniques, where the surgeon actually performs the operation with tiny instruments and the aid of a microscope. Such operations, designed to rejoin the severed Fallopian tubes, take four to six hours, cost anywhere from $6,000 to $8,000, and have approximately a 50-60 percent chance of restoring the woman's fertility.[54] The success of such operations depends on a number of factors, including the age and health of the woman, the man's sperm count, and the extent of the damage done to the Fallopian tubes in the original sterilization procedure. Physicians generally advise their patients to consider the tubal ligation process an irreversible one, since there is no assurance, even with the most sophisticated techniques of micro-surgery, that fertility can be restored should the woman's attitude or family circumstances change.

Vasectomy. An increasingly common method of male contraception, vasectomy is undergone by some 750,000 American men each year.[55] This represents a dramatic increase since 1969, when 212,000 men underwent this sterilizing procedure.[56]

A vasectomy, which can be done in a doctor's office or clinic, takes about twenty minutes and typically costs around $200. Such elective sterilizations have been legal in all fifty states since 1972, when the state supreme court of Utah, the last state banning such operations, struck down a law prohibiting the operation for other than "medical reasons."[57]

The vasectomy procedure involves the surgical excision of the vas deferens, the sperm-carrying duct. Due to the presence of residual sperm, a sterile condition does not result immediately. According to a study published in *The Journal of the American Medical Association*, vasectomy cannot be relied upon to provide 100 percent protection against pregnancy for at least six months after the operation. Researchers found that eight of 400 postvasectomy patients had transient reappearance of sperm in the semen from one to four months after the operation. All the patients studied became sterile seven weeks to six months after the operation.[58]

Vasectomies were first performed in the latter part of the nineteenth century for medical rather than purely contraceptive reasons. The operation was performed in order to prevent inflammation of the area behind the testes, which sometimes occurred in connection with surgery on the prostate gland.[59] During the early part of the twentieth century the operation was employed as part of a eugenic program to sterilize men who were suffering from hereditary disorders and who were considered unfit to propagate offspring.[60] In the 1940s and 1950s the Human Betterment Association, later called the Association for Voluntary Sterilization, crusaded for the social acceptance of the practice. The association made a grant in 1969 to the Margaret Sanger Research Bureau in New York, where the first vasectomy clinic was opened. Within six months, some fifty other clinics, many sponsored by Planned Parenthood, were in operation around the country.[61]

The general opinion in medical circles is that vasectomy is a safe and effective means of contraception with no significant harmful side effects. There have been a few physicians and medical researchers, however, who have raised questions about the effects of the procedure. Dr. H. J. Roberts, who practices internal medicine in West Palm Beach, Florida, has expressed concern about evidence that men who have vasectomies can develop immune reactions to their own sperm. "I know of no other operation performed on normal individuals that evokes immunologic responses of such magnitude," Roberts observed.[62] Dr. Roberts thinks that long-range studies are needed to probe the possible dangers of this procedure. "The medical profession, by assisting in population control through mass vasectomy in the absence of definitive long-term epidemiologic data, puts itself at great risk," he warns.[63]

This immune response to vasectomy is part of the body's effort to eliminate some of the 50,000 sperm that are produced each minute. According to Dr. John B. Henry, Professor of Pathology at the State University of New York Medical Center, the antibodies produced in reaction to the man's own sperm after a vasectomy could prove to be "an important component in the evolution of autoimmune disease," though such a connection has not been definitely established.[64]

Some studies, but not all, have indicated a possible link between vasectomy and the risk of prostate cancer. While this possible link has not been firmly established, there is certainly cause for "discussion . . . and further research," according to Dr. Stuart Howards at the American Urological Association.[65]

In the most comprehensive study of the long-term effects of vasectomy to date, Dr. Edward Giovannucci and his colleagues examined the medical histories of 14,607 men who had undergone this procedure. They concluded that vasectomy was not associated with higher risks of heart disease or cancer in general.[66] However, the researchers found that 20 years or more after vasectomy there was an increased risk of prostate and lung cancer.[67] Given this evidence of increased risk, "more study is clearly warranted," observed Dr. Giovannucci.[68]

Such caution seems in order, given other examples in recent medical history where harmful side effects came to light only years after the introduction of a "safe" drug or treatment. During the 1950s and 1960s it was not uncommon for doctors to prescribe diethylstilbestrol (DES) to pregnant women who were in danger of having a spontaneous abortion or miscarriage. It has since been discovered that daughters born to women who were given that drug are more susceptible, fifteen or twenty years later, to a rare form of vaginal cancer. About 220 cases of such cancer have come to light in recent years, all of them associated with women whose mothers were given DES during pregnancy.[69]

There are possible psychological as well as medical side effects to be considered in relation to vasectomy. Dr. Harold Lear of the Mount Sinai School of Medicine in New York notes that optimistic surveys indicate a potential 3 percent psycho-sexual casualty rate, and other researchers have reported much higher incidences of psychological complications.[70] Men who have had problems with sexual dysfunction or histories of emotional instability before the operation are likely to find these conditions exacerbated afterward, warns Dr. Lear.[71]

While men with healthy egos and self-confidence can apparently accept the condition of sterility without psychological damage, that is not necessarily the case for men with marital or emotional problems. Shirley Southwick, a staff supervisor at a family service organization in Worcester, Massachusetts, notes that social workers around the country are beginning to report cases in which vasectomies have compounded sexual difficulties, increased anxieties and tensions, and helped to break up marriages. In a study of 26 couples done for the Family Service Association of America, it was found that in problem marriages "vasectomy represented a real threat to the marriages . . . leading in some cases to divorce, in some cases to emotional separation and in most cases to less effective handling of their emotional problems."[72]

Vasectomy generally produces permanent sterility, but recent developments in micro-surgery now raise the possibility that the operation can be reversed and fertility restored. Such operations are long and expensive, few surgeons have the necessary training and skill, and even under the best of circumstances, success is not assured. Urologists estimate that the chances of achieving pregnancy after such reversals are no more than 50 percent.[73] In addition to the problems of rejoining the severed vas deferens, there is the very real possibility that antibodies produced as a result of the vasectomy will attack and inactivate the sperm, causing infertility in spite of the attempted reversal.

"There are changes in the quantity and the quality of sperm that has been obstructed, as well as immunological changes in the body. In nine out of ten men, the tubes can be sutured together so that they are open once more, but that won't necessarily achieve the goal of getting a woman pregnant," warns New York urologist Gerald Zelikovsky.[74] Consequently, those who seek vasectomies should do so with the knowledge that there is no certainty of reversing their sterile condition, in the event that either their attitudes or marital circumstances change subsequent to the operation.

NATURAL FAMILY PLANNING

Natural family planning is being promoted by leaders in Roman Catholic circles as an alternative to the artificial methods of contraception prohibited by the Church's teaching. According to Lawrence Kane, executive director of the Human Life and Natural Family Planning Foundation of Washington, instruction in natural family planning is available in all fifty states.[75] It is estimated that there are now more than 100,000 people who have been trained in such methods. According to its proponents, these natural methods of birth control are 100 percent medically safe, have no side effects, require no surgery, chemicals, drugs, or mechanical devices, are completely reversible, and cost the users nothing.

Newer techniques such as the "basal body temperature method" and the "sympto-thermal method" have made the older "rhythm method" obsolete. The basal body temperature method is based on the fact that a woman's basal body temperature rises by a small but measurable amount, approximately three-tenths to four-tenths of a degree, after she has ovulated. This rise in temperature is caused by the release of progesterone following ovulation. A temperature rise that has been sustained for three days tells the woman not only that the time of ovulation has definitely passed, but also that the egg—which lives only for 12 to 24 hours—is no longer viable. Conception cannot occur once the post-ovulatory rise in temperature has been clearly established.[76]

Unlike the older "rhythm method," which was based on observation of the woman's past menstrual cycles, the B.B.T. method is based on observation of the present cycle and hence is not invalidated by the irregular menstrual patterns experienced by some women.

The sympto-thermal method combines the observation of the woman's body temperature with observation of the changing patterns of the woman's vaginal mucus. Drs. John and Evelyn Billings, husband and wife physicians, discovered that these external vaginal secretions of mucus change as the woman approaches ovulation, reflecting the rising levels of estrogen that precede the actual time of ovulation. As ovulation approaches, these secretions become thin, slippery, and clear, somewhat like runny egg white. At other times, the mucus is in a thick, gummy "barrier" condition, which makes it difficult for the sperm to penetrate, and the vagina has a dry feeling. Consequently, if conception is to be avoided, the couple should abstain from intercourse when the vaginal mucus is thin and the rising body temperature indicates that ovulation has occurred.[77]

Scientists working in London for the World Health Organization have developed a new device that may be of considerable interest to those who favor natural family planning methods. The researchers connected an electronic thermometer to a clock with a computer chip that monitors the woman's temperature during the menstrual cycle. A green light signals time of infertility. Dr. Heinz Wolff, one of the inventors of the device, expressed optimism that the device would be received favorably in Roman Catholic circles. It is not really a form of artificial contraception, he noted. "We've simply computerized something that people have been doing using paper and pencil charts for years." During a trial run, the researchers claimed that the device flawlessly tracked the menstrual cycles of 500 women. They hope that mass production will eventually reduce its cost to about $24, and that future versions could be made small enough to fit inside a necklace or another small object.[78]

Support for natural family planning methods has come from some rather unexpected circles. Said one committed feminist, "You know, I rather like this ovulation method of fertility control taught by the Catholics. . . . I think that it is very positive about women."[79] Such methods have found favor with many because they seem to fit in well with an interest in ecology, nutrition, and herbal medicines. Other feminists have found the methods appealing because they impose a certain amount of discipline on the man.[80] Unlike other methods, which often leave responsibility entirely to the woman, these natural methods make it a shared discipline.

MORAL DIMENSIONS OF CONTRACEPTION

THE ROMAN CATHOLIC TRADITION

The Roman Catholic understanding of contraception developed as a reaction against the widespread promiscuity and general decline in family life that characterized the Greco-Roman world into which the church was born.[81] Adultery, divorce, abortion, infanticide, declining fertility rates, and childlessness were common during the declining centuries of the Roman Empire. In the face of such social trends, the church strongly affirmed the sanctity of the marriage bond and the duty of procreation as an essential aspect of marriage.

According to Clement of Alexandria (c. 150-c. 215), for couples to have sexual relations in marriage "other than to procreate children is to do injury to nature" (*Pedagogus* 2.10-95.3). Clement and other Christian writers of the period were responding not only to tendencies in pagan society to deny the procreative dimension of marriage, but also to "Christian" Gnostics who were denying the role of procreation in matrimony, or were taking very libertine views of what "Christian freedom" in sexual matters meant. It was in this context that the fathers adopted the Stoic view (e.g., Musonius Rufus, *Reliquiae*, sec. 63), that procreation was the purpose of sexual intercourse, and that any other purpose was contrary to nature and therefore wrong.

The single most influential figure in setting the basic direction of the Catholic tradition in these matters was St. Augustine (354-430), whose theological influence has been massive in both the Roman Catholic and Protestant streams of Christianity. Prior to his conversion at the age of 29, Augustine had been a follower of the teachings of the Manicheans, a religious sect whose founding prophet, Mani, had been put to death in Persia. The Manichees taught that human beings had originated from the lustful sexual relations of the princes and princesses of darkness after they had devoured the sons of the King of Light.[82] Within each human being were particles of light, which longed to be free but which remained imprisoned as long as man continued his procreative sexual activity. The Manichees did not prohibit sexual intercourse, but did favor contraception, including coitus interruptus and contraceptive drugs. Procreation itself was discouraged and even excluded by the Manichean theology. After his conversion, Augustine reacted strongly against both the antiprocreative teachings of the Manichees and the sexual licentiousness that was so common in the pagan Roman society of the day.

According to Augustine, marital relations, in order to be entirely free from the stain of sin, had to have procreation in view (*The Good of Marriage* 16.18). In his view, since original sin was transmitted through sexual generation, the concupiscence or sexual desire involved in the act had to be balanced by the positive good of procreative in-

tent; otherwise, sexual relations, even within marriage, would be ve-
nially sinful. An intent to prevent procreation through the use of contraception turns "the bridal chamber into a brothel" (*Against Faustus*
15.7). Husbands and wives who used "poisons of sterility" to systemat-
ically exclude conception were "not joined in matrimony but in seduc-
tion" (*Marriage and Concupiscence* 1.15.17).[83] Augustine taught that the
sin of Onan described in Genesis 38, where Onan spilled his seed on
the ground rather than raise up offspring for his deceased brother's wife,
according to the levirate custom, was the sin of contraceptive marital
intercourse, "and God killed him for it" (*Adulterous Marriages* 2.12.12).[84]

Augustine thus forged a strong presumption in Catholic teaching
against contraception by combining elements from Stoicism, the Old
Testament, and his own reaction to Manicheanism and the sexual excesses of Roman society. His position was to set the course of Catholic
thinking in such matters for centuries to come.

During the Middle Ages, Catholic theologians developed themes
in the Christian understanding of marriage that helped to modify somewhat the rather one-sided Augustinian view, which focused almost exclusively on procreation. St. Paul had taught that Christian husbands
and wives have mutual conjugal responsibilities toward one another (I
Cor. 7:3-6). This passage pointed to the dimension of companionship
as an essential aspect of marriage, in addition to the procreative element. Hence the satisfaction of such conjugal rights could be virtuous
even when procreation was not in view, for example, when the wife was
beyond the age of childbearing (Aquinas, *On the Sentences* 4.32.1.2).
William of Auxerre (d. 1231) taught that the "good of offspring" meant
not merely their procreation, but also their education and nurture as rational, spiritual beings (Summa 4,f.287v).[85] This broader view of the
purpose of marriage was only to come into its own during the twentieth century, especially in the teachings of the Second Vatican Council,
where the companionate aspect of the marriage relationship was fully
recognized.

The twentieth century manifested both continuity and development in the Roman Catholic understanding of contraception. On December 31, 1930, Pope Pius XI issued the encyclical *Casti connubi*, a major statement on the nature of marriage. The encyclical was evidently
prompted by a number of factors: the vote of the Anglican bishops at
the Lambeth Conference of August 15 of that same year, in which the
bishops very cautiously affirmed the legitimacy of artificial contraception; calls for revision of the traditional Catholic teaching in the

Catholic religious press in Germany; and a growing sense that priests were not enforcing the Church's teaching at the parish level.[86]

In *Casti connubi,* Pius XI steadfastly reaffirmed the traditional ban against contraception: "Any use whatever of marriage, in the exercise of which the act by human effort is deprived of its natural power of procreating life, violates the law of God and nature, and those who do such a thing are stained by a grave and mortal flaw."[87]

Pius XI did, however, introduce a new dimension into the official teaching by making reference to the use of sterile periods in one sentence in *Casti:* "Nor are those considered as acting against Nature who in their married life use their right in the proper manner, although on account of natural reasons of time or of certain defects, new life cannot be brought forth."[88] This somewhat cryptic statement, which reflected the growing knowledge of the female menstrual cycle, a knowledge accumulating for over a century, seemed to indicate that a "rhythm method" of contraception based on a knowledge of the woman's naturally infertile periods might be acceptable in the light of Catholic moral teachings. For some twenty years, however, the ambiguity remained unresolved, while some moral theologians held that Pius XI had actually endorsed the "rhythm method," and others held that the reference was only to marital intercourse when the wife was beyond the age of childbearing, or when either husband or wife was sterile because of untreatable medical conditions.

These ambiguities were resolved in a 1951 address by Pope Pius XII to the Italian Catholic Society of Midwives, a group specializing in maternity cases. In this speech Pius XII publicly endorsed the rhythm method as an option for all Christian couples. While persistently avoiding the duty of procreation was sinful, there nevertheless were serious "medical, eugenic, economic, and social" indications to be considered. "It follows," he stated, "that observance of the sterile period can be licit."[89] This position represented a significant development in Catholic thought beyond that of Augustine, one that had in fact been maturing for centuries.

The next major pronouncement from the Holy Office came on July 25, 1968, with the publication of Paul VI's encyclical *Humanae vitae.* Many observers in the Church, encouraged by the new spirit of openness manifested at the Second Vatican Council (1963-65), expected Paul VI to take the next step beyond the rhythm method by endorsing the legitimacy of other means of birth control. But that was not to be. Paul VI, in spite of the recommendations of the majority of the papal commission appointed to study the matter, reaffirmed the ban on all forms of artificial contraception. While observance of natural rhythms is legitimate, ". . . the Church, calling men back to the observance of the norms of the natural law, as interpreted by their constant doctrine, teaches that each and every marriage act must remain open to the transmission of life."[90]

During the next decade, Catholic reaction to *Humanae vitae* continued to be very mixed. According to the liberal priest and writer Andrew Greeley, the encyclical was a "dead letter." On the other hand, John Cardinal Carberry wished to offer the Holy See a statement of gratitude for these "courageous conclusions."[91] Traditional Roman Catholic moral theologians such as Charles McFadden continued to appeal to the natural law in defense of the ban on all forms of artificial contraception: "Any use of man's reproductive powers is immoral when the use is of such a nature that it impedes attainment of the very purposes for which God created these organs."[92]

In a statement of December 15, 1981 Pope John Paul II reaffirmed the ban of *Humanae vitae* on all forms of artificial contraception. The use of such means "degrades human sexuality" by permitting couples to act as "arbiter of the divine plan."[93] John Paul did further commend methods of natural family planning, but it appeared, at least in the near future, that no significant changes were to be expected in the Church's official teachings on the matter.

The papal ban on artificial contraception has extended even more emphatically to voluntary sterilization. According to Pius XI, in *Casti connubi*, "Private individuals . . . are not free to destroy or mutilate their members, or in any other way render themselves unfit for their natural functions, except when no other provision can be made for the good of the whole body."[94] The "principle of totality" allowed, in cases of medical necessity, the sacrifice of one bodily organ in order to preserve the life of the individual as a whole. Thus the removal of a cancerous uterus, even though such an operation would produce sterility, was normally licit.

In 1968, in *Humanae vitae*, Paul VI stated that "equally to be excluded [together with abortion] . . . is direct sterilization, whether perpetual or temporary, whether of the man or the woman."[95] Tubal ligations, hysterectomies, and vasectomies for strictly contraceptive reasons were excluded. This exclusion was repeated in a statement issued from the Vatican in 1975, in which it was affirmed that sterilization is "harmful to the dignity and inviolability of the human person."[96] Considerable numbers of Roman Catholic laity were in fact practicing artificial means of contraception, and even sterilization; but they were not doing so with the official approval of the Church.

THE PROTESTANT POSITION

In important respects the Protestant Reformation did not represent a decisive break with the medieval tradition in the areas of marriage and family ethics. Luther and Calvin and the other leading Protestant Reformers nowhere give explicit endorsement to what would be considered modern attitudes toward contraception. In other respects, however, the Reformers opened the way to a new understanding of the nature of marriage.[97] Marriage was no longer considered a sacrament of the church; mandatory priestly celibacy was repudiated as being out of accord with Scripture; and companionship in marriage was given new emphasis, though not at the expense of the procreative dimension. The emphasis on companionship was not entirely new, of course; the scholastic theologians had pointed to it as an element of the Christian ideal. With Luther and Calvin, however, it assumed greater weight, and helped to open the way centuries later for a different understanding of human responsibility for the procreative process.

Not until well into the twentieth century did the major Protestant bodies publicly affirm the moral legitimacy of artificial contraception. Prior to this, medical and popular opinion had begun to change in response to new inventions in contraceptive technology and the efforts of social activists such as Margaret Sanger. As is often the case, ecclesiastical opinion followed public opinion and practice rather than shaping it. In 1908 and again in 1920 at the Lambeth Conference the bishops of the Anglican Church condemned contraception. In 1925 the bishops of the Protestant Episcopal Church in the United States also rejected its moral legitimacy.[98] In 1930, however, the Anglican bishops broke with the past and affirmed, in the face of a vigorous minority dissent, artificial contraception in the following cautious formulation:

> Where there is a clearly felt moral obligation to limit or avoid parenthood, the method must be decided on Christian principles . . . where there is a morally sound reason for avoiding complete abstinence, the conference agrees that other methods may be used, provided this is done in light of the same Christian

principles. The Conference records its strong condemnation of the use of any methods of conception control from motives of selfishness, luxury, or mere convenience.[99]

It was not until the 1950s and 1960s that the major Protestant bodies, following the lead of the Anglican bishops at the Lambeth Conference of 1930, set forth positive statements on contraception with developed theological rationales to support them. Such statements were issued by the Reformed Church of the Netherlands in 1952, the National Christian Council of India in 1953, the Augustana Evangelical Lutheran Church in 1954, and again the Lambeth Conference of 1958, the last in the form of a report titled "The Family in Contemporary Society."[100] In 1969 a group of conservative Protestant scholars issued an "Affirmation on the Control of Human Reproduction," which even included therapeutic abortion as a possible means of birth control in certain cases.[101]

During this same period contraception began to receive special attention from the Protestant theologians. Karl Barth discussed the issue in volume III/4 of his massive *Church Dogmatics*, in relation to the doctrine of creation. Barth recognized the divine command to "be fruitful and multiply" (Gen. 1:28), but noted that "a general necessity in this regard cannot be maintained on a Christian basis."[102] Barth seemed to be saying that, while there was a general human obligation to propagate the race, this obligation did not apply in the same way to all people at all times, irrespective of circumstance. Barth also stressed the dimension of personal decision and responsibility within marriage. Procreation is not merely a natural or biological phenomenon, but "must be understood as a responsible action on the part of those concerned."[103]

The prominent Lutheran theologian Helmut Thielicke, like Barth, sees human responsibility, rather than the "laws of nature," as the morally crucial variable in the discussion. Man, he argues, "is not merely another natural being, but unlike the other natural beings is in a relationship of responsibility to God. . . . the Creator . . . calls him to act in responsible freedom."[104]

Critics of such Protestant positions could point out, of course, that appeals to "responsible freedom" do not in themselves decide the question. The real question remains: By what standard does one determine what constitutes "responsible freedom"? And, does Scripture actually see responsible freedom in these terms?

The "Protestant Affirmation of the Control of Human Reproduction," drafted by a conservative group of American scholars in 1969, states that "the prevention of conception is not itself forbidden or sinful providing the reasons for it are in harmony with the total revelation of God for married life. . . . The method of preventing pregnancy is not so much a religious as a scientific and medical question to be determined in consultation with the family physician."[105] This statement, issued in the wake of the public concern generated by *Humanae vitae* in 1968, endorsed the legitimacy in some cases of sterilization and abortion as means of birth control.

An evangelical Protestant understanding of contraception must in the last analysis be derived from the explicit teaching of Scripture, and from legitimate biblical principles regarding the nature of human sexuality and the divine purposes for the institution of marriage.[106] The Scriptures have very little explicit teaching concerning contraception, but much concerning sexuality, marriage, and procreation, and it is from the latter passages that the decisive moral considerations must be drawn.

From the very beginning mankind is given the mandate to "be fruitful and multiply, and fill the earth and subdue it"(Gen. 1:28). This command is repeated to Noah and his sons after the flood (Gen. 9:1). The promise of fruitfulness in procreation is an important feature of the Abrahamic covenant, repeated on a number of different occasions (Gen. 12:2; 13:16; 15:5; 17:6; 18:18; 22:17, 18; to Isaac in 26:4, 24; and to Jacob in 28:14; 35:11).

In Genesis 38:9-10 Onan, one of the sons of Judah, spills his seed on the ground rather than raise up offspring for his deceased brother's wife, according to the custom of levirate marriage, by which the family line was perpetuated in such cases. It is recorded that God struck Onan dead for his action.

In Leviticus 18:19 sexual intercourse is prohibited with a woman during her menstrual flow. The time of menstruation produced a seven-day period of ritual uncleanness (Lev. 15:19-24). It has been pointed out that this regulation would actually have an anti-contraceptive effect, since intercourse would take place during the time in the menstrual cycle when conception would be more likely.

In Deuteronomy 23:1 it is stated that "he whose testicles are crushed or whose male member is cut off shall not enter the assembly of the Lord." This probably refers not to states of infertility produced by illness or accident, but to deliberate acts of castration at times associated with pagan worship in the ancient Near East.[107]

In the Psalms there are a number of significant expressions of the Old Testament outlook on procreation. "Lo, sons are a heritage from the

Lord, the fruit of the womb a reward" (Ps. 127:3). The family that fears God will be blessed: "Your wife will be like a fruitful vine within your house; your children will be like olive shoots around your table. Lo, thus shall the man be blessed who fears the Lord" (Ps. 128:3). In Hebrew culture childbearing was considered a blessing, and infertility a curse.

The Old Testament closes on this same note, with the prophet Malachi reminding the Israelites of his day that the Lord desires "godly offspring" (Mal. 2:15).

It seems evident, then, that the Old Testament expresses a clearly pro-natalist philosophy. At first glance, it would not seem easy to justify contraception on the basis of the Old Testament outlook. To what extent is the Old Testament outlook still valid in the New Testament era? Are there significant social or theological differences between the Testaments on this matter? Or do both Testaments share basically the same outlook on procreation and childbearing? These are some of the questions that arise as we survey the New Testament passages relevant to this issue.

In the New Testament the Hebraic emphasis on procreation and childbirth is somewhat modified, though not abandoned or denied, by a greater recognition of celibacy as a legitimate state for some within the covenant community. In a discussion on divorce and marriage, Jesus tells the disciples that there are eunuchs who are so by accident of birth, others who have been made eunuchs by men, and yet others who have chosen such a state for themselves for the sake of the kingdom of God (Matt. 19:10-12). This last condition probably refers to a voluntary state of celibacy (like that of the apostle Paul) undertaken for a spiritual purpose, rather than literal emasculation, although the latter meaning cannot be totally excluded.[108] The text refers to celibacy as an alternative to marriage, and not contraception within marriage, which is nowhere explicitly recommended as an option in the New Testament.

In I Corinthians 7:7 Paul expresses the wish that "all were as I myself am," i.e., celibate. Such a state frees one from the normal cares of the married life and allows one to concentrate one's full attention on the work of the kingdom of God. But Paul recognizes that not all have been given the gift of celibacy, and those that have not should marry (vv. 7-9).

A third reference to the celibate state is found in Revelation 14:1-5, where John sees a vision of the 144,000 that follow the Lamb, who stands on Mount Zion. It is expressly stated that the 144,000 are virgins, who have not defiled themselves with women (v. 4). Given the visionary character of the passage, and the symbolic nature of the Book of Revelation, it is difficult to know with what degree of literalness this passage is to be taken. Is the reference to virginity/celibacy merely a symbolic reference to the spiritual purity of the redeemed? On such an interpretation, the reference would mean that the 144,000, symbolic of the entire church, had not been defiled through spiritual intercourse with the pagan world system.[109] In any case, it is true that the writer considers celibacy an appropriate illustration of a spiritual point, and in so doing gives the concept additional visibility within the Christian community.

In I Corinthians 7:5, in a discussion of marriage and celibacy, the apostle Paul writes to married couples, "Do not refuse one another [conjugal rights] except perhaps by agreement for a season, that you may devote yourselves to prayer." While this passage does not mention contraception, it does carry important implications for the discussion. Here it seems evident that God's will for the Christian couple is not "maximum fertility," i.e., the maximum number of conceptions biologically possible during the course of a Christian marriage. By mutual agreement, sexual relations may be renounced for a time in order to pursue spiritual objectives—in this case, prayer. The larger principle would be that Christian couples have the right to choose to "override" the usual responsibility to procreate (Gen. 1:28) for a season in order to pursue a spiritual good.

In Galatians 5:20, in the context of a list of the sins of the flesh, Paul includes the term *pharmakeia*. This word, from which our word *pharmacy* is derived, is commonly translated "sorcery" in our English versions. John T. Noonan has argued that the term is more properly translated as "medicine" in the sense in which a North American Indian medicine man makes "medicine."[110] In the ancient world, "medicine" was associated with religion and the occult in a way that is difficult for the modern mind to appreciate. *Pharmakeia* is generally used of drugs, potions, and spells, and hence can include sorcery, but is not limited to it. In at least one case, it is used by the second century A.D. Greek physician Soranus of Ephesus, sometimes called the "father of gynecology," to refer to abortifacient drugs.[111] Consequently, Noonan would appear to be correct in saying that the word used by Paul in Galatians 5:20 is broad enough to include abortifacient drugs, though the term is certainly not limited to that meaning. Thus certain types of contraception, such as the IUD, the "morning after pill," and prostaglandin drugs, all of which can cause the abortion of the fertilized ovum, would not be licit for the Christian. Such devices would fall into the category of abortifacients rather than contraceptives.

Elsewhere in his epistles Paul admonishes the younger widows to remarry, to bear children, and to rule their households, in order to maintain a good Christian witness to the community (I Tim. 5:18). Here it is clearly implied that the general creation mandate to procreate (Gen. 1:28) still applies in the Christian era. The new life in Christ is not so utterly "spiritual" that the propagation of the race through human sexuality is transcended. This understanding of "spirituality" was encountered by the early church in its struggle with the Gnostics and was firmly repudiated. While voluntary celibacy is recognized in the New Testament, neither Paul nor any other New Testament writer envisions any Christian couple voluntarily remaining childless for the duration of marriage. God still desires "godly offspring" (Mal. 2:15) as a fruit of Christian marriage.

In summary, then, it would appear that there is no explicit endorsement of artificial contraception in either Testament. The Old Testament is clearly pro-natalist in its general outlook. The New Testament, though allowing for voluntary celibacy, does not envision permanent childlessness as a matter of choice for married couples. It would appear that the burden of proof rests on those who advocate contraception, given the general drift of Scripture.

There is, however, no explicit condemnation of contraception in Scripture. The case of Onan in Genesis 38:9-10 is most likely to be understood in terms of God's condemning Onan not for a contraceptive act per se, but for his willful refusal to perform his levirate duty to his deceased brother's wife. The general mandate to be fruitful and multiply (Gen. 1:28) does admit of some exceptions, as the cases of Jeremiah, Paul, and Jesus attest. The advice of Paul in I Corinthians 7:5 implies that Christian couples have the right to abstain from the normal conjugal relations (and the possible procreative consequences involved) in order to pursue a higher spiritual good. This higher spiritual good could certainly be broadened to include the good of the family as a whole and the welfare of children already born.

The command to procreate in Genesis 1:28 must be seen in terms of the immediate context of 1:26, where it is taught that men and women are made in the image and likeness of God. This means that men and women are different not only in degree but also in kind from the rest of the animal kingdom. Man is not just a part of nature, but is called to be a responsible ruler and steward of nature on God's behalf.

Man, as a conscious being, is to direct all his powers, including his pro-creative ones, toward their appointed goals, with the guidance of the principles revealed in Scripture. Man's calling is not simply to let "na-ture take its course," but to *consciously* redirect nature toward the ful-fillment of the divine plan. Just as God himself created the human race and recreated a fallen humanity according to a conscious plan, so it would follow that man, as God's vice regent on earth, should imitate God by exercising his procreative gifts according to a conscious plan. God did not create by a blind act of passion and will; neither should those made in his image.

It may be argued, then, that contraception can be justified in terms of the general teachings of Scripture concerning the nature of man and Christian marriage. It does not follow, however, that the use of contra-ception would be right in all circumstances. A legitimate use of such means presupposes that contraception is being used within marriage, and not just as a means of escaping the consequences of fornication; and that the contraception is not being used selfishly to avoid permanently the obligation to raise up a godly seed *within* marriage. Further, certain devices that destroy a human life already conceived (e.g., the IUD), rather than merely preventing the conception of new life, are not morally licit for Christian use. Any decision concerning the use of ar-tificial contraception must be done with an informed awareness of the possible harmful side effects to the husband, the wife, or any children conceived. If, for example, there was a reasonable possibility that cer-tain spermicidal agents could increase the likelihood of birth defects, then it would be wrong to take such risks. Considerations of either *fact* or *personal intent* might raise questions about the legitimacy of contra-ception under certain circumstances.

The question of contraception by sterilization is even more com-plex. A distinction should be made between *voluntary sterilization*, which is at issue here, and *involuntary sterilization*, for eugenic or demographic reasons, of certain classes of persons by government authority.

Compulsory sterilization has not been unknown in the American tradition. During the years 1907-17, laws were passed in 16 states man-dating compulsory sterilization for some 34 different categories of "mis-fits," including rapists, drunkards, drug addicts, epileptics, and the in-sane.[112] Such laws providing for involuntary sterilization were eventu-ally in force in 29 states. In 1927 they received the approbation of Supreme Court Justice Oliver Wendell Holmes when he made the state-ment, "The principle that sustains compulsory vaccination is broad enough to cover cutting the Fallopian tubes. . . . Three generations of imbeciles are enough."[113]

Similar sentiments can still be heard in our own day. Professor Garrett Hardin of the University of California, in a biology textbook still in use, urged the sterilization of persons with low I.Q. scores and suggested that "more spectacular results could be obtained by preventing the breeding of numerous members of the subnormal classes higher than the feeble-minded."[114]

Beginning in 1966, the U.S. government began funding the sterilization of the working and welfare poor under Title XIX of the Social Security Act.[115] By 1974 at least 100,000 poor persons had been sterilized with federal welfare support.[116] In one South Carolina county, more than one-third of the women who had had illegitimate children at Medicaid expense were said to have been sterilized.[117] Such procedures aroused considerable public outcry when it became apparent that many of these women may have been coerced into accepting the operation through veiled threats that their welfare payments would be cut off if they refused sterilizing surgery.

Such involuntary sterilizations represent a violation of the basic rights and dignity of a human being and must be firmly rejected as morally illicit. If free and informed consent is essential for even minor forms of surgery, it is even more crucial in operations that affect a person's procreative powers.

Even the case of voluntary sterilization is fraught with difficulty. It is not simply another case of surgery; the power to procreate life itself is at stake. While in principle the argument for contraception can be extended to sterilization as a special case, several factors call for special ethical reflection. Sterilization represents a much more pervasive intervention into the integrity of the body than do other forms of contraception. As yet unknown, long-range side effects—particularly in the case of vasectomy—need to be carefully pondered as possible hazards. Sterilization should be considered an irreversible procedure; there is, given the present state of medical knowledge, no assurance that such operations can be reversed so as to restore fertility. Circumstances such as the death of a spouse, divorce and remarriage, the death of a child, or changes in one's outlook on childbearing could lead a person to regret a decision to permanently erase his or her fertility. While a case can be made for the moral legitimacy of such operations (in light of the age of the spouses and a large number of children), such procedures should not be lightly considered or encouraged within the Christian community.

RELATED ISSUES

PREMARITAL SEX

When the "pill" became readily available in the early 1960s, there was concern that the widespread availability of such a contraceptive drug would lead to a sharp rise in teen promiscuity. In retrospect, there appears to have been justification for that concern. On any account, premarital sex is very widespread today and is almost taken for granted. The language routinely used in the media and in educational circles makes its own value judgments: teens are no longer "promiscuous," much less engaging in "fornication," but rather have chosen to become "sexually active." Such language is neither neutral nor objective, but implies the legitimacy of sex outside of marriage. "Active" is such a strong and positive word that the "sexually inactive" must be unhealthy or abnormal or "hung up," or so it would seem.

According to Dr. Aaron Hass, supervisor of UCLA's Human Sexuality Clinic, 43 percent of the boys and 31 percent of the girls in the U.S. lose their virginity by age 16.[118] Given the strong social and media pressure in this direction, it is somewhat surprising that the figures are not higher. Teenage girls account for 18 percent of the sexually experienced women in the country, but are responsible for 46 percent of out-of-wedlock births and 31 percent of all abortions.[119] Teen promiscuity clearly constitutes one of our society's major problems.

The biblical teaching on the illicitness of sexual intercourse outside of marriage is clear and unequivocal. The authors of the article on "fornication" in the *Theological Dictionary of the New Testament* conclude that the New Testament is characterized by an "unconditional repudiation of all extra-marital and unnatural intercourse."[120] O. J. Baab, writing in the *Interpreter's Bible Dictionary*, concurs: "In the New Testament the words for 'fornication,' 'to practice fornication,' etc. refer to every kind of sexual intercourse outside of marriage."[121]

These conclusions are easily confirmed by an inspection of representative New Testament texts. No fornicator has any part in the kingdom of God (I Cor. 6:9; although repentance and forgiveness mean a new start, v. 11). Fornication and sexual uncleanness are repeatedly mentioned in the lists of vices the Christian is to avoid (Rom. 1:24-32; I Cor. 5:10f.; 6:9f.; II Cor. 12:20f.; Gal. 5:19-21; Col. 3:5, 8f.). Toleration of the fornicator endangers the spiritual well-being of the church (I Cor. 5:1f.). God's will for the believer is sanctification and sexual purity (I Thess. 4:1-5). The believer is a temple of the Holy Spirit (I Cor. 6:19) and should glorify God in the body (I Cor. 6:20). Problems of sexual immorality are rebuked in the church of Pergamum (Rev. 2:14) and at Thyatira (Rev. 2:20). The author of the Revelation warns that the persistent and unrepentant fornicator is in danger of the second death (Rev. 21:8; 22:15).

Human sexuality within the bounds of marriage is to be an image of the pure and devoted love of Christ for his church (cf. Eph. 5:23-33). Promiscuous intercourse denies the permanence, purity, exclusiveness, and deep commitment that God intended human sexuality in marriage to represent. Promiscuous intercourse separates the unitive and the procreative functions of human sexuality, which God intended to be joined in marriage.

The "sexual revolution" that swept the country during the 1960s is now beginning to encounter problems. "Liberation" has brought in its train new epidemics of sexually transmitted diseases. It has been estimated that as many as twenty million Americans now suffer from recurrent genital herpes, for which there is no known cure.[122] Although this infection generally does not cause death in adults, it can be fatal or cause serious neurological damage in newborn infants.[123]

Dr. Robert W. Kistner, speaking at an annual clinical congress of the American College of Surgeons, noted a striking correlation between the incidence of cervical cancer and promiscuous intercourse. In 1950, women under 25 constituted 30 percent of the total population with cervical cancer, and nearly 93 percent in 1967.[124] According to Kistner, the younger the woman is at first intercourse, the more frequently she engages in the activity, and the greater the number of partners, the higher is her risk of cervical cancer.[125] "About 10 years ago I declared that the pill would not lead to promiscuity. Well, I was wrong," Kistner remarked, commenting on the growing numbers of teenagers in his area who lived communally and had intercourse five or six times a day with multiple partners.[126]

A recent study by the National Center for Health Statistics has documented a disturbing rise of infertility among younger women in the United States. Among women between the ages of 15 and 29 and with one child or no children, the percentage considered medically infertile rose from 6 to 9 percent between 1965 and 1976. The report suggested that one reason for the rise in sterility may be the tripling between 1965 and 1976 in the reported cases of gonorrhea, which can cause sterility.[127]

There are 1-2 million new cases of gonorrhea each year in the United States.[128] In addition each year there are some 4 million new cases of chlamydia, .5-1.0 million cases of pelvic inflammatory disease, and .5 million new cases of genital herpes.[129]

These disturbing trends in American public health confirm the Bible's teaching that those who sow to the flesh will from the flesh reap corruption (Gal. 6:8). Persistent violation by any society of the basic principle of the moral law will eventually reap its consequences. As the modern proverb has it, in the long run, we don't break God's laws; they break us.

History confirms in the life of nations the wisdom of the moral law that is written upon the hearts of all men (Rom. 2:14, 15). The British anthropologist J. D. Unwin concluded, on the basis of a comprehensive study of ancient and modern civilizations, that "the whole of human history does not contain a single instance of a group becoming civilized unless it has become absolutely monogamous, nor is there any example of a group retaining its culture after it has adopted less rigorous customs."[130]

Thus history confirms what the Bible teaches: unless human sexuality is carefully channeled within its proper bounds, the energies of an individual and a society are dissipated, and decline eventually follows. Promiscuous sexual intercourse is contrary to the divine law, can endanger the health and childbearing capacity of the individual, and, when widespread as a societal phenomenon, contributes to the decline of a civilization.

SEX EDUCATION

The controversies over sex education in the public schools and the dispensing of contraceptives to unmarried teenagers by federally funded clinics have made contraception a matter of public policy debate. The drive for comprehensive sex education programs in public schools in the United States began in the late 1960s and was spearheaded by Mary Calderone and the Sex Information and Education Council of the United States (SIECUS), and backed by grants from the Department of Health, Education and Welfare (now Health and Human Services).

Although in public debates the proponents of sex education argued that such programs were necessary to reduce the numbers of illegitimate births and unwanted children, in reality there was a larger agenda at stake. The sex educators saw their programs as the means for bringing about more "enlightened" attitudes toward human sexuality in our society. According to Herbert Otto, editor of *The New Sex Education: The Sex Educator's Resource Book*, "Today, sexuality is seen as an important aspect of healthy personality functioning, as enhancing the quality of life and fostering personal growth, and as contributing to human fulfillment."[131] This new philosophy was to be fostered by the use of sexually explicit films, class discussions, exercises in "values clarification," and presentation of such "alternative lifestyles" as homosexuality, lesbianism, and bisexuality as legitimate options in a pluralistic society. In this context, "values clarification" clearly implied a rejection of the idea that any one code of morals, such as that taught by the Bible, could be considered as finally authoritative.

Leaders in the sex education movement evidently considered themselves more competent than parents and religious leaders to provide this sensitive information to impressionable young minds. Parents, however, generally did not agree. According to a national poll conducted by Yankelovich, Skelly, and White, eight out of ten parents of teenage children felt that it was the responsibility of parents to educate their children about birth control. Only one in ten assigned this responsibility to the schools.[132] The sex educators were creating a supply of a product for which there was little demand.

It has been frequently claimed that sex education programs reduce the number of illegitimate births, but the facts do not support that contention. In Sweden, sex education became compulsory in 1956. Subsequently, the illegitimacy rate, which had been declining, rose for every age group except the oldest group, which had not received the sex education. By 1975, Swedish births out of wedlock amounted to 31 percent of all births, the highest proportion in Europe.[133] Sex education without strong moral teaching was interpreted by many Swedish teenagers as permission from the authorities to engage in premarital sex.

Since 1970, the federal government has expended some $3 billion to promote contraception and "safe sex."[134] As these figures indicate, sex education has been part of a significant growth industry, providing lucrative contracts and income to various consultants, educators, and sex education interest groups.

The results have paralleled the Swedish fiasco. Since the federal government began its contraception program in 1970, unwed pregnancies have increased 87 percent among 15- to 19-year-olds.[135] Abortions among teenagers have increased 67 percent, and unwed births have risen 61 percent.[136]

Susan Roylance, national vice president of United Families of America, in testimony before the Senate Labor and Human Resources Committee, commented that giving federal funds to groups such as Planned Parenthood, who ostensibly want to solve the teenage pregnancy problem, "is like trying to stop a raging forest fire by pouring gasoline on it."[137] Mrs. Roylance presented to the Committee convincing evidence that as family planning expenditures have increased, so has the teen pregnancy rate. The experience of both Sweden and the United States has demonstrated that sex education programs that abandon Judeo-Christian values exacerbate the problem of illegitimacy rather than solve it.

WORLD POPULATION

Concern over world population growth has given strong impetus to the drive for government-funded birth control programs. Such programs not only touch the lives of people in this country, but through the Agency for International Development affect the lives of countless people in the Third World.

Environmentalists such as Professor Paul Ehrlich consider population growth a "cancer" that needs to be "cut out." If necessary, says Ehrlich, the United States government should use its power "to halt the growth of American population."[138] Exactly how this would be done, Ehrlich does not state. Such a perspective seems to assume that population growth is out of control, that population growth inevitably leads to poverty, and that "zero population growth" is a moral necessity.

Recent demographic developments, however, give sufficient reason to reexamine the assumptions of the "ZPG" mentality, which has become so pervasive in our society since the late 1960s. A case can now be made, especially in our own country, for the *benefits* of population growth.

In the developing nations, fertility rates are declining at a dramatic rate, according to a comprehensive study funded by the United Nations and the U.S. Agency for International Development. Dr. Phyllis Pietrow, director of the Population Information Program at the Johns Hopkins University, stated that the survey showed that "there is a demographic revolution—birth rates are coming down much faster than anyone expected."[139]

Earlier predictions of a planet suffocating with "wall-to-wall people" and endangered by imminent, massive starvation are now seen to have been overdrawn. According to a study conducted by the Population Reference Bureau, "In the world as a whole, there appears to be enough land and water to meet food demands during the next half century."[140] The problems now appear to be more political in nature, involving questions of distribution, rather than of the physical exhaustion of resources because of overpopulation.

Here in the United States, the postwar "baby boom" has turned into the "baby bust." U.S. fertility rates have been trending generally downward since 1800, but the process began accelerating in 1921. During the 1950s the fertility rate for American couples reached a high point for the century, 3.8 children per woman, but then began to decline dramatically. By 1976, the nation's bicentennial, the fertility rate had plummeted to fewer than 1.8 births per woman, the lowest level in American history.[141] As of 1982, the rate was hovering around 1.9, still well below the replacement rate of 2.2.[142]

Given present attitudes among American women concerning childbirth, it does not seem likely that the low fertility rates that have characterized the past few decades will be dramatically reversed. A June 1980 census study found that young single women expected to bear an average of only 1.8 children, and as many as 21.4 percent said they expected to have no children at all.[143] According to Professor Charles Westoff of Princeton, "Unless there is a radical change in the attitude toward big families, which I don't see now, the prospects are for a continuing low degree of fertility."[144]

The reality of the "baby bust" has serious social and economic implications for America's future. Declining fertility rates are producing a rapidly aging population. Between 1980 and 1990 the 15- 19-year-old age group shrank by 14 percent; during this same period, the number of those 65 and older increased by 21 percent.[145]

The "graying of America" has ominous implications for the Social Security system. As an editorial in the *Wall Street Journal* put it, "In 30 years or so, the baby boom bulge will start trading in its Perrier for Geritol."[146] In 1950 the ratio of workers paying into the system to retirees drawing benefits was 16 to 1. Today the ratio is 3.5 to 1. By the time the baby boom generation is ready to retire, the ratio will be down to 2 to 1. Increasingly heavy tax burdens will be placed on younger workers to keep the system solvent. Heavier tax burdens are a sure-fire recipe for social conflict. According to Professor Peter Drucker, an astute observer of social trends, "The conflict between older and younger people, rather than between management and labor, will be the central social conflict of the next 50 years."[147]

The aging of the American population has serious implications not only for the Social Security retirement system, but also for Medicaid and Medicare. Older people tend to require more medical care than do the young, and with a higher proportion of older people in the population, that means greater medical costs for the society as a whole. The problem is exacerbated by both increasing lifespans and the high costs of "high-tech" medical care.

Present demographic trends could also have an adverse impact on the labor market. The retirement age group is growing at a rate almost four times that of the population as a whole. More and more workers will be leaving the employment "pipeline" at the retirement end, and fewer will be entering employment. Beginning in 1983, each successive graduating class was expected to be 2 to 3 percent smaller than the previous one, while retirement losses were expected to grow at 6 percent a year.[148] Shortages of younger skilled workers for entry-level positions were considered likely as a result.

The shrinking number of young people aged 15-24 also has serious implications for the armed forces. As an article in *The Futurist* notes, "With lower unemployment and higher wages in store for the baby-bust cohort, the armed forces will find it even more difficult to attract and retain recruits in the coming years."[149] In order to maintain the armed forces at their present levels, either higher salaries will be needed, which would imply higher taxes, or else the idea of an all-volunteer armed forces would have to be reconsidered. Neither idea is socially appealing or politically popular.

These considerations relative to Social Security, health care, the labor force, and the armed forces show that higher fertility rates, which would slow the trends toward an aging population, could have positive social benefits. The "baby bust," rather than a "population explosion," is America's real population problem.

There is a widely held misconception that population growth and high population densities inevitably lead to poverty, pollution, and crime. An examination of selected nations around the world will show that this assumption is simplistic at best, and utterly false at worst. The Netherlands, for example, has a population density *seventeen times* that of the United States: 1,002 persons per square mile versus 64 persons per square mile.[150] Yet it is obvious that the people of the Netherlands enjoy a very high quality of life. On the other hand, Afghanistan, with a population density of 56 persons per square mile, though lower than that of the United States, has a far lower standard of living.

It is simply not the case that high population density leads to poverty, and low population densities lead to prosperity. The issues are far more complex: social values, religious traditions, attitudes toward work, educational levels, and technological sophistication have a far greater impact on per capita income than does population density.

South Korea, with a population density of 973 per square mile, almost twice that of India (519), has at the same time a higher per capita income. South Korea has in fact become one of the world's leading producers of black-and-white television sets. Highly populated societies such as Singapore, Taiwan, and Hong Kong are becoming leaders in the world of high-tech manufacturing. Their energetic, hardworking populations are an asset in labor-intensive and knowledge-intensive fields.

Demographic experts are now beginning to give greater recognition to the positive long-range benefits of population growth. As Professor Julian Simon of the University of Illinois has stated, "People bring not only mouths and hands into the world but also heads and brains."[151] Additional persons can be the source of technological advance by "inventing, adapting, and diffusing new productive knowledge."[152] Japan is a good case in point. Japan's high population density (810 per square mile), over twelve times that of the United States, is an asset rather than a liability in the new high-tech world of the information age. Japan's educated, highly energetic people are a real asset in its drive to become the world leader in the "fifth generation" of "supercomputers" and machines that display artificial intelligence.[153]

Population growth can create new business opportunities and markets and can facilitate change. Such growth makes expansion investments more attractive by reducing risks and increasing the total demand for goods and services. Larger populations lead to economies of scale that make large social investments such as highways, bridges, railroads, irrigation systems, and ports less expensive on a per-person basis.[154]

These considerations mean that Christians who have larger families, and who raise their children well, are making a contribution of great significance to both society and the kingdom of God. Such Christian families produce young people of character and diligence who will contribute to the solution of the difficult problems facing the Social Security system and other facets of American life. Christians who have larger families are also contributing to the expansion of God's kingdom in the world. Humanists who consistently practice the "ZPG" philosophy are literally breeding themselves out of existence. Christians, on the other hand, who have a philosophy of positive population growth, will, under the blessing of God, achieve a position of cultural dominance over the course of several generations. American evangelicals are quite aware—at least in principle—of the biblical mandate for the Great Commission (Matt. 28:19-20). They need to rediscover the relevance of the Cultural Mandate to "be fruitful and multiply" (Gen. 1:28). God wants his kingdom to expand through evangelism and through the raising up of a godly seed (Mal. 2:15).

CHAPTER 3

Reproductive Technologies

"Oh, this is a crushing blow, to be left out of this sperm bank. I felt badly enough when I only made it into President Nixon's second enemies list." That was the reaction of biologist George Wald of Harvard, winner of the Nobel Prize in 1967, when he was informed that he had not been invited to contribute to the Repository for Germinal Choice, the so-called Nobel sperm bank established by California businessman Robert K. Graham.[1] Graham said that he was merely fulfilling the dream of the geneticist Hermann Muller, a 1946 Nobel Prize winner, who had advocated the storage of the sperm of brilliant men in order that carefully selected women might later have the opportunity of producing "superior" children.[2]

Responses to the creation of a Nobel sperm bank have been very mixed. Many have seen in such developments steppingstones toward the world of *1984* or *Brave New World*. Noted Fr. Richard McCormick, Professor of Christian Ethics at Georgetown University, "When we do that we turn ourselves into shoppers and our children into purchases. A people that does that is on its way to doing a lot more that civilized people ought not to do."[3]

ARTIFICIAL INSEMINATION

The Nobel sperm bank is one of the more flamboyant examples of the use of artificial insemination, a reproductive technology that has come into widespread use in the United States in the twentieth century, and especially in the last decade. It has been estimated that there are more than 250,000 people in this country whose lives began through the use of this technique.[4] Each year some 15,000-20,000 babies are said to be conceived in the United States through artificial insemination.[5] Exact figures are difficult to obtain, since the whole procedure is usually veiled in secrecy.

There are at least a dozen commercial sperm banks operating around the country, which buy, sell, and store frozen sperm, in addition to many others associated with universities and fertility clinics. The largest of these businesses is Idant in New York City, where more than 30,000 vials of frozen sperm from more than 3,000 men are in storage.[6]

According to an article in *Advertising Age,* two commercial sperm banks fill over 100 orders per month, and one is preparing to market sperm directly to consumers. In the near future it is quite possible that do-it-yourself "home insemination kits" could be available for purchase off the shelf.[7]

Discussions of artificial insemination usually distinguish between artificial insemination by husband (AIH) and artificial insemination by donor (AID). It is the latter practice that raises the most acute ethical questions. Some observers have noted that the term "donor" is something of a misnomer, inasmuch as the typical "donor" is not donating his sperm at all, but rather selling it to a commercial firm for $25 or so per sample. One young graduate student at UCLA, for example, earned $50 every week by stopping by at the Southern California Cryobank twice a week in order to masturbate and sell two samples of his sperm. Says "Gregg," (not his real name), "Without sounding too conceited, I'm healthy. I'm intelligent. I have good genes, and I'd like to pass them along."[8]

The demand for artificial insemination has been increasing in recent years for a number of reasons. Because of legalized abortion and declining levels of fertility, as well as a growing tendency of unwed mothers to keep their children, there has been a shrinking supply of babies for adoption. Couples with fertility problems are increasingly turning to other means. In 1970, for example, the state of California had some 5,500 babies under six months of age up for adoption through its various agencies. In 1978, the number was only 818.[9]

Another significant factor in the increasing demand for AID is the increase in male infertility. It is estimated that one man in ten in the United States is sterile. Fifty to one hundred million sperm cells per cubic centimeter of semen was common among healthy American males fifteen years ago; today the figure may be about half that.[10] Various reasons for this decline have been suggested, including environmental factors such as the increasing use of pesticides, chemicals in food, and heightened levels of stress, but the exact cause or causes are not known.

Many of the increasing number of American men who are choosing vasectomy as a means of permanent birth control are also choosing to take out "insurance" in the form of a deposit of their sperm in a commercial sperm bank. It is their hope that should their marital status or attitude toward procreation change, their frozen semen could be used to generate new human life.

A new twist in the artificial insemination scene was introduced by the opening of a "feminist sperm bank" in October of 1982 in Oakland, California. Opened as the latest program of the ten-year-old Feminist Women's Health Center, the sperm bank offers artificial insemination not only to married couples, but to "a broader group of women" as well. Said Barbara Raboy, assistant director of the center, "This is the first program that is really geared toward different populations, including lesbians."[11] According to the director of the sperm bank, Laure Brown, "Women are not only going to control their bodies through abortions, but they will also be able to control when they have children."[12] Raboy stated that of the first 300 inquiries received by the bank, about one-third were interested in artificial insemination for medical reasons, while the vast majority were interested for reasons of "lifestyle and sexual preference."[13] Of the women in the latter category, about half were heterosexuals without partners and half were lesbians.

Studies of the practice of artificial insemination at the national level suggest that the use of AID by unmarried women is not limited to California. A 1977 survey of 379 physicians who performed AID disclosed that 10 percent of the cases involved single women.[14] "Five years ago, an unmarried patient requesting insemination was unheard of," stated Dr. Jaroslav Marik, director of the Tyler Medical Clinic in Los Angeles. "Now we do have some coming in. We have no policy of refusing or accepting them. It depends on the situation."[15]

An unmarried mother who gave birth to a healthy 7-pound, 2-ounce baby boy in Milwaukee in April of 1982 said that she had chosen artificial insemination because she didn't want a man in her life and she didn't like the idea of a casual sexual encounter. "It's not fair to the baby," she was quoted as saying. "I'm not going to run out and find someone real quick because my time for being fertile is running out."[16]

Lesbians whose requests for artificial insemination have been refused by physicians have turned to feminist or homosexual organizations such as the one in Oakland or others elsewhere in the United States. According to Linda Gryczan of the Lesbian Mothers' Defense Fund in Seattle, "We've had gay men call and offer to be donors. . . . When the father is gay, he may act as coparent. The child may live sometimes with the man and sometimes with the woman and another party not biologically involved."[17]

THE HISTORY OF ARTIFICIAL INSEMINATION

The history of artificial insemination dates back to the latter part of the eighteenth century in the case of humans, and possibly as far back as the fourteenth century for animals. It is said that Arabian horse breeders in the fourteenth century successfully inseminated a mare with the semen of a stallion.[18] In 1776 the Italian priest and biologist Lazzaro Spallanzani succeeded in producing tadpoles by pouring semen on the eggs of a frog.[19] Spallanzani performed the experiment to disprove ideas that were then current concerning sexual reproduction. It was believed that flies and worms arose through spontaneous generation from decaying matter; that birds and reptiles were generated from the eggs of the female alone; and that the higher animals were produced by the male semen, incubated in the female. Four years after his experiments with frogs, Spallanzani successfully artificially inseminated a dog.[20]

The first successful experiment in human artificial insemination was performed by an English surgeon, John Hunter, in 1790.[21] An American, Marion Sims, performed such an insemination in 1866, but was forced to abandon the practice because of the public outcry it produced.[22]

Artificial insemination techniques for horses, cattle, sheep, and pigs were refined in Russia during the first decades of the twentieth century. Such techniques have become commonplace since the 1930s. In Denmark about 95 percent of the dairy cattle are produced in this way, and in England and Wales about 70 percent.[23] In the United States it is about 65 or 70 percent.[24]

The use of artificial insemination in animal breeding achieved a new plateau with the discovery in 1949 that semen could be frozen for storage and easily transported in this form. It has led to superior stocks and increased productivity. The semen from one superior bull can be used to inseminate thousands of dairy cattle. According to William M. Durfee of the National Association of Animal Breeders in Columbia, Maryland, the number of dairy cattle "has actually declined, but . . . we now produce as much milk as we did 25 years ago, with half as many cattle."[25] Such artificial insemination techniques hold considerable promise for increasing milk and meat production in the developing nations. Whether such technologies should be extended to human beings in order to produce "superior stocks" is, of course, an entirely different question and continues to generate much debate both in scientific circles and in the public at large.

MEDICAL CONSIDERATIONS

While the ethical ramifications of artificial insemination are complex, especially insemination by donor, medically it is a simple procedure. The ejaculate, usually obtained by masturbation, is placed in a syringe, inserted into the vagina, and squirted in the direction of the uterus as close as possible to the time of ovulation. The success rate for this procedure commonly ranges from 50 to 60 percent.[26]

The desire for artificial insemination can arise from a number of medical considerations. A woman's inability to conceive through normal sexual intercourse may result from vaginal tumors, scarring of the vagina, an abnormal position of the uterus, a small cervical opening, or obesity. A man's impotence, malformed penis, low sperm count, or obesity may hinder the normal reproductive process.[27] In a significant number of cases couples request artificial insemination by donor when it is known that the man is a carrier of a genetically transmitted disease such as hemophilia, cystic fibrosis, Huntington's chorea, or certain forms of muscular dystrophy.[28]

In recent years the use of frozen sperm has become more common in the insemination procedure. Dr. Armand M. Karow, Jr., of the Medical College of Georgia, speaking at a 1979 meeting of the American Association for the Advancement of Science, estimated that 10-20 percent of all inseminations now make use of frozen sperm.[29] Karrow was quoted as saying that "if you can bake a cake, you can freeze donor sperm. . . . It's exceptionally simple if you just follow the recipe."[30] The sperm is treated with glycerol to protect it, placed in plastic straws, and then immersed in a liquid nitrogen bath at –196 degrees centigrade.

The frozen sperm can be tested for genetic defects and contagious diseases that could harm either the mother or the child. According to Dr. Karrow, "Artificial insemination with thawed semen results in far fewer miscarriages and in fewer birth defects than one finds in the general population."[31]

The increasingly common use of vasectomy as a birth-control measure has led a growing number of men to regard sperm banks as a form of "fertility insurance." Dr. Alan Guttmacher of Planned Parenthood has issued some cautionary advice in this regard. "I am less sanguine than others about the storage of pre-vasectomy specimens," he noted. "In some cases, it would act as a psychic crutch and persuade immature or poorly motivated individuals to undergo a procedure for which they are poor candidates."[32]

A number of studies have examined the possible impact of artificial insemination on sex ratios—the relative numbers of male and female births. One British study, based on combined data from the United States and several European countries, found that artificial insemination with fresh semen significantly increased the prevalence of male births to 57.7 percent, whereas insemination with frozen semen decreased it to 49.7 percent.[33] The normal rate of male births is 51.1 percent.

Few medical complications arising from artificial insemination have been reported in the literature. There has been some concern, however, that donor insemination could in some cases be implicated in the transmission of venereal disease.[34] According to Dr. Herbert W. Horne, Jr. the transmission of disease through donor sperm may be more of a problem than the literature suggests and may be a contributing factor in the increase in spontaneous abortions he has observed among his own AID patients.[35]

Questions have also been raised about the psychological impact of AID upon the couple, especially the man, and upon the child conceived in this fashion. Horne notes that "unjustified A.I.D. can lead to unhappiness on the part of the husband and may negatively affect the marriage as well as the husband's relationship with the child."[36] Further study of the long-range impact of AID on all involved is certainly needed. "Until 25 years have passed and the treated couples and at least some of their artificially induced offspring have been questioned, the rightness or wrongness of A.I.D. will not become clear," concludes Horne.[37]

A nationwide study based on responses from 379 physicians who practiced AID raised serious questions about the lack of uniform standards in this area. Screening of potential donors was somewhat haphazard, and some of the physicians displayed a rather poor knowledge of genetics. Most of the physicians surveyed did not keep accurate records of the donors, recipients, or offspring, which made it difficult to gather reliable information for future studies. One respondent reported that he had used the same donor in more than 50 pregnancies, raising the small but nevertheless real possibility of unwitting incestuous marriages in the future.[38]

LEGAL IMPLICATIONS OF ARTIFICIAL INSEMINATION BY DONOR

As with other modern reproductive technologies, artificial insemination raises many complex legal questions, many of which remain unresolved. The legal trend in the United States today is to recognize as legitimate a child conceived through AID when the mother's husband has given consent to the procedure. Oklahoma's 1967 law was the first such piece of legislation to this effect. As of 1981, 20 other states—Alaska, Arkansas, California, Colorado, Connecticut, Florida, Georgia, Kansas, Louisiana, Maryland, Michigan, Montana, New York, North Carolina, Oregon, Tennessee, Texas, Virginia, Washington, and Wyoming— had passed similar legislation.[39]

These laws reflect the changing moral climate of our society. In a 1921 case in Ontario, Canada, *Orford v. Orford,* Justice John F. Orde held that the mother of an AID child was guilty of adultery.[40]

While state legislatures are recognizing AID children as legitimate, much legal ambiguity remains in this entire area. Do single women have a "right" to AID, as an implication of the so-called "right of privacy"? Are physicians liable for medical malpractice should the child be born with a serious birth defect? Should states impose stringent requirements for the screening of sperm donors? These are only some of the unresolved legal dilemmas that arise in relation to AID.

In 1980 Professor Jeffrey Shaman observed that it would be only a matter of time until "AID children begin to file lawsuits claiming the right to know the identity of their biological fathers, the donors of semen for AID."[41] One such person is Suzanne Rubin of Southern California, born in 1950 as a result of AID. She is now searching for her biological father, because she wants to ask him "why he was so casual about fathering children."[42] Rubin felt betrayed and angry when she discovered that her "father" was a $25 vial of sperm. She believes that AID children, like those who are adopted, should be told the truth about their biological beginnings. In her case, she sensed as a child that her parents were keeping an "ugly, unspeakable secret," and she believes that the deceptions involved "warped the [family] relationships and poisoned them beyond repair."[43] The plight of Suzanne Rubin is likely to become more common during the years ahead as a generation of AID children come of age and seek to know the truth of their own biological origins.

THE MORAL DIMENSION

As with other issues involving human procreation, an ethical analysis of the nature of artificial insemination transcends medical and legal considerations alone, although these factors are essential and must be taken into account. From a Christian perspective, an analysis of the morality of artificial insemination must take seriously the divine purpose for human sexuality and the institution of marriage. This *personal* dimension must be given a central place in the discussion; otherwise the generation of human life is placed on the same level as animal husbandry merely because the technical possibilities are similar.

According to official Roman Catholic teaching, both AIH and AID are morally illicit. Pope Pius XII, in an address to the Fourth International Convention of Catholic Physicians in October of 1949, stated in reference to artificial insemination outside of marriage that "the natural law and the divine law are such that the procreation of a new life may only be the fruit of marriage."[44] A child conceived by such means would be illegitimate.

With respect to the use of AID within marriage, Pius XII went on to say that it was likewise illicit, inasmuch as "only marriage partners have mutual rights over their bodies for the procreation of a new life, and these rights are exclusive, nontransferable, and inalienable."[45]

Even the use of AIH within marriage is illicit, since it is wrong to use unnatural means to achieve a worthy end. Moreover, Pius XII went on to state, "It is superfluous to indicate that the active element can never be lawfully obtained by acts that are contrary to nature." AIH thus is illicit according to official Roman Catholic teaching because it is not the expression of the natural conjugal act between the husband and the wife, and because it involves an act of masturbation.

In recent years some Roman Catholic theologians have argued for the legitimacy of AIH. Roger Van Allen, for example, has argued that masturbation, when undertaken by a husband "out of necessity for the artificial insemination of his wife, when viewed as a human action rather than a biological occurrence, can lose its character of self-abuse and become an unselfish act ordered toward procreation and therefore may be considered licit."[46] Van Allen and other Roman Catholic theologians and ethicists have tended in recent years to move away from the so-called "physicalism" of traditional Catholic ethics toward a more "personalistic" view, which sees the physical act as part of the whole fabric of human relationships.

Protestant opinion on artificial insemination has been diverse. In 1945, a special commission appointed by the archbishop of Canterbury recommended that Parliament pass legislation making AID a criminal offense.[47] In 1957, G. Aiken Taylor, writing in *Christianity Today*, concluded that AID was "intrinsically a breach of marriage."[48] In 1959 a group of British churchmen, in an opinion submitted to the government, concluded that AID could be right under some circumstances, but should only be used as a means of "last resort."[49] The General Assembly of the United Presbyterian Church passed a resolution in 1962 calling upon synods, presbyteries, and individual Presbyterians to work for the passage of "uniform state laws . . . protecting couples and physicians and also the rights of children in cases of artificial insemination involving an anonymous donor."[50]

Joseph Fletcher has been one of the more outspoken proponents of the legitimacy of artificial insemination by donor. Writing in his 1954 book *Morals and Medicine*, Fletcher argued that AID is morally right inasmuch as the fidelity of marriage is a personal bond between husband and wife, rather than a legal relationship; similarly, the parent-child bond is a moral, rather than a merely material or physical one.[51] Marriage is not an absolute sexual monopoly. Christian ethics elevates the meaning of love above the determinism of biological necessity and moralistic legalism.[52] In Fletcher's perspective, AID cannot constitute a form of adultery when both partners freely consent to the use of that technique. "Legalism" must give way to the welfare of persons. If AID contributes to the well-being of persons, then it is morally right, according to Fletcher.

Within evangelical Protestant circles AID has been given a qualified endorsement by Norman Geisler, Professor of Systematic Theology at Dallas Theological Seminary. Geisler concludes that "artificial insemination by mutual consent of married couples does not appear to be a moral evil. Indeed, it could in some cases be a great good."[53] While artificial insemination without the free consent of all the parties involved would be wrong, the practice of AID does not really constitute adultery, according to Geisler, since no act of sexual intercourse is involved. The act of masturbation is wrong insofar as it involves lust or becomes an enslaving habit; neither of these considerations need apply in the case of AID. Geisler also believes that the Old Testament practice of levirate marriage (Deut. 25:5-10), in which a brother was to raise up seed for his deceased brother's wife, provides a biblical precedent for "artificial" insemination. Consequently, according to Geisler, when artificial insemination promotes "complete and whole personhood," it can be morally right, but when it violates either free consent or the intrinsic value of personhood, it is morally wrong.[54]

The German Lutheran theologian Helmut Thielicke addressed the question of artificial insemination in his 1964 book *The Ethics of Sex*. Thielicke concluded that the arguments against AIH are not compelling. Condemning the practice on the grounds that it involves an act of masturbation does not take adequately into account the context and intent of the act, which in this case is to further the bonds of marriage, rather than to subvert them.[55] Neither is the "unnaturalness" of the means employed a compelling objection, since man, as the image of God, is called to subdue and transcend nature, rather than to be simply a part of nature. The practice of medicine in the proper sense involves constant intervention into the "course of nature." The question is not so much whether interventions are ever appropriate, but rather "what are the *limits* and in what *kind* of nature interventions are possible."[56]

Artificial insemination by donor is, however, another matter. The problem "is presented by the fact that here a third person enters into the exclusive psychophysical relationship of the marriage, even though it is only his sperm that 'represents' him."[57] The biological dimension of marriage cannot be split apart from the "personal." The practice of AID introduces a significant imbalance into the relationship, since it involves a fulfillment of motherhood that is not accompanied by a fulfillment of fatherhood and thus "breaks down the personal solidarity of the married couple."[58] Consequently, while AIH can be morally licit, AID is not.

Of the three Protestant ethicists whose positions have been reviewed, it would appear that Thielicke's analysis is most in keeping with the biblical outlook on human sexuality and marriage. While AID does not, strictly speaking, involve an act of adultery, since no act of intercourse is involved, and both husband and wife consent, it nevertheless does involve the intrusion of a third party into the intimacy of the marriage relationship. This intrusion may be effected by rather impersonal means, but nevertheless, the presence of a third party in the marriage is a reality in both the biological and the emotional realms. The biblical understanding of man does not separate the "personal" from the physical, as AID does by its very nature; man in Scripture is a psychophysical whole.

The appeal to Deuteronomy 25:5-10 and the practice of levirate marriage does not really provide a good analogy for the practice of AID.[59] In the case of levirate marriage, it was not merely a case of *inseminating* the deceased brother's wife; actual *marriage* was in view. The levirate custom, unlike AID, did not involve an anonymous "donor" who took no further responsibility for the woman or the child conceived. The practice of levirate marriage took place within the household (v. 5, "when brothers dwell together"), and presupposed the solidarity of the family unit. The similarity of AID and the levirate custom is so remote it is almost nonexistent.

As Thielicke has noted, AID introduces an imbalance into the relationship between the husband and the wife. Her maternal functions have been fulfilled, but his paternal function has not. The AID child remains as a constant reminder of his biological failure, and the shadow of an anonymous third party clouds the relationship. The deception that may be involved concerning the child's true origin—involving the parents and friends, the parents and the child, and the child and the siblings—can introduce unhealthy and even destructive currents into the family relationship, as the case of Suzanne Rubin has demonstrated. AID endangers the one-flesh unity (Gen. 2:24) that God has willed for human marriage. Although artificial insemination by husband can be consistent with the divine outlook on marriage, it must be concluded that artificial insemination by donor is not.

SURROGATE MOTHERS: WOMBS FOR RENT

> Childless couple—wife unable to conceive looking for white female who would volunteer to be artificially inseminated with semen of husband and then give child to couple. All responses confidential. All expenses paid. Kindly direct responses to Noel P. Keane, attorney, 1129 Parklane Towers East, Dearborn, Michigan 48126. (313) 336-9290.

The above classified ad, which appeared in the December 22, 1980 issue of the *Boston Globe,* points to one of the most exotic of recent developments in artificial insemination: surrogate motherhood. According to Lori B. Andrews, a research attorney for the American Bar Foundation, as of 1983 some 60 children had been born to surrogate mothers in the United States, and ten states were considering laws that would legalize the practice.[60] There are currently at least eight for-profit services in this country that for a fee will match infertile couples with potential surrogates.[61]

Dr. Myron Gordon, chairman of the ethics committee of the American College of Obstetricians and Gynecologists sees the phenomenon as a significant social trend, even though it may never involve great numbers of people. "I don't think surrogate mothering will become a major mode of obtaining children," he observed, "but then no one would have predicted five years ago that 100 in vitro fertilization clinics would open up in this country by 1983."[62]

Dr. Richard Levin of Louisville, Kentucky is one obstetrician who has become deeply involved in the surrogate-motherhood business. He has advertised extensively for women to participate in his Louisville Surrogate Parenting Associates. Levin's involvement began during his treatment of an infertile couple. The wife had severe tubal pathology, and had had unsuccessful surgery in New York and Chicago. "After 10 years of battle, of being left hanging, she came to me and asked me 'what can we do?'" related Levin.[63] "I see these people every single day," said Levin. "You get very tired of people sitting on the other side of your desk crying."

In Kentucky, the waiting period for the adoption of a healthy infant, black or white, can be five to seven years.[64] Desperate couples can see in the surrogate-mother option a solution to their dilemma. This solution can be an expensive one, however. According to Levin, the fees for medical costs, the surrogate's fee, hospital expenses, legal fees, and transportation can range from $13,000 to $20,000.[65]

Who are the women who choose to be surrogates, and how does the experience affect them emotionally? "Elizabeth Kane" (a fictitious name) came to Louisville under the auspices of Dr. Levin's surrogate parenting service to be inseminated with the sperm of "Ralph Lansdale." On November 9, 1980, "Neil Ransdale," a healthy 8-pound, 10-ounce boy, was born, the first child known to be born to a paid surrogate under a legal contract with the natural father.[66] Kane has been quoted as saying, "I never think of it as mine. . . . I am simply growing it for him (the natural father)."[67] Kane became such a celebrity that her husband's insurance firm reached the conclusion that the notoriety generated by his wife's actions was not compatible with his continuing employment.[68]

Jacquelyn Burkhart, a nursing student at Portland State University, placed an ad in the newspaper, offering to "rent" her womb to a childless couple for $15,000. She saw this as a good opportunity to help pay her school expenses. "In essence, I am selling a baby," Ms. Burkhart stated, "but I don't feel bad about it. I'm doing someone a service. . . . I'm just growing it for them, renting out—for a high fee—my uterus."[69]

Since she has had fairly easy pregnancies and deliveries, she decided it would be "a fairly easy way to make money." Ms. Burkhart was married at 17 and was divorced from her husband shortly after the birth of her first child, Heidi. After the divorce, she decided that she wanted another child, so she performed artificial insemination on herself using sperm donated by a friend. The result was her second child, Jeffrey.[70]

Some women apparently see surrogate motherhood as a way of atoning for the guilt of having had an abortion. Alice G. responded to an ad in the paper offering $10,000 plus expenses for the services of a surrogate. "I killed a baby," she explained. "Now I can make up for it by giving one to a needy and loving family."[71]

Dr. Philip Parker, Clinical Instructor in Psychiatry at Wayne State University, did a study of 50 respondents to an ad for surrogate mothers. The average age of the respondents was 25; half were married, 25 percent single, and 25 percent divorced; half were Protestant, and half Roman Catholic. More than 40 percent were unemployed or receiving some form of financial assistance such as welfare or Medicaid. Half said they would participate only if a married couple unable to have a child was involved; one sixth, for either a married or an unmarried couple; a sixth, for a single man; and a sixth for anyone for any reason.[72]

Surrogate motherhood is presently in a legal quagmire. Bernard Hirsh, formerly general counsel for the American Medical Association, notes the courts and legislatures "have barely begun to confront even the most elementary of the myriad, complex legal issues raised by new reproductive technologies."[73] Professor George Annas of the Boston University Schools of Medicine and Public Health stated that while there were no state or federal laws dealing with the subject, there were laws that made it a crime to accept payment for placing a child up for adoption. Most surrogate arrangements have involved such payments, and thus would appear to be in violation of the law. On January 26, 1981, the attorney general of Kentucky issued an opinion that Dr. Richard Levin's Surrogate Parenting Associates was violating state law by offering such payments to surrogates.[74]

A committee of the American Medical Association called for study of the issue, noting such potential problems of legal liability as genetic problems, the birth of a deformed child, health complications, or the death of the adopting parents prior to the child's birth.[75] That these problems are not merely theoretical was dramatically demonstrated in the case of Christopher Ray Stiver, a baby born to Judy Stiver of Lansing, Michigan after Alexander Malahoff, a 46-year-old accountant from

Middle Village, New York had agreed to pay $10,000 for the surrogate child produced with his sperm. Young Christopher, unfortunately, was born with an abnormally small head (microcephaly) and the possibility of mental retardation. Malahoff disavowed the child and threatened to sue the Stivers for having intercourse during the insemination period. Blood and tissue tests later showed the child's genetic makeup to be different from Malahoff's. Said Mrs. Stiver after the tests were announced, "I'm probably a little disappointed, but I'll have to live with it."[76]

What happens if the surrogate mother changes her mind and decides to keep the child? Denise Lucy Thrane of Arcadia, California contracted with Mr. and Mrs. James Noyes of Rochester, New York to be artificially inseminated with Mr. Noyes' sperm. She became pregnant in June of 1981 with sperm that had been frozen and flown to Los Angeles from New York. During the sixth or seventh month of her pregnancy, Thrane decided that she wanted to keep the child. A paternity-custody lawsuit then developed, in which the Noyeses attempted to compel Thrane to honor the original agreement.[77]

These cases do not exhaust the list of possible legal complications. If the baby should die prior to birth, could the adoptive parents sue in order to force the surrogate to become pregnant again? What if the surrogate decided to have an abortion? Could the adoptive parents do anything to prevent her? If the father changed his mind, could he then be compelled to give his semen? Could a child born through this process later sue in order to learn the identity of the surrogate mother? At present there are no clear answers to these questions, and those who seek the surrogate option are walking into a legal minefield.

The *moral* considerations relating to surrogate motherhood are similar to those concerning artificial insemination by donor. Surrogate motherhood is almost the "mirror image" of AID, except that the female "donor" sells her ovum, her womb, and her time, whereas the man sells his sperm. If one has concluded that AID is inconsistent with biblical teachings on human sexuality and marriage, then similar conclusions will follow for this practice. In both cases, a third party intrudes both biologically and emotionally into the sanctity of the marriage bond. One marriage partner, but not the other, is biologically fulfilled through the process. In a surrogate arrangement, it is the wife who is reminded by the presence of the surrogate child of her biological inadequacy, while the man's potency is affirmed.

This *asymmetry* in the adoptive parents' relationship to the child is the factor that distinguishes the surrogate case morally from simple adoption. In a normal adoption, both parents bear the same biological relationship to the child—none. The possibilities for tension and conflict that exist in the surrogate arrangement do not arise in the same way.

The problems of secrecy and deception that can surround AID also accompany surrogate motherhood. Should the child be told the truth about his biological origins? If so, when? Does the child have a legal right to know the identity of his biological mother? Should the surrogate tell her family and friends the true circumstances of her pregnancy? Should the adoptive parents tell their family and friends the whole story? The same tensions that can arise from the "unspeakable secret" in the case of AID can arise here as well.

It has been suggested that the case of Sarah and Hagar in Genesis 16 provides a biblical justification for surrogate parenting. When Sarah proved to be infertile, she urged Abraham to have intercourse with her Egyptian maid Hagar. According to the custom of the time, the child to be born of Hagar would legally be reckoned as Sarah's. Abraham took his wife's advice, and in due course Ishmael was born (Gen. 16:1-6).

Under closer examination, however, it can be seen that this account does not really provide a moral justification for the current practice of surrogate motherhood. It should first be observed, as a general principle, that not all practices *described* by Scripture are thereby *endorsed* by Scripture as moral ideals. Solomon had many wives, but that constitutes no endorsement of polygamy; monogamy is clearly the divine standard. In a fallen world, God has tolerated certain practices, such as polygamy and slavery, which, from the larger context of Scripture, can clearly be seen as falling short of the divine ideal. The precepts and commands of Scripture have priority over the narrative passages in discerning the moral law.

In the more immediate context of Genesis, it is evident that Abraham erred in following Sarah's suggestion. God had promised him a son, but his impatience and the weakness of his faith led him to "take matters into his own hands" in an attempt to bring about the fulfillment of the promise in a purely natural way. The birth of Ishmael led to strife and envy between Sarah and Hagar (16:4), and the descendants of Ishmael—the Arabs of the present day—proved to be the constant antagonists of the covenant people. In the larger context of the Abrahamic narrative, then, it seems evident that the passage teaches not the moral propriety of surrogate arrangements, but Abraham's foolishness to participate in such a practice. It should also be noted that Hagar was part of the household, and legally under the authority of Abraham; such is not the case with modern-day surrogates.

Then also, surrogate arrangements bring mercenary considerations into the generation of human life. That may not seem problematic when the child is born healthy, but the case of the unfortunate Christopher Stiver brings the problems to light. From the time of his birth on January 10, 1983, Christopher was regarded "as a piece of inferior merchandise, an imperfect creature come into the world as damaged goods," observed Roger Rosenblatt.[78] Surrogate parenting can degenerate into commerce in human souls, and that, among other reasons, is sufficient to make it an illegitimate solution to one's infertility.

SEX SELECTION

"I explain that we're not guaranteeing anything," says Dr. Ferdinand Beernink of the East Bay Fertility Ob-Gyn Medical Group in Berkeley, California. "And I tell them that, at worst, their chances of having a boy are 50-50 but that we are confident there is some gain over that." This is the counsel given to parents who come to the clinic in hopes that new prenatal sex-selection techniques will help to fulfill their desire to have a boy in the family.[79]

Beernink uses a technique developed by reproductive physiologist Dr. Ronald Ericsson, based on the ability of the sperm bearing Y chromosomes to swim faster than the X-bearing sperm. The female egg always carries an X chromosome; if it is fertilized by an X sperm, a girl results; if by a Y sperm, a boy is conceived. Ericsson's technique involves placing drops of semen onto a solution of albumin, a dense fluid found in blood plasma. By allowing the sperm to swim through several layers of albumin "screens," the proportion of faster-swimming Y sperm is increased to 75 percent, giving the couple three out of four chances of having a boy.[80]

Techniques such as Ericsson's, which take the technology of artificial insemination one step further, have brought closer to reality the age-old desire of many parents to have some control over the sex of their children. In the fifth century B.C. the Greek philosopher Parmenides suggested that wives who wanted boys should lie on their right side after intercourse. An old German folk tradition recommended that men take an ax along to bed in order to produce males, and that the ax be left in the woodshed if a girl was desired.[81] Such recommendations remained strictly in the realm of folklore, of course, since detailed knowledge of the physiology of human reproduction dates only from the nineteenth century.

During the 1960s Dr. Landrum B. Shettles of the Columbia University College of Physicians and Surgeons, noting the difference in swimming speeds of X- and Y-bearing sperm, suggested that the timing of intercourse relative to the moment of ovulation could influence sex determinations. Shettles hypothesized that if intercourse was timed shortly after ovulation, when the egg was still high in the Fallopian tube, there would be a greater probability that the faster-swimming Y sperm would reach the egg first, and consequently produce a boy. Shettles' hypothesis has received some confirmation through the work of a Polish physician, Dr. Franciszek Benendo. Based on his studies of the experience of 322 couples, Benendo concluded that if ovulation occurred before or within a day of intercourse, the birth of a boy was favored, while if ovulation occurred three or more days following intercourse, the birth of a girl was more likely.[82] The implication of this research is that couples desiring the birth of a boy might choose to have intercourse as near to the time of ovulation as possible. The moment of ovulation is signaled by a slight but measurable rise in the woman's body temperature.

The technique of *amniocentesis* has been seen by some couples as a method of sex selection. Amniocentesis involves removing a sample of the amniotic fluid by means of a hypodermic syringe inserted through the abdominal wall, and then subjecting the sample to genetic analysis. Some women, after learning the sex of their unborn children in this manner, have chosen abortion as a solution to the problem of the "wrong" sex.[83] Needless to say, this is not a legitimate option for the Christian. Amniocentesis followed by abortion destroys a human life already in existence; the other techniques attempt to influence the circumstances of conception of a life not yet in existence.

Research on sex selection is also receiving considerable attention in the area of animal breeding. One research group at the University of Kentucky has succeeded in changing the normal 50-50 ratio in rabbit litters to 75 percent female. Similar efforts are being made with cattle, but thus far with less success.[84]

Researchers in animal studies have taken two approaches to the matter of sex selection. One approach involves the separation of X- and Y-bearing sperm—a technique parallel to that used for humans. Another method involves the identification of the sex of the animal embryo after fertilization, and discarding the embryos of the undesired sex. Farmers, for example, generally prefer milk-producing cows to grain-consuming bulls. Chicken farmers prefer hens, and mink farmers prefer males for their better pelts. According to Dr. Robert Foote of Cornell University, such sex selection techniques could "considerably improve the production of eggs, milk, and meat."[85] Discarding *human* embryos is, of course, another matter indeed. As a form of abortion, it would be ethically unacceptable.

While techniques presently in use for human sex selection favor male births, new research in Japan may soon give parents the option of selecting either a girl or a boy. Dr. Rihachi Iizuka and other researchers at the universities of Kyoto and Tokyo observed that the X- and Y-bearing sperm carry slightly different electrical charges. By introducing the sperm into cultures with varying electrical charges, the Japanese scientists have been able to separate the female-producing X chromosomes with 100 percent effectiveness and the male-producing Y chromosomes with 85 percent effectiveness. Iizuka suggested that the new techniques might be ready for use by human subjects within two to three years.[86]

The technology for sex selection is already on the scene and is being improved in its efficiency and accuracy; moral reflection on the matter, however, is still in a very rudimentary state. According to Professor Roberta Steinbacher of Cleveland State University, speaking at a symposium sponsored by the American Association for the Advancement of Science, "It is clear the sex-selection research has far outdistanced serious discussions of its ethical, social, legal and demographic implications."[87]

At the personal level, it would seem that such techniques are a legitimate extension of the moral argument for the proper use of contraception. Men and women as the image bearers of God have the responsibility to exercise their procreative powers for the glory of God and the advancement of his kingdom, and this includes exercising those powers in the light of rational planning and forethought. This right of dominion would extend to the choice of seeking a desired gender balance within the family. Some qualifications are in order, however. It is clear that some selection techniques—specifically, amniocentesis followed by abortion—are not morally acceptable. This "search and destroy" mentality is not consistent with the Bible's teaching on the value and sanctity of human life. And parents should be prepared to accept in love the birth of a child not of the desired sex, given the fallibility of all human means. Such an attitude recognizes that in the last analysis God is sovereign in such areas. Furthermore, parents should recognize the present experimental nature of such techniques. No long-range studies exist that show that such techniques do not, for example, increase the incidence of birth defects. While no data clearly indicate such risks, the burden of proof rests on the advocates of the new reproductive technology to give *positive evidence* of its safety. Parents who seize the existing technical possibilities in the absence of definitive studies showing their safety must be prepared to bear the possible consequences.

At the societal level, there are other possible problems to be considered. Some scholars have expressed concern that an imbalance of males stemming from widespread use of such technologies could lead to serious social problems. Dr. Hans Zeisel, Professor of Law and Sociology at the University of Chicago, foresees "more homosexuality, more adultery, more rape, more crime in general—altogether a profound conflict between individual whims and the interests of a healthy society."[88] Studies during the last 30 years have disclosed a parental preference for sons, both in the United States and in the developing countries.

On the other hand, other researchers have noted that societies have had gender imbalances in the past without serious adverse consequences. Washington, D.C. has a significant preponderance of females, and Alaska a significant preponderance of males. Research conducted by Charles F. Westoff of Princeton and Ronald Rindfuss of the University of Wisconsin, based on interviews with 5,981 married women, found that wide use of sex selection would, during the first several years, lead to an imbalance favoring men. This would be followed, however, according to their calculations, by a wave of female births to achieve balance, and such oscillations would continue until the sex ratio returned to what it is at present.[89]

So in reference to balance, it would not appear that societal considerations present compelling arguments against sex selection techniques.[90] Christian parents would be advised, however, to approach this entire area with great caution, inasmuch as conclusive information regarding the long-term safety of such methods is not yet available.

IN VITRO FERTILIZATION

"We've got some beautiful eggs," said Dr. Georgeanna Jones, after a successful recovery of human ova from the ovaries of a patient at the in vitro fertilization clinic at the Eastern Virginia Medical School in Norfolk.[91] The clinic in Norfolk was the first among many such clinics to begin operation in the United States.[92] There are currently about 250 in vitro fertilization clinics in the United States, up from only 30 in 1985, and the treatment of infertility is now a $1 billion business in America.[93]

Louise Brown of Oldham, England, was the world's first in vitro baby, born on July 25, 1978. Fertilized in a petri dish and implanted as an embryo into her mother's womb, Louise was born after 100 unsuccessful implantations by Drs. Patrick Steptoe and Robert G. Edwards. In an early stage of the research, human embryos were placed in rabbit oviducts in an attempt to find an environment conducive to the early stages of an embryo's cell division.[94]

In vitro fertilization of a human egg is a fairly recent idea, apparently first achieved by Edwards, Steptoe, and Bavister in 1969. Only nine years later did the first live birth occur as a result of this process.[95] Research on in vitro fertilization with marine animals dates back to 1893, but the first unequivocal success in fertilizing an animal's egg outside its natural environment was achieved with rabbits in 1959.[96] It has only been in the last several decades that a detailed knowledge of the hormonal factors that govern human ovulation and implantation of the fertilized egg in the uterus, and of the complex biochemistry of the culture medium needed to support cell division of the human embryo, has been available to researchers. Without this knowledge, successful births from the in vitro process were not a realistic possibility.

The widespread public interest in "test tube" fertilizations may in part be a reflection of increasing levels of infertility among American couples of childbearing age. According to Dr. Ralph Dougherty, Professor of Chemistry at Florida State University, during the last 50 years the sperm count of American males has fallen 30 percent, from 90 million sperm per cubic centimeter to 65 million per cubic centimeter. Possibly more than 10 percent of American men have sperm counts low enough to make them "functionally sterile."[97]

Infertility is on the rise among American women as well. "Because more young women are having sex with a variety of partners and sustaining low-level gynecological infections that may go untreated and damage the reproductive system," says Professor Robert T. Francoeur of Fairleigh Dickinson University, "as many as one in four women between the ages of 20 and 35 are now infertile."[98] It would be wrong to assume that women who seek in vitro fertilization have been sexually promiscuous, since infertility can be caused by a very broad range of physiological conditions. Nevertheless, the increasing incidence of sexually transmitted diseases is contributing to a noticeable rise in female infertility in this country.

According to a study by the National Center for Health Statistics, there appear to be about 4.3 million women of childbearing age who are infertile for one reason or another, and at least 2 million of these women would like to have children.[99] These figures suggest that Francoeur's figures may overstate the problem, but infertility nevertheless remains a serious social and medical problem. As a result, many childless couples are seeking "state of the art" solutions such as in vitro fertilization.

THE MEDICAL TECHNOLOGY

In vitro fertilization (IVF) has most commonly been resorted to when the woman's Fallopian tubes are blocked or damaged, thus making impossible the normal passage of the egg from the ovaries to the place of fertilization. IVF has also been used when artificial insemination has been unsuccessful in producing pregnancy during a twelve month period, and when infertility resulting from unknown causes has persisted for four or more years.[100]

According to Dr. Howard Jones and his associates at the Norfolk clinic, IVF not only has proved to be a helpful technique in the treatment of infertility, but promises to be a source of valuable scientific information about human reproduction. Jones expects that new knowledge concerning the details of the maturation of the human egg in the ovaries, the nature of the egg-sperm interaction during fertilization, and the early cleavage of the human embryo will be derived from IVF operations.[101]

The woman's egg is recovered through the use of a laparoscope, a small telescope inserted into the abdominal cavity through a small incision in the abdominal wall. This fiber optics device allows the physician to inspect visually the internal organs and to carefully harvest the eggs. Although under normal conditions only one ovum matures during a given menstrual cycle, fertility hormones are usually administered as part of the IVF process in order to induce "superovulation." Thus several eggs are available for fertilization in vitro.[102]

During the harvesting process, it is not simply a matter of finding and removing the ova without physical damage, but of removing them at the proper time as well. If the removal is done too soon, the eggs may be immature and incapable of normal fertilization. But if the physician waits too long, spontaneous ovulation may occur and the eggs may be lost somewhere in the abdominal cavity.[103]

As the egg is being removed, some of the fluids that normally surround it are inevitably lost. Thus, notes Dr. Gary Hodgen, a researcher at the National Institutes of Health, "Essential biochemical interactions occurring within the gamete and surrounding ovarian support-cells may be interrupted."[104]

A fresh semen sample is obtained by masturbation approximately ninety minutes before the fertilization is to be attempted. The sperm sample is washed and centrifuged in a culture medium in order to concentrate the sperm for insemination. After the eggs have been cultured for five or six hours in the laboratory in order to provide additional time for maturation, the fertilization is actually done in a petri dish. After fertilization has occurred, embryonic cell division takes place in the laboratory culture medium designed to duplicate natural conditions. But, notes Dr. Hodgen, "Though certain media and in vitro conditions may be superior to others in supporting embryonic cleavage, none is able to replicate satisfactorily that provided by nature—the female reproductive system."[105]

The embryo or embryos are then implanted into the uterine cavity with a slender teflon catheter passed through the neck of the uterus. The researchers at the Norfolk clinic have reported pregnancy rates of 20 percent with single-embryo implants, 27 percent with double implants, and 39 percent with the implantation of three embryos.[106] The use of multiple implants is evidently both a response to criticisms from Right-to-Life groups that "surplus" embryos were being "flushed down the drain," and an outgrowth of a purely technical concern to increase the success rate of the process.

The technology of IVF raises the possibility of yet more exotic variations on the normal reproductive process. Usually, eggs from the infertile woman and sperm from her husband are used. Insemination may be accomplished, of course, with the use of donor sperm, thus combining the techniques of AID and IVF. More recently, "adoptive pregnancies" have been achieved by Australian physicians where both eggs and sperm have been donated.[107]

In California physicians achieved two pregnancies with a technique known as "ovum transfer." The donor egg of an anonymous volunteer was fertilized *in utero* by artificial insemination, using the sperm of the husband of an infertile married couple. The fertilized egg was then flushed out of the volunteer's uterus, and implanted in the womb of the infertile woman. Such "ovum transfers" have been successfully used in animal breeding for many years. "The basic research had been done before we got there," commented Dr. John Buster, head of the UCLA team that designed the transfers.[108] Because the fertilized egg develops in a natural setting rather than in a petri dish, Buster and his associates hope for a higher pregnancy rate than is presently achieved by IVF techniques.

Controversy erupted in Australia when it became known that researchers were freezing embryos and then thawing them for implantation in infertile women. According to Margaret Tighe, president of the Victoria Right to Life Association in Australia, the human embryos were being treated "with as much respect as frozen peas."[109] Researchers have pointed out that the freezing of embryos has been successfully used in animal husbandry for some time, and the freezing of "spare" embryos eliminates the need to subject the woman to another egg-recovery operation should the initial IVF implant fail.

The Australian researchers did admit, however, that serious problems could arise from the freezing and thawing process. In one case there was clear evidence that cells in one embryo were damaged by ice crystallization prior to implantation. Dr. Alan Trounson, one of the members of the Australian research team, raised a number of very pertinent questions: "What happens if the embryo is damaged during freezing or thawing? If a resulting child were deformed, could the child or its parents claim compensation, and from whom?"[110] Questions such as these show how the technology of in vitro fertilization is raising ethical and legal questions that are running ahead of society's ability to formulate answers.

IN VITRO FERTILIZATION AND THE LAW

IVF technology raises a host of legal questions that are at present unresolved in American law. In vitro fertilization has already given rise to at least one lawsuit. In 1978, the same year that Louise Brown was born in England as the first IVF baby, Doris Del Zio and her husband were bringing suit against Columbia Presbyterian Medical Center, Columbia University, and Dr. Raymond Vande Wiele, chief of obstetrics and gynecology at Columbia. Mrs. Del Zio had undergone an IVF procedure in New York, but Dr. Vande Wiele had intervened, charging that such work was unethical and that proper clearance had not been obtained from Columbia Presbyterian Medical Center. As a result of the disagreement, the embryo perished. Mrs. Del Zio went into a state of depression, and the suit was heard in the Federal District Court in New York. After a seven-week trial the jury brought in a verdict in favor of the Del Zios and awarded them $50,000 in damages.[111]

Since its inception, in vitro fertilization has been largely unregulated by state or federal law. As of 1979 the Department of Health, Education and Welfare (now Health and Human Services) had a regulation relating to applications for federal funding of research in this area, but that regulation was merely administrative in nature and had no legal force in terms of civil and criminal actions.

The closest legal analogies are provided by state laws dealing with artificial insemination and fetal experimentation. If the courts followed the reasoning of existing statutes dealing with artificial insemination by donor, then it would be expected that an IVF child born through the use of donor sperm would be considered the legitimate offspring of the infertile couple, assuming that informed consent was given by all parties to the case.

A Minnesota statute expressly forbids certain types of fetal experimentation: "Whoever uses or permits the use of a living human conceptus for any type of scientific, laboratory research or other experimentation except to protect the life or health of the conceptus, or except as herein provided, shall be guilty of a gross misdemeanor."[112] This law would forbid, for example, the freezing of a "spare" IVF embryo simply for the purpose of obtaining new information about the effects of freezing.

One California law explicitly recognizes the legal rights of the unborn: "A child conceived, but not yet born, is to be deemed an existing person, so far as may be necessary for its interest in the event of its subsequent birth."[113] Under this law a child who suffered prenatal injury as a result of the negligence of a third party could recover damages after birth.

Physicians and researchers who are working in the area of IVF could be subject to malpractice suits in the event of the birth of a child with birth defects. Dr. Mark Evans and attorney Alan Dixler, writing in the *Journal of the American Medical Association*, warned that "a malformed child of the in vitro process could recover damages if the physician were negligent and that negligence proximately caused the deformities. The potential damages for life of deformity are staggering."[114] It is conceivable that in such a case a jury could require the doctor to pay compensation for the entire lifetime of the person "malconceived" through IVF.

Many other questions that arise in connection with IVF are yet unresolved. What would happen if the mother changed her mind and decided not to accept the embryo? What legal status do "spare" embryos have? Do researchers have a right to freeze such embryos? What would happen to the embryo in the event that both mother and father were accidentally killed before implantation could be accomplished? It seems only a matter of time before some of these unresolved legal questions become matters of litigation in the courts.

ETHICAL CONSIDERATIONS

"I condemn in the most explicit and formal way experimental manipulations of the human embryo, since the human being, from conception to death, cannot be exploited for any purpose whatsoever," stated Pope John Paul II in an October 1982 address to scientists attending the annual seminar of the Pontifical Academy of Sciences. The pope did not specifically mention in vitro fertilization, but his remarks were evidently broad enough to include that technique.[115]

Other reactions from the Roman Catholic Church have been guarded. Bishop Walter F. Sullivan of Richmond, Virginia—the diocese in which the Norfolk IVF clinic is located—was quoted as saying, "I'm not against the birth of babies, but I do think there's need for dialogue on the procedure that is being done."[116] Fr. Richard McCormack, a Professor of Ethics at Georgetown University, noted that because of the unknown hazards of laboratory transfers of human embryos, in vitro fertilization represents a "potentially hazardous experimentation" on a human subject without his consent.[117]

Various observers have raised concerns about the impact of such technology on the institutions of marriage and the family. According to Professor Donald DeMarco, "By removing the origin of the child from the personal context of conjugal love . . . a decisive step is taken which necessarily depreciates that love.[118] In a similar vein, Professor Albert S. Moraczewski, another Catholic ethicist, argues that IVF violates the proper family environment for the generation of human beings. IVF "displaces the human act which is the essential bonding act of the family."[119]

Such arguments do not appear to be persuasive to other ethicists, who argue that such reasoning places too much emphasis on the physical act of sexual intercourse and not enough weight on the larger relational context of marriage. Given a firm commitment of the husband and wife to the obligations of parenthood, it could be argued, the exact means by which human generation takes place becomes of secondary importance. The analogy of adoption might be suggested in this regard: the parents' love for the child is not necessarily dependent on the circumstances of origin. Nevertheless, in light of the great pressures that exist in modern society on the institutions of marriage and family, any development that could further depersonalize human relationships must be viewed with concern.

The crucial variable in the moral analysis would appear to be the question of the extent to which the IVF process increases the risk of birth defects among children conceived in this way. Even though some 200 children around the world have been born as a result of IVF, there is not yet enough data available to draw firm conclusions regarding its safety. According to Joan E. Densberger of the Boston University School of Public Health and Sharon Schwartz of the University of Massachusetts, "No definitive statements can be made about the safety of IVF to the potential child because some birth defects do not become evident until the child is up to five years old."[120]

Expert witnesses who appeared before the Ethics Advisory Board to testify on in vitro fertilization agreed that there has been insufficient animal research designed to study the long-range effects of IVF and embryo transfer.[121] In particular, such research has not been conducted with primates, the animals physiologically most similar to man. The board's report noted that the lack of primate research is "particularly noteworthy in view of the opportunity provided by primate models for assessing subtle neurological, cognitive and developmental effects of such procedures."[122]

Concerns have also been expressed about the fertilization process itself. Natural fertilization occurring in the female genital tract may have a "filtering" effect on abnormal sperm. That is not so with fertilization in vitro. According to Dr. John Biggers of the Harvard Medical School, "Fertilization of ova in vitro with spermatozoa that have not passed through the female genital tract may be associated with an increased risk of fertilization with abnormal spermatozoa. The extent of this risk is an open question."[123]

There is also the possibility that the concentration of sperm used in IVF may increase the probability that the ovum will be fertilized by more than one sperm, producing chromosomal aberrations. Such an effect has been observed in the in vitro fertilization of mice.[124]

A study of 1,581 children born to British parents through IVF and 2,536 such children in Australia and New Zealand did not find a higher incidence of birth defects. However, the multiple births often resulting from IVF can be associated with increased incidence of low birthweights and jaundice in the newborn. "No evaluation of the long-term health and development of the children has yet been performed," cautions Dr. V. Beral and his colleagues, and there are not yet sufficient numbers of children to draw firm conclusions about the risks of specific types of birth defects.[125]

While all the above factors may involve relatively small risks, still the judgment of Protestant ethicist Paul Ramsey would appear to be sound: "A small risk of grave induced injury is still a morally unacceptable risk."[126] Further research is needed to establish definitively the safety of in vitro fertilization for those conceived in this manner. Until such evidence is available, IVF represents a form of experimentation on human subjects, who are being exposed to as yet unknown risks.

CHAPTER 4

Divorce and Remarriage

"What's happening to kids is just a howling shame," stated University of Chicago law professor Franklin Zimring.[1] The comment was in reference to the fact that one out of every two marriages in the United States ends in divorce, and children are involved more than half the time.[2] Forty-eight of the fifty states now have no-fault divorce laws, and for the last several years there have been approximately one million divorces in this country.[3] The divorce rate in the United States has doubled since 1960.[4]

During most of the 1970s and 1980s approximately one million American children a year watched their parents' marriages dissolve.[5] Studies in the United Sates and Canada have shown that, compared to teens from intact homes, adolescents from nonintact families are more likely to engage in premarital sex, and to use alcohol, tobacco, and illicit drugs.[6] The sense of rejection, loneliness, and impaired academic achievement experienced by many children of divorce is an often-overlooked need for ministry when churches confront the emotional trauma created by divorce.

In the United States the divorce rate is highest among those who marry young.[7] Among white males the divorce rate is three times greater for those who never attend religious services than for those who attend at least two or three times a month.[8] The divorce rate is moderately higher for Protestants than for Catholics; lower for Jews than for Catholics; highest for those stating no religious preference.[9]

HISTORICAL TRENDS

Divorce can be defined as the legal or customary decree that a marriage is dissolved.[10] The term is derived from the Latin *divortium*, from *di-*

vertere, divortere, "to separate." Divorce is distinguished from annulment, in which it is declared by some authoritative body that the marriage attempted by a couple was invalid according to the rules of society, and that as a consequence a true marriage never existed.

Since early in the twentieth century the United States has had the highest divorce rate of any modern society. The divorce rate, computed as the number of divorces per 1,000 population, was 2.4 in 1960.[11] This compared with rates ranging from 0.6 to 0.8 in France, West Germany, England, and Japan, and less than 0.1 in Portugal.[12] The divorce rate in the United States was 0.3 in 1870 and 0.7 in 1900.[13] During the last fifty years, the number of divorces in the United States has increased by 700 percent.[14]

In the early church, the view of Augustine that adultery is the only permissible ground for separation, but that even this does not dissolve the marriage bond, gradually became the dominant view. That view was endorsed by the eleventh synod of Carthage in 407.[15]

The civil law of the empire did not, however, immediately reflect the views developed in the Catholic Church. From Constantine to Justinian there was little influence on civil law from the side of the church. In England and Gaul full divorce with remarriage was allowed on various grounds.[16] It was not until 1164, in the fourth book of the "Sentences" of Peter Lombard, that there was a clear recognition of the "seven sacraments," including marriage.[17]

The Council of Trent in 1564 made the dogma of the indissolubility of marriage a matter of faith. According to session xxiv, canon v, "If anyone shall say that the bond of matrimony can be dissolved for the cause of heresy, or of injury due to cohabitation, or of wilful desertion, let him be anathema."[18] Martin Luther had stated that "marriage is a worldly thing," rather than a sacrament of the church, and he allowed for full divorce in cases of adultery and willful desertion.[19] Martin Bucer of Strasbourg was willing to extend the grounds for divorce to include cruelty and refusal of conjugal duty.[20] Luther, Calvin, and other Reformers had protested against the situation in the medieval church that allowed the wealthy to use the ecclesiastical courts to obtain annulments, but not the less fortunate.

The Protestant Reformation laid the groundwork for a more moderate view of divorce, but its views were only very slowly reflected in the civil law. In England, for example, full divorce was not recognized until 1857. Prior to that, only a decree of separation from bed and board was obtainable from the ecclesiastical courts, and this only in the cases of adultery and cruelty.[21]

Recent Roman Catholic practice in the United States has seen a dramatic increase in the number of annulments granted. For all practical purposes, this amounts to a recognition by the Church that the marriage bond does in fact dissolve in a sinful world. In 1968, only 338 annulments were granted by the Catholic Church in the United States. In 1970, the Church began recognizing psychological grounds for annulment. In 1978, more than 27,000 were granted—an increase of 8,000 percent since 1968.[22] The approximately eight million Catholics in this country who have received civil divorces cannot remarry in the Church unless their former marriages have been declared annulled.[23]

THE BIBLICAL DATA

The most important Old Testament text relating to divorce is Deuteronomy 24:1-4:

> If a man marries a woman who becomes displeasing to him because he finds something indecent about her, and he writes a certificate of divorce, gives it to her and sends her from his house, and if after she leaves his house she becomes the wife of another man, and her second husband dislikes her and writes her a certificate of divorce, gives it to her and sends her from his house, or if he dies, then her first husband, who divorced her, is not allowed to marry her again after she has been defiled. That would be detestable in the eyes of the Lord. Do not bring sin upon the land the Lord is giving you as an inheritance. (NIV)

This Mosaic provision was not intended to be a divine endorsement of divorce, but merely a concession to human sinfulness and "hardness of heart" (Matt. 19:8). The intention was to regulate and mitigate an existing custom, rather than to set forth God's ideal for human marriage from the time of creation (cf. Matt. 19:8b, "But it was not this way from the beginning").

The certificate of divorce mentioned in verse 1 was evidently intended to protect the reputation and rights of the woman, including the right to remarry. The Mishnah (Gittin 9:3) stated that a divorce certificate was not valid unless it was said explicitly by the husband, "Thou art free to marry any man."[24]

The meaning of the term "something indecent" (*ervath dabar*) in verse 1 has been the subject of much debate. Already in the time of Jesus rabbinic opinion was divided on the issue. The conservative school of Shammai took it to refer to immodest behavior, while the liberal Hillelites explained it as anything displeasing to the husband, including even so trivial a matter as spoiling his food.[25] Both Philo (De. spec. leg. III, 30) and Josephus (Ant. 4.253) knew of the Hillelite view and agreed with it.[26] This permissive interpretation of the law was evidently the prevailing view in first-century Judaism and is the viewpoint sharply challenged by Jesus in the New Testament.

The term *ervath dabar* cannot be taken to mean adultery, since the Pentateuch prescribed the death penalty rather than divorce for adultery (Lev. 20:10; Deut. 22:22). It has been suggested that the term might refer to some physical deficiency such as the inability to bear children, but this interpretation lacks support by other Old Testament usage.[27]

John Murray notes that this exact phrase occurs elsewhere only in Deuteronomy 23:14, in reference to human excrement, and he concludes that the term means some indecency or impropriety of behavior. While falling short of adultery or illicit sexual intercourse, it may have referred to some shameful conduct connected with sex life.[28]

Abel Isakkson argues that the term refers to the wife's having exposed herself voluntarily or involuntarily.[29] He cites the account of Michal's despising David when in his dance before the ark he accidentally exposed himself to the crowd (II Sam. 6:12-20). In Ezekiel 23:18 it is said that a man's soul turns away from the wife who exposes her nakedness. According to the school of Shammai, a wife who went out with her hair unbound, spinning in the street or talking to a strange man, was guilty of indecent or immodest behavior.[30] This interpretation of the *ervath dabar* as "indecent or immodest behavior" seems to fit the text and the general Old Testament outlook on human sexuality and personal modesty.[31]

Malachi 2:10-16 is another crucial passage in the Old Testament that relates to divorce. Writing in the first part of the fifth century, probably just prior to the time of Ezra and Nehemiah, the prophet addresses the issues of mixed marriages and divorce, both of which were serious problems at that time:

> Have we not all one Father? Did not one God create us? Why do we profane the covenant of our fathers by breaking faith with one another? . . . the Lord is acting as the witness between you and the wife of your youth, because you have broken faith with her, though she is your partner, the wife of your

marriage covenant. Has not the Lord made them one? In flesh and spirit they are his. And why one? Because he was seeking godly offspring. So guard yourself in your spirit, and do not break faith with the wife of your youth. "I hate divorce," says the Lord God of Israel, "and I hate a man's covering himself with violence as well as with his garment," says the Lord Almighty. (NIV)

Some modern scholars have argued that "divorce" in this passage is to be taken in the symbolic sense of Israel's unfaithfulness to her covenant with Yahweh, but that interpretation does not appear to be the most natural or convincing one.[32] It would require, for example, God to be understood as the *wife* of Israel in verse 14. While the prophets describe Israel as the bride of Yahweh, nowhere is God described as the wife or bride of Israel. It is more natural to take the text in the usual sense of literal divorce.

Malachi teaches that husbands and wives are to be faithful to one another because they have one God as their Father, because their relationship rests on a solemn covenant, and because God desires their unity for the benefit of a godly offspring. Malachi sets forth the theological framework within which the personal relationship of marriage is to be understood. While God might tolerate divorce under some circumstances (Deut. 24), he hates the sinful conditions that produce it. In this text the prophet reaches back beyond the concessions of Deuteronomy 24:1-4 to the creation accounts of Genesis 1-2 and anticipates the teachings of Jesus set forth in Matthew 5:31-32 and 19:4-9.[33]

An examination of the teachings of Jesus on divorce as recorded in the synoptic Gospels immediately confronts the reader with the question of whether Matthew's "exception clauses" are original to Christ or are later additions:

Matthew 5:31, 32: "It has been said, 'Anyone who divorces his wife must give her a certificate of divorce.' But I tell you that anyone who divorces his wife, except for marital unfaithfulness, causes her to commit adultery, and anyone who marries a woman so divorced commits adultery."

Matthew 19:9: "I tell you that anyone who divorces his wife, except for marital unfaithfulness, and marries another woman commits adultery."

Mark 10:11, 12: "Anyone who divorces his wife and marries another woman commits adultery against her. And if she divorces
her husband and marries another man, she commits adultery."

Luke 16:18: "Anyone who divorces his wife and marries another
woman commits adultery, and the man who marries a divorced
woman commits adultery."

Mark and Luke do not record the phrase "except for marital unfaithfulness" (*parektos logou porneias*, 5:32; *me epi porneia*, 19:9) included
by Matthew.

Many modern scholars argue that the exception clauses are
Matthew's editorial addition, rather than the original teaching of Jesus.[34]
It is said that emphatic, unqualified ethical statements are characteristic of the teaching style of Jesus, and that for this reason it is more likely
that Mark's and Luke's forms of the saying are closer to the actual words
of the Master.

But that conclusion does not necessarily follow. It is likely that Jesus, like most preachers and teachers, repeated the same material in
slightly different forms on various occasions. The differences would reflect not a fundamental change in content, but an adaptation of the
message to different contexts and audiences.

As A. W. Argyle has suggested, Matthew may be including what
Mark and Luke took for granted, namely that unchastity was a possible
grounds for divorce.[35] Krister Stendahl has noted that Matthew's Gospel
has the formal features of a church manual, and such an exception clause
would be expected in the context.[36]

It is also interesting to recall in this connection Jeremiah 3:8,
where Yahweh is said to divorce Israel for her spiritual adultery (idolatry): "I gave faithless Israel her certificate of divorce and sent her away
because of all her adulteries." If God himself can properly divorce his
bride because of adultery, then, given Christ's unqualified adherence to
the authority of the Old Testament, it seems difficult to conclude that
Jesus would have allowed for no exceptions whatever.

Several features of the divorce texts in Matthew 5 and 19 call for
special exegetical comment. R. C. H. Lenski has noted that English
translations [including the NIV] tend to overlook the *passive* forms of the
verbs *moicheuthenai* and *moichatai* in 5:32 and 19:9, giving them an active sense unwarranted by the forms themselves. He suggests that the
passive infinitive *moicheuthenai* be translated, "He brings about that she

is stigmatized as adulterous," and the passive finite verb *moichatai* as, "He is stigmatized as adulterous."[37] Matthew 5:32 would then be rendered as follows:

> "But I say to you that every man releasing his wife without cause of fornication brings about that she is stigmatized as adulterous; and he who shall marry her that has been released is stigmatized as adulterous."

This somewhat unusual translation does have the merit of reflecting grammatical features overlooked by most translations and commentaries.

There has been much debate in scholarly circles concerning the meaning of *porneia* in Matthew 5:32 and 19:9. Some Roman Catholic scholars have argued that the term refers to incestuous unions prohibited by the Mosaic law (cf. Lev. 18).[38] Mark Geldard takes the term to refer to premarital sexual unfaithfulness.[39] According to Donald Shaner, *porneia* most likely refers to "persistent and unrepentant adultery."[40] The problem with Shaner's view is that Matthew does not use the specific word for adultery (*moicheia*) in 5:32 or 19:9, and Matthew seems to imply a distinction between the two in 15:19.

In view of the New Testament usage it seems best to take the term in the wider sense of unchastity that includes "every kind of unlawful sexual intercourse."[41] The word can include adultery but is not limited to it. Paul uses *porneia* in reference to incest (I Cor. 5:1) and intercourse with prostitutes (I Cor. 6:13; cf. vv. 15, 16). Unlawful sexual intercourse would also include premarital unchastity (cf. Matt. 1:18, 19), homosexual practices (Lev. 18:22; Rom. 1:26-28; I Cor. 6:9), bestiality (Lev. 18:23). As Stott notes, such acts of sexual immorality violate the "one flesh" principle, which is fundamental to the unity and exclusivity of marriage as divinely ordained.[42]

In a valuable exegetical article Carroll D. Osburn has elucidated the sense of *moichatai* ("commits adultery") in Matthew 19:9, a verb in the present indicative.[43] In this context the present indicative is an example of a "gnomic present" or "present of general truth," and continuity of action is not necessarily under consideration.[44] Another example of a gnomic present in Matthew is found in 7:17, "Every good tree bears [*poiei*] good fruit"; i.e., it is characteristic of a good tree to bear good fruit, though not necessarily continuously throughout the year. In the case of Matthew 19:9, the sense of *moichatai* as a gnomic present would imply that while divorce and remarriage apart from unchastity constitute an *act* of adultery, they do not necessarily constitute a continuing *state* of adultery. This conclusion should encourage churches in their efforts to restore to full fellowship those couples whose divorces and subsequent remarriages were in violation of the divine standards.

Scholarly discussions of Mark 10:11, 12 often focus on the statement of verse 12, "And if she [the wife] divorces her husband and marries another man, she commits adultery." While in Jewish law a woman could sue for divorce, the right of divorce remained the husband's.[45] William L. Lane has argued convincingly that the Western and Caesarean families of Greek manuscripts, which speak of desertion and remarriage rather than divorce, preserve the original reading, and that the Alexandrian texts assumed by the RSV [and NIV] may represent an adaptation of the words of Jesus to the legal situation prevailing in Rome and elsewhere in the empire.[46] Understanding the original text in terms of desertion and remarriage seems natural in light of Mark's having given special attention to Herodias, who had deserted her husband Philip to marry Antipas (cf. Mark 6:16-29). Jesus' words in 10:12 would then be a vindication of John the Baptist's denunciation of this adulterous union.[47]

Luke's form of the divorce saying (16:18) is quite similar to Mark 10:11. By placing the saying immediately after verses 16 and 17, which speak of the law, Luke may be emphasizing the continuing validity of the law, but in the new form given to it by Jesus.[48]

There has been considerable debate among biblical scholars concerning the thrust of Jesus' sayings on divorce. Were they intended to be binding legal precepts for conduct, or merely moral ideals intended to shape the attitudes of the heart?

M. J. Down has pointed to the distinction in Jewish theology between *halakah* and *haggadah*: *halakah* is legal and prescriptive, instruction about good conduct; *haggadah* is affective and imaginative, using poetry, figures of speech, and stories to inculcate attitudes.[49] He argues that the divorce sayings are intended as *haggadah*—statements intended to shock the Jews out of their complacency over divorce by categorizing it as adultery. According to Down, neither the statement in Matthew 5:29 about plucking out the right eye that causes one to sin nor the following statement in 5:31, 32 about divorce is a literal legal prescription; both are deliberately shocking statements intended to challenge existing attitudes.[50]

While there is no doubt that the divorce sayings bear some similarity to Jewish *haggadah*, their legal or *halakic* elements should not be minimized. In Matthew 19:3-9 the context of the discussion is precisely that of the proper interpretation of the Old Testament law of divorce (Deut. 24:1-4). As A. D. Verhy has noted, in Matthew's Gospel "the impression here of Halakah, of legal interpretation of the precepts of Torah to govern external behavior, is unavoidable and probably correct."[51] Luke deliberately places the divorce saying (16:18) immediately after sayings about the continuing authority of the law (16:16, 17). While Jesus was without question concerned about attitudes that promoted divorce, it cannot be denied that he also wished to discourage it in the strongest terms as a specific form of behavior. The interpreter does not have to choose between the categories of *halakah* and *haggadah;* the statements share characteristics of both.

Paul's teachings on divorce are found in I Corinthians 7:10ff. In this passage he deals with issues involving both Christian couples and mixed marriages:

> To the married I give this command (not I, but the Lord): A wife must not separate from her husband. But if she does, she must remain unmarried or else be reconciled to her husband. And a husband must not divorce his wife. To the rest I say this (I, not the Lord): If any brother has a wife who is not a believer and she is willing to live with him, he must not divorce her. And if a woman has a husband who is not a believer and he is willing to live with her, she must not divorce him. . . . But if the unbeliever leaves, let him do so. A believing man or woman is not bound in such circumstances; God has called us to live in peace.

In speaking of divorce in relation to Christian couples (vv. 10, 11), the apostle refers to the teachings of Jesus ("not I, but the Lord"). Does the verb "separate" (*chorizo*) in verses 10 and 11 mean "separate" in our modern sense, or divorce?[52] While in the Septuagint *choristhenai* is used of separation of place, in the Greek papyri it is clearly used as a technical term for divorce.[53] The term is linked in the immediate context (v. 11) with *aphiemi*, which clearly means divorce. In Matthew 19:6, "let not man separate" (*anthropos me chorizeto*) is in antithesis to "what God has joined together" (*ho oun ho theos sunezeuzen*), and clearly divorce and marriage are in view. Paul, who travelled extensively, was no doubt aware that in the Gentile world the wife had the legal right to initiate a divorce proceeding.[54] These considerations make it clear that Paul is in fact referring to divorce in verses 10 and 11.

In verses 12-16 the apostle addresses the issue of mixed marriages. Even in spite of the religious incompatibility involved in such a relationship, the believing spouse is not to seek a divorce (vv. 12-14). But if the unbelieving partner insists on divorce, the believer may acquiesce; in such a case, the believer is not bound (v. 15). What is the exact force of the language "not bound" (*ou dedoulotai*, lit., "has not been enslaved," perfect passive of *douloo*)?

Some interpreters have argued that the language implies that the believer may acquiesce in a divorce when the unbelieving partner insists upon it, but that the right to remarry is not necessarily included.[55] This, however, seems inconsistent with the forceful language of not being "enslaved" by the conflicts of an unworkable mixed marriage.

In Romans 7:2, 3 Paul uses similar language in relation to marriage, speaking of being "bound" (*dedetai*, from *deo-*) and "released" (*eleuthera*) from the relationship. In this text "not bound" is equivalent to "release," and the one who is "released" is free to remarry (v. 3). The implication is that the one who is "not bound" in I Corinthians 7:15 is likewise free to remarry. It is true that Romans 7:2, 3 speaks of the *physical* death of the spouse, but in I Corinthians 7:12-16, the spouse's unbelief and desire to desert the believing partner produces a similar result, the death of the marriage relationship.

The conclusion, then, is that in the case of desertion by an unbelieving spouse, the Christian may acquiesce to divorce and subsequently may remarry. An important question of interpretation and pastoral application arises at this point: What circumstances constitute *desertion*? Is the term to be narrowly or broadly defined? Physical abandonment of the spouse and long-term absence from the household would certainly qualify as desertion, but could the term also be extended to cases of persistent physical abuse, drunkenness, lack of financial support, or denial of conjugal rights?

It might be argued that there is a basis in I Corinthians 7:12-16 for the broader interpretation of desertion. For the mixed marriage to be viable, the unbelieving partner must be "willing" (vv. 12, 13: *suneudokei*) to live with the believer. The verb used here by the apostle appears six times in the New Testament, and can mean "agree with, approve of, consent to, or sympathize with."[56] Behavior such as persistent physical abuse is a violation of the marriage covenant and is a *prima facie* indication that true consent is not being given to living in harmony with the believing spouse. Such persistent behavior could be construed as a de facto desertion of the marriage covenant. In such cases the believer who is being abused has the right to say to the unbelieving spouse, "If you intend to continue this marriage, then change your irresponsible behavior and fulfill your marriage vows." If the abusive spouse shows no willingness to change the irresponsible and destructive behavior, he or she is then in fact not demonstrating willingness to live in harmony (cf. v. 13).

Even in such hard cases, however, the church should not encourage divorce. If all attempts at reconciliation fail, legal separation is available as a remedy to protect the abused spouse. Given the general thrust of I Corinthians 7:10-16, which is to discourage divorce, it seems wiser to understand the desertion mentioned in verse 15 in the more narrow and literal sense.

Similarly, inability to engage in conjugal relations due to sickness or physical incapacity would not constitute "desertion." The traditional marriage vows speak of a commitment to faithfulness "for better [or] for worse . . . in sickness and in health." Conditions of illness or physical incapacity do not inherently negate a fundamental intention to honor the spirit of the marriage covenant.

SUMMARY AND CONCLUSIONS

God hates divorce (Mal. 2:16). This emphatic statement should always be kept in mind in the midst of discussions of the many tragic circumstances that contribute to the disintegration of marriage relationships. Divorce is always a consequence of sinful human attitudes and behavior and should not be encouraged or promoted by any Christian leader.

At the same time, Scripture recognizes that not all divorces are in and of themselves sinful. As the foregoing study has shown, sexual infidelity and desertion by an unbelieving spouse make divorce morally permissible (though not obligatory). Under such circumstances God permits divorce as the exception to the divine ideal of lifelong, heterosexual, monogamous marriage. Divorce should always be seen as a measure of the last resort, to be accepted only when all reasonable attempts at reconciliation have been exhausted.

With respect to remarriage, it is commonly held in evangelical circles that in cases of divorce occasioned by sexual infidelity or desertion by an unbelieving spouse, the offended party has the right to remarry.[57] The bonds of the marriage have been broken by the act of unfaithfulness or desertion, and remarriage is then possible subsequent to divorce.

What can be said about the status of the guilty party in such a divorce?[58] May such a person legitimately remarry? Here the answer would be in the affirmative, if the guilty party has truly repented and attempted to make restitution for personal and financial obligations that may have been forsaken during the dissolution of the marriage.

True repentance means a fresh start in the eyes of God, freedom from the guilt of past sins, and new possibilities for the future (cf. I Cor. 6:9-11). If God has truly forgiven a sinner, then the church should no longer speak of the "guilty" party; in Christ he is now innocent.[59] The church should, of course, have good reason to judge that repentance is genuine, based on the observation of changed life and attitudes, and should counsel such persons in the biblical standards of marriage prior to giving its blessings to a subsequent remarriage.

Questions also arise in regard to professing Christians who are divorced on unscriptural grounds, i.e., for reasons other than sexual infidelity or desertion. Are such persons in a position to legitimately remarry?

In such cases the improperly divorced believer is obligated to repent of the divorce and the sinful behavior that contributed to it, and to seek reconciliation with the spouse (I Cor. 7:11), assuming the spouse has remained unmarried. The process of reconciliation would include making restitution for personal and financial obligations that may have been abandoned, and seeking the offended spouse's forgiveness. If the spouse persistently refuses all attempts at reconciliation, he has de facto placed himself in the position of an unbelieving,[60] deserting spouse, and the partner who has been seeking reconciliation is free to remarry another. If either of the spouses remarries without seeking reconciliation and forgiveness—in violation of I Corinthians 7:11—he or she commits adultery against the former partner (Matt. 19:9; Mark 10:11). The spouse remaining single may then be free to remarry, after having sought forgiveness for any wrongs committed in the prior marriage.

A final question of application relates to divorced persons and eligibility for leadership positions in the church. In I Timothy 3:2 Paul states that the church leader must be above reproach, "the husband of but one wife" (*mias gunaikos andra*). Does this stipulation bar divorced persons from serving as elders or pastors?

The language prohibits the ordination of a practicing polygamist. Polygamy was known in first-century Judaism, and Roman laws from the third and fourth centuries A.D. witness to its existence among the Jews.[61] If the apostle had specifically intended to bar divorced persons from leadership positions in the church, he could have made his point clearly and unambiguously by writing *me apolelumenon* ("not divorced"), rather than *mias gunaikos andra*.[62] The language the apostle actually chose can well be rendered by such expressions as "a man of one woman" or "a one-woman man"; it emphasizes the faithfulness and stability of the present marriage, rather than any sins or failures of the past.[63]

In the New Testament divorce is not considered an unforgivable sin. The grace of God in Jesus Christ and the sanctifying power of the Holy Spirit are able to cleanse the believer from past sexual sins (I Cor. 6:11).

Paul himself was a blasphemer and persecutor of the church (I Tim. 1:13) and had consented to the death of Stephen (Acts 8:1), and yet God later used him in a most remarkable way in the missionary expansion of the church.

In Christ Jesus the sinner is a new creature (II Cor. 5:17). The divorced person, through repentance, forgiveness, and the transforming presence of the Holy Spirit, may likewise transcend the failures of the past and win acceptance in the eyes of God's people for a fruitful ministry of leadership and service.

CHAPTER 5

Homosexuality

"It is not a simple task for any of us to meet adequately the obligations of either public or private life, let alone both. But these challenges are made substantially more complex when one is, as I am, both an elected public official and gay."[1] This statement by Representative Gerry Studds (Dem., Mass.), after the House Ethics Committee had recommended an official reprimand by the full chamber for Studds' having had sexual relations with a teenage male page, vividly dramatized the high visibility of homosexuality in recent American life.

Just how prevalent is homosexuality in America today? Is it a consciously learned behavior, or is it perhaps related to inherited hormonal and genetic influences? Is homosexuality a condition that can be changed by appropriate psychological treatment? Is the traditional bias in Western civilization toward heterosexuality primarily due to the influence of the Judeo-Christian Scriptures, or is this bias also widespread in non-Western cultures? How should the Christian church respond pastorally to the homosexual? Should Christians support the decriminalization of private acts between consenting adult homosexuals and calls for ensuring the "civil rights" of those with such a sexual orientation? These are some of the crucial questions on the subject of homosexuality, which call for careful reflection by evangelicals in America today.

HISTORICAL AND ANTHROPOLOGICAL PERSPECTIVES

In this book a *homosexual* is understood as one who in adult life is motivated by "a definite preferential erotic attraction to members of the

95

same sex and who usually (but not necessarily) engages in overt sexual relations with them."[2] This definition acknowledges that some individuals, e.g., prison inmates, may engage in sporadic homosexual acts, though not on the basis of a persistent homosexual orientation.

Homosexuality is a very ancient phenomenon, being evidenced in prehistoric art, as well as in the pictographs and hieroglyphs of ancient cultures.[3] The ancient Hebrews, Egyptians, and Assyrians had laws against homosexual practices.[4]

From the sixth century B.C. onward, homosexuality is increasingly referred to in the art and literature of Greece: in the poetry of Sappho and Anacreon, the prose of Plato, and the plays of Aeschylus.[5] It would be a mistake, however, to conclude that ancient Greek culture ever accepted homosexuality as a societal norm. Aristotle, Herodotus, Aristophanes, and many later Stoic and Cynic philosophers expressed moral disapproval of such practices.[6] A minority in the Greek upper classes may have tolerated or even encouraged homosexuality, but Greek society as a whole disapproved of it and held to traditional heterosexual norms. As Arno Karlen has observed, the "acceptance" of homosexuality in ancient Greece remains "common knowledge," that is, "to all who have not read the primary sources."[7]

The existence of homosexuality in ancient Roman society is attested in the writings of Suetonius, in the *Satires* of Juvenal, and in the poetry of Catullus and Martial.[8] As in ancient Greece, visibility of the practice did not imply general social approval.

There is no evidence that the Vikings, Visigoths, Celts, or Vandals approved of homosexuality; some of these pagan cultures in fact punished it severely. Visigoth law condemned the practicing homosexual to be burned at the stake.[9] Evidence such as this shows that hostility toward homosexuality in the West did not originate with the Christian church; the church's teaching merely reinforced convictions that were already present in Europe.

Between the years 1000 and 1500, as Europe began to experience greater urbanization, evidence of homosexual activity increased. From the late sixteenth to the early nineteenth century, sexual deviation grew in England and France.[10]

In recent American history, especially since the 1970s, the homosexual subculture has been increasingly visible and militant. In 1973 homosexual activists persuaded the board of trustees of the American Psychiatric Association to remove homosexuality from its list of mental disorders. The condition was replaced by the terminology of "sexual orientation disturbance," a compromise between the view that it invariably represents a mental disorder and the view that it is merely a normal sexual variant.[11] A poll conducted in 1977 by the medical journal *Medical Aspects of Human Sexuality* found that 69 percent of the member psychiatrists of the APA considered homosexuality a pathological rather than normal condition, with less than 13 percent undecided.[12] Such results indicate the persistence of the longstanding bias toward heterosexuality, even after years of "gay" activism in this society.

Studies in cross-cultural anthropology have shown that the bias toward heterosexuality is more than a Western cultural convention rooted in the Judeo-Christian tradition. The most comprehensive research on homosexual behavior in various cultures, that of Ford and Beach (*Patterns of Sexual Behavior*, 1951), based on data from 77 different cultures, found that "all known cultures are strongly biased in favor of copulation between males and females as contrasted with alternative avenues of sexual expression."[13] As Karlen has noted, some societies may permit sporadic homosexual behavior for some individuals at certain times of life, but no known cultures permit preferential homosexuality for most adults for the predominant portion of the life cycle.[14]

Warren J. Gadpaille, a secular psychiatrist at the University of Colorado Medical Center in Denver, states that "from an evolutionary perspective, homosexuality as a preferential or obligatory mode must by definition be biologically deviant."[15] From a purely biological perspective, it is clear that any human society that did not encourage heterosexual marriage and childbearing over homosexual activity would, in the course of time, fail to reproduce itself. Biologically, preferential homosexuality is a maladaptive sexual orientation. Gadpaille states further that there is both "evolutionary and neurophysiological evidence for an innate heterosexual bias."[16] Far from being a mere convention of certain human cultures, masculine/feminine differences and "heterosexual preferences are quite consistent up through the phylogenetic scale."[17] Gadpaille concludes that the cross-cultural data clearly show that adult homosexuality "does not naturally develop . . . in human cultures or families in which the innate heterosexual bias is allowed expression and is fostered."[18]

These conclusions are supported by the earlier work of British anthropologist J. D. Unwin, in an important 1927 article, "Monogamy as a Condition of Social Energy." After a comprehensive study of both

Western and non-Western cultures throughout human history, Unwin concluded that the record of mankind "does not contain a single instance of a group becoming civilized unless it has been absolutely [heterosexually] monogamous, nor is there any example of a group retaining its culture after it has adopted less rigorous customs."[19] Unwin observed that a society's adoption and maintenance of heterosexual monogamy as a social standard "has preceded all manifestations of social energy, whether that energy be reflected in conquest, in art and sciences, in the extension of the social vision, or in the substitution of monotheism for polytheism, and the exaltation of the conception of the one true God."[20] Unwin's conclusions, based on cross-cultural data, anticipated the later conclusions of Ford and Beach and Gadpaille: preferential homosexuality, if adopted as a standard by any society, will eventually prove to be socially counterproductive.

MEDICAL ASPECTS

INCIDENCE

The most extensive surveys concerning sexual behavior in the United States were conducted by Alfred Kinsey and his associates in the late 1940s. According to Kinsey's data, the incidence of predominant homosexuality or bisexuality is about 9 percent among males and approximately 2 percent for females.[21] Dr. Paul Cameron, Professor of Psychology at the Fuller Graduate School of Psychology in Pasadena, has pointed out, however, that Kinsey's data may be biased. His samples were not representative of the general population, and in many of the calculations sexual explorations in childhood were granted the same status as acts in adulthood.[22] Other surveys conducted in the 1970s indicated incidences in the range of 2-4 percent for males and 1-4 percent for females.[23]

It is interesting to note, however, that whatever the methodological limitations of Kinsey's earlier work, no significant increases in homosexual behavior were found for the period between 1890 and 1950, in spite of the considerable changes in sexual attitudes in the society at large. And despite the growing visibility of the homosexual subculture during the 1970s, it has been questioned whether or not the incidence of predominant homosexuality actually increased during that period in America.[24]

CAUSES

The question of the causes of homosexuality is hotly debated in research circles. It has been suggested that some persons are predisposed toward homosexuality by genetic and chromosomal factors for which they can be assigned no personal responsibility. On the basis of the available literature, however, Dr. John Money, a researcher at the Johns Hopkins University and leading authority on the physiological aspects of human sexuality, concluded that there is no evidence to support the hypothesis that "homosexuals or bisexuals of any degree or type are chromosomally discrepant from heterosexuals."[25]

Imbalances in the sex hormones have also been suggested as a possible cause for or contributing factor to homosexual behavior. It has been pointed out, however, that while the sex hormones are crucial for the physiological development of the organs needed for the sexual act and for increasing their sensitivity to stimulation, *psychological* factors are the crucial elements that influence the choice of the sexual *partner* and the intensity of sexual emotions.[26] As Tourney has pointed out, there is no evidence that treating male homosexuals with male hormones significantly alters the sexual preference.[27] The clear implication of these results is that sexual preference is predominantly a socially learned response, not an orientation fixed from the outset by genetic or hormonal factors.

The East German researcher G. Dorner, drawing on studies performed on rats, has suggested that hormonal irregularities during the fourth to seventh months of prenatal development may predispose one toward homosexuality. His studies have not been replicated, however, by other scientists.[28] According to Dr. Money, prenatal hormonal determinants, if they are indeed a factor, "probably do no more than create a predisposition on which the postnatal superstructure of psychosexual status differentiates, primarily, like native language, under the programming of social interaction."[29]

Family psychopathology has often been suggested as a possible cause of homosexuality. There is some evidence to suggest that the combination of a domineering mother and a father who is detached or hostile can contribute to this condition. It should be noted, however, that evidence does not appear to indicate that such a constellation of factors is either a *necessary* or a *sufficient* condition for the genesis of homosexual behavior. Some homosexuals do not have such family backgrounds, and persons with such family pathologies do not necessarily develop homosexual tendencies.[30] Evelyn Hooker is probably correct in seeing *multifactorial* causation at work in the etiology of homosexuality. The diverse forms of adult homosexuality, she concludes, "are produced by many combinations of variables, including biological, cultural, psychodynamic, structural, and situational."[31] If this analysis is correct, one could say, from a biblical perspective, that the genesis of homosexuality is not a matter of "nature" to the exclusion of "nurture," or vice versa, but rather a combination of both. Man brings a fallen human nature into a social environment that itself bears the marks of sin, and homosexuality is one of the distortions that can result from that interaction. The Bible has no illusions about the perfection of either human nature or the social environment, but it does hold man morally responsible for the way he interacts with his world.

TREATMENT

Regarding treatment of homosexuality, it is sometimes argued that such sexual orientations are innate and not subject to change. That view is not supported, however, by current clinical data. "Contrary to some of the arguments I have heard," states Dr. David Barlow, Professor of Psychology at the State University of New York at Albany, "there is no evidence that homosexuality or any sexual preference is learned by the age of three and cannot be changed after that."[32] One's sense of gender is learned very early, but that is not the same as sexual object preference. With the development of modern psychological techniques, notes Dr. Barlow, "changing sexual preference is not particularly difficult for those who make that choice."[33] Such change is possible even in the so-called "Kinsey 6" or "obligatory homosexual" who has never experienced heterosexual relations.

Barlow's testimony is supported by that of Dr. Armand M. Nicholi, a faculty member of Harvard Medical School's Department of Psychiatry. "No society, past or present, has ever tolerated the institutionalization of homosexuality," noted Nicholi, "for to do so would be to sow the seeds for its own extinction because homosexuality undermines the basic unit of society—the family—and of course precludes procreation, which means extinction of the human race."[34] According to Nicholi, the claim that homosexuality is an irreversible condition is patently untrue and flies in the face of a massive body of clinical research. The studies of Anna Freud, Bergler, Bychowski, Lorand, Hadden, Ovesey, Eber, Socaidles, Glover, Bickner, Hatterer, and others show that homosexuality can be reversed.[35]

The extensive clinical research of William Masters and Virginia Johnson supports the same conclusion. According to their studies, which included a five-year follow-up period, there was a 66 percent success rate in changing homosexual orientation.[36] These and the foregoing studies represent, of course, success rates with purely *human* means. If the resources of divine grace and the power of the Holy Spirit become part of the therapeutic process, then who can say that the homosexual who desires change has no real hope of success?

HEALTH COMPLICATIONS

No consideration of the medical aspects of homosexuality would be complete without some attention given to the serious public health problems in the United States today resulting from such practices. Homosexuality is associated with higher than normal incidences of sexually transmitted diseases.

According to Drs. Edward J. Artnak and James J. Cerda, writing in the medical journal *Current Concepts in Gastroenterology,* the male homosexual "is responsible for the majority of new cases of sexually transmitted diseases."[37] The Centers for Disease Control have reported that approximately 50 percent of new cases of syphilis occur in the homosexual population. "On a national basis," notes the center, "the homosexual is five times more likely to contract syphilis than his heterosexual peer."[38]

Three recent studies have documented the prevalence of rectal gonorrhea in homosexual men.[39] This condition is thought to be associated with the homosexual practice of anal intercourse. Also associated with homosexual anal intercourse is the transmission of the hepatitis B virus, which has become a common infection among homosexual men.[40] And according to Dr. Bruce Voeller, anal intercourse may lead to a higher incidence of rectal cancer among homosexual men.[41]

For the last several years the correlation of homosexuality and AIDS (acquired immune deficiency syndrome) has received a great deal of attention in the mass media, as well as in the medical community. This condition, which appears to be almost always lethal, has been strongly associated with homosexual practices. As of 1991, homosexuals and intravenous-drug abusers accounted for 76.4 percent of all AIDS cases reported in the United States.[42] The possibility that the disease could be contracted from infected blood donated by homosexuals has further increased public concern about AIDS.

Medical research has disclosed that the higher than normal incidence of sexually transmitted diseases in the homosexual subculture is related to the promiscuous practices of many of its population. A study by Drusin and his colleagues found that college-age homosexuals had eight times the number of different sex partners as their heterosexual classmates.[43] Homosexual men who patronized Denver's steam baths reported an average of 7.9 different sex partners per month; one-third reported more than 10 different partners per month.[44] In a study of 575 homosexual men interviewed in the San Francisco Bay area, Bell and Weinberg found that 43 percent of their respondents said they had had at least 500 different sex partners during their lifetimes.[45] Medical research such as this, together with the striking correlation between homosexuality and sexually transmitted diseases, shows very clearly that such practices, far from being merely a "private matter between consenting adults," represent a public health problem of serious proportions, which touches the general interests of society at large.

THE WITNESS OF SCRIPTURE

"Only towering cynicism can pretend that there is any doubt about what the Scriptures say about homosexuality," writes Michael Ukleja.[46] Until somewhat recently, the general consensus in scholarly circles would have been heavily in support of this position. In general terms, such a consensus still exists, but some scholars, such as D. S. Bailey and John J. McNeill, have attempted to revise the received view, and their arguments will call for close attention below.[47]

Foundational for any Christian understanding of human sexuality is the creation account in Genesis 1-2. God's original creative intent is manifested in the creation of *male* and *female* in his own image and likeness (Gen. 1:27). Human sexuality is reflected in the differentiation of two, not three or four, sexual genders, nor some androgynous combination of the two. It was not good for the man to be alone (Gen. 2:18), and so God created the woman to be man's counterpart and co-laborer in the fulfillment of the dominion mandate to subdue the earth (Gen. 1:28). Sexual differentiation is the basis of human marriage, procreation, and family life, which is the primal form of human community. As Don Williams has put it, in the plan of God "the primal form of humanity is the fellowship of man and woman."[48]

Homosexual relationships cannot fulfill the procreative dimensions of human sexuality and marriage, which are part of the divine intention for mankind. "Be fruitful and multiply, and fill the earth and subdue it" (Gen. 1:28). While the procreative dimension does not exhaust the meaning and significance of marriage, neither may it in principle be divorced from it, as in a homosexual relationship.

The book of Genesis also tells us that human life, including sexuality, no longer reflects fully the original divine intent, because man's life is disordered by sin. Man, as a consequence of disobedience, is marked by the curse (Gen. 3:16-19). His labor and his sexual life reflect the disordering and rupturing of the divine-human relationship. The marriage relationship between image bearers, intended to be a reflection of God's love for man, is instead marked by lust, violence, and the struggle for dominance and power. Homosexuality is simply one expression among many of the basic disordering of human life; all lust, whether heterosexual or homosexual, violates the divine law and reflects man's fallen nature. The Bible looks not to the social environment for the source of the human dilemma, but to the heart of man himself.

The first reference to homosexuality in the Bible is found in Genesis 19:1-11, where Lot entertained the two angels sent to Sodom to investigate the outcry against the sins of that city and Gomorrah (cf. Gen. 18:20-22). Lot received the angels into his house, and at evening the men of the city surrounded the house and demanded to see his visitors. "Where are the men who came to you tonight? Bring them out that we may know them" (19:5).

D. S. Bailey argues that the demand to "know" the strangers was nothing more than a desire to get better acquainted; it was no more than a matter of a breach of hospitality.[49] The word *yada* appears some 943 times in the Old Testament, notes Bailey, and only on 12 occasions does it clearly mean "to have intercourse with"; elsewhere it means "to get acquainted with" or "to have knowledge of."

The problem with Bailey's argument is that mere word counting is no criterion of meaning; the use of a word in its specific context is the decisive consideration. In the book of Genesis, the word *yada* is used 12 times, and in ten of those instances it denotes sexual intercourse.[50] Even more to the point, in the immediate context in 19:8 *yada* is used in a way that unmistakably refers to sexual intercourse. Lot said to the men of Sodom, in a desperate attempt to protect his guests, "Behold, I have two daughters who have not known man; let me bring them out to you, and do to them as you please; only do nothing to these men, for they have come under the shelter of my roof." Whatever one might conclude about Lot's judgment in this case, it is clear that he was offering his virgin daughters as a substitute to the men of Sodom who were demanding homosexual intercourse with his guests.

Both Christian and Jewish commentators on this passage have seen in it a clear reference to homosexual activity. The writer of the Book of Jude noted that "Sodom and Gomorrah and the surrounding towns gave themselves up to sexual immorality and perversion"(v. 7).[51]

A rabbinic commentary on Genesis 19:9 states that "Rabbi Menahema said in Rabbi Bibi's name: The Sodomites made an agreement among themselves that whenever a stranger visited them they should force him to sodomy and rob him of his money; even him of whom it is written, *That they may keep the way of the Lord, to do righteousness and justice* (Gen. 18:19), we should use him bestially and rob him of his money."[52]

Philo, a Jew of Alexandria who lived c. 25 B.C.-c. A.D. 45, characterized the country of the Sodomites as "full of innumerable iniquities. . . . gluttony and debauchery." The men of Sodom "lusted after one another, doing unseemly things, and not regarding or respecting their common nature. . . . the men became accustomed to be treated like women."[53]

The Jewish historian Josephus, in reflecting on the Genesis 19 passage, stated that "the Sodomites, on seeing these young men of remarkably fair appearance whom Lot had taken under his roof, were bent only on violence and outrage to their youthful beauty. . . . Lot adjured them to restrain their passions and not to proceed to dishonor his guests. . . . God, therefore, indignant at their atrocities, blinded the criminals."[54]

In his *First Apology* Justin Martyr, writing in the second century, noted that "Moses related that Sodom and Gomorrah were cities, filled with impious men, which God burned and devastated with fire and brimstone."[55]

In the third century Origen, in his fourth homily on Genesis, wrote of the Sodomites, "No one besides Lot is found who would repent, no one would be converted. . . . he alone is delivered from the conflagration. . . . No one wished to know the mercy of God; no one wished to take refuge in his compassion."[56]

Methodius of Olympius (A.D. 260-312) wrote that the inhabitants of Sodom "were goaded on to an unnatural and fruitless desire for males."[57]

The medieval Jewish commentator Rashi (d. A.D. 1105), in his comment on Genesis 19:5, "that we may know them," stated that this means "by pederasty."[58]

Thus it is clear that both the immediate context of Genesis 19:5 and a long history of both Jewish and Christian interpretation point unmistakably to the true meaning of the text: homosexual practices. Bailey's misinterpretation of the text, which has become a stock argument in pro-homosexual circles, simply cannot be sustained.

Homosexual practices are strongly condemned in the Mosaic law. "You shall not lie with a male as with a woman; it is an abomination" (Lev. 18:22). Such offenses carried the capital penalty: "If a man lies with a male as with a woman, both of them have committed an abomination; they shall be put to death, their blood is upon them" (Lev. 20:13).

The word *abomination (toebah)*, used five times in Leviticus 18, is a term of strong disapproval, meaning literally something detestable and hated by God (cf. Prov. 6:16; 11:1).[59]

Some have suggested that the prohibition of sexual intercourse with a woman during her menstrual flow (Lev. 18:19) shows that the prohibition against homosexual intercourse, which closely follows it in the text (18:22), is likewise cultic rather than moral in nature. That argument, however, is clearly untenable in that the prohibition appears with others of a clearly moral nature, e.g., prohibitions against adultery (18:20), child sacrifice (18:21), and bestiality (18:23). Sacrificing children to Molech violated not one but two provisions of the moral law, namely, the prohibitions against idolatry (Exod. 20:3) and murder (Exod. 20:13).

Judges 19 also contains explicit references to homosexuality. In many respects this narrative is similar to the one in Genesis 19, but the events described in Judges 19 are clearly intended to be understood as distinct from those that transpired in Sodom.

A Levite was traveling with his concubine and spent the night in the town of Gibeah in Benjamin, accepting the offer of hospitality of an elderly man from Ephraim who was sojourning in the area at that time (19:16-21). That evening "base fellows" from the city surrounded the house and said to the old man, "Bring out the man who came into your house, that we may know him" (v. 22, RSV; NIV, "so that we can have sex with him"). The man seized the Levite's concubine, put her outside the house, and the men of the city "knew her, and abused her all night until the morning" (v. 25, RSV; NIV, "and they raped her and abused her throughout the night").

The use of the same Hebrew word, *yada* ("to know"), in verses 22 and 25 shows unmistakably that in verse 22 the men of the city were demanding homosexual intercourse with the visiting Levite. The rest of the text also shows that more was at stake than mere hospitality. The men of the city are described in verse 22 as *bene beliyyaal* ("base fellows," RSV; lit., "sons of wickedness"). This phrase, which appears about 27 times in the Old Testament, denotes here, as in I Samuel 1:16, "human beings who act in disregard of all laws, whether human or divine."[60] One modern scholar has suggested that the phrase could well be paraphrased in the current vernacular as "the local hell raisers."[61]

In verse 23 the request by the men of the city is characterized as "this vile thing" (RSV; "this disgraceful thing," NIV: *nebalah*). Keil and Delitzsch point out that the word is used to denote "shameful licentiousness and whoredom, as in Genesis 34:7 and Deuteronomy 22:21."[62]

The language of the narrative, then, clearly shows that Judges 19 contains an explicit reference to homosexuality, and that such practices are viewed with abhorrence.

The Jewish abhorrence of homosexuality reflected in the Old Testament Scriptures is also found in the rabbinical writings. References to such practices are relatively infrequent in the Talmud, evidently because such sins were rare in Israel.[63] According to the rabbis, "Israel is suspected of neither pederasty nor bestiality."[64] According to the Talmud, two brothers are allowed to bathe together because homosexuality is not expected.[65] There is one brief incident described in the Jerusalem Talmud, however, about a righteous man who warned two homosexuals to desist from their acts, and who in response was threatened with murder.[66]

While the rabbis believed that homosexuality was very rare in Israel, they considered matters to be quite otherwise among the heathen. One talmudic tractate prohibited leaving animals in the care of heathens, because "heathens frequent their neighbor's wives, and should one by chance not find her in, and find the cattle there, he might use it immorally."[67] This rather harsh judgment is somewhat softened in another passage, which states that "this is their real sentiment but they think it beneath their dignity to show it."[68]

Thus it is clear that even though homosexuality is not mentioned often in the rabbinic writings, it is nevertheless considered with the same moral disapproval that characterizes the Old Testament Scriptures.

The New Testament contains prohibitions against homosexuality in three places: Romans 1:26, 27; I Corinthians 6:9; and I Timothy 1:10. Of these three references, the one in Romans is theologically the most significant, since it discusses homosexuality in the larger context of man's relation to God and God's general revelation in nature.

In Romans 1:18-32 the apostle Paul was concerned to establish the Gentile world's guilt before God and their need for the gospel. The Gentile world's alienation from God is evidenced in the sphere of human sexuality: because they turned away from the true worship of God, "God gave them over to shameful lusts. Even their women exchanged natural relations for unnatural ones. In the same way the men also abandoned natural relations with women and were inflamed with lust for one another. Men committed indecent acts with other men, and received in themselves the due penalty for their perversion" (vv. 26, 27).

In verse 26 Paul used the words *pathe atimias*, "shameful lusts," literally, "passions of dishonor." The term *pathos* means "passion" or "passionate desire," the ungoverned aspect of evil desire. The word *atimia* denotes "dishonor" or "disgrace."

In verse 27 he used the word *exekauthesan*, the aorist passive of *ekkaio*, "to set on fire"; here, "to be consumed or to be inflamed." The term *aschemosune* means "shameless," "disgraceful"; "obscenity." Paul's moral judgment on such practices is clear.

It will not do to suggest that the apostle was condemning only "irresponsible" or "promiscuous" homosexual acts. Given the context in the passage, it is quite evident that homosexuality per se is contrary to the will of God.

According to the apostle, such activity is inexcusable, because men are sinning against the light of creation and conscience (Rom. 1:18-20; 2:14, 15). They instinctively realize—with an awareness that they repress (1:18)—that such conduct is contrary to the holy and righteous character of God and is even worthy of death in his eyes (1:32). In Romans 1, homosexuality is seen not merely as a violation of some Jewish or Christian sectarian code, but as a transgression of the basic moral law of God known in all cultures.

It is also significant that in the Pauline analysis homosexual practices derive ultimately not from the social environment, but from the human heart or inner disposition, which has turned away from God, its ultimate good, and turned toward the mutable goods of creation, including the self. The inward and invisible apostasy of the heart eventually becomes visible in false religions and immoral, antisocial behavior. "Idolatry," notes Ernst Kasemann, "opens the floodgates for vices which destroy society and turn creation back into terrible chaos."[69] The various forms of sexual immorality are consequences of an earlier apostasy and at the same time God's judgment on that apostasy: "*Therefore God gave them up in the lusts of their hearts to impurity. . . .*" The spread of homosexuality in a society is in itself a sign of that society's apostasy and of the impending judgment of God.[70]

In I Corinthians 6:9 Paul used two terms, *malakoi* and *arsenokoitai*, generally considered to refer to homosexual practices. "Do not be deceived; neither fornicators, nor idolaters, nor adulterers, nor effeminate [*malakoi*] nor homosexuals . . . shall inherit the kingdom of God" (vv. 9, 10, NASB). Both C. K. Barrett and Hans Conzelmann, in their commentaries on I Corinthians, take *malakoi* and *arsenokoitai* to refer respectively to the passive and active partners in male homosexual relations.[71]

There has been some debate, however, about the proper translation of these two terms, and this measure of uncertainty is reflected in the renderings of the English translations. The translators of the King James Version read "effeminate" and "abusers of themselves with mankind." The New International Version reads "male prostitutes" and "homosexual offenders." The New English Bible simply refers to "homosexual perversion."

The pro-homosexual scholar John Boswell has argued that neither term connoted homosexuality in the time of Paul or for centuries thereafter.[72] In his view *malakos* refers to general moral weakness, with no specific reference to homosexuality; *arsenokoitai* refers to active male prostitutes.[73] According to Boswell, early Christian writers did not use the terms to refer to homosexuality.[74]

It is true that both terms are relatively infrequent in the New Testament. The first, *malakos*, appears four times, and in three of those instances (Matt. 11:8, twice; Luke 7:25) it refers to those who are clothed in soft raiment. There is also the connotation of a luxurious and even decadent style of life. The fourth occurrence is in I Corinthians 6:9, a text that has become the subject of scholarly debate. Adolf Deissmann, however, has pointed to an occurrence of the word in the Greek papyri that clearly bears the meaning "effeminate." The word occurs in a letter from Demophon, a wealthy Egyptian, to Ptolemaeus, a police official (c. 245 B.C.) in Egypt. The term is an allusion to the foul practices by which the musician Zenobius eked out his living.[75] This evidence is contradictory to the claim of Boswell cited above.

The term *arsenokoitai* is used in the New Testament only in I Corinthians 6:9 and in I Timothy 1:10. The word is a compound formed from *arsen*, "male," and *koite*, a word with definite sexual overtones (cf. Rom. 9:10; Heb. 13:4); in one instance it has the connotations of licentiousness and debauchery (Rom. 13:13). The literal etymology of this compound term suggests "males who go to bed with males." Even if the reference were *restricted* to male cult prostitutes who engaged in homosexual intercourse, it is nevertheless clear from the context that such activity is morally blameworthy. The entire section in I Corinthians 6:9f. is keynoted by the term *adikoi:* "Do you not know that the *unrighteous* will not inherit the kingdom of God?" In verse 9 the two terms in question are found in association with other sexual offenders, namely fornicators (*pornoi*) and adulterers (*moichoi*). These considerations of etymology and the immediate context are weightier than the arguments from silence adduced by Boswell. The conclusion, supported by both the textual evidence and the great majority of commentators, is that I Corinthians 6:9 does refer to homosexuality, and that it considers it a morally blameworthy activity that can exclude the persistent practitioner from the kingdom of God.

The term *arsenokoitai* is also used in I Timothy 1:10: ". . . the law is not made for a righteous man, but for those who are lawless and rebellious, for . . . immoral men and homosexuals" (vv. 9, 10, NASB). The King James reads, "for whoremongers, for them that defile themselves with mankind"; the New International Version, "for adulterers and perverts." The same considerations that applied in the discussion of this word in I Corinthians 6:9 are relevant here. The list of vices given by Paul in I Timothy 1:9, 10 are all examples of things "contrary to sound doctrine" and the gospel of Jesus Christ (vv. 10, 11). Donald Guthrie comments that the references to "whoremongers" and "them that defile themselves with mankind" (KJV) are perhaps given as extreme examples of violations of the seventh commandment, just as the other vices listed are examples of other violations of the stipulations of the Decalogue.[76]

With respect to I Corinthians 6:9-10 and I Timothy 1:10 Michael Ukleja writes, "Only wild speculation can avoid the conclusion that Paul knew exactly what he meant and how he should be understood when he used these terms."[77] Both the Old and the New Testament are unequivocal in their teaching that homosexuality is contrary to the moral law of God, and only the most forced and arbitrary modes of biblical interpretation can conclude otherwise.

THEOLOGICAL AND PASTORAL ISSUES

A number of modern theologians readily admit that the Bible condemns certain homosexual acts, but they contend that the writers of Scripture do not recognize "constitutional" homosexuality as a *condition* that is intrinsic to the personality of certain people and consequently not morally blameworthy. This distinction between "act" and "disposition" is found, for example, in the thought of the Roman Catholic theologian John McNeill. According to McNeill, the Bible condemns perverse homosexual activity by *heterosexuals*,[78] but has nothing to say about "responsible" relationships between "constitutional" homosexuals.

It is simply not true, however, that the biblical understanding of man and human behavior does not recognize the distinction between "act" and "disposition." A man's disposition ("heart") is the ultimate driving force behind his outward actions: "Out of the heart are the issues of life" (Prov. 4:23). Man's "flesh," i.e., the totality of his fallen human nature, is the spring of the vices that disrupt his relationships with God and the neighbor (Gal. 5:19). A man may appear to be socially acceptable in the sight of his peers, and yet in the sight of God, his heart may be full of hypocrisy and iniquity (Matt. 23:28). Men are drawn away from godly behavior by their own lusts, which then conceive and bring forth sin (James 1:14, 15).

Greg Bahnsen is surely correct in his observation that "an inner, inherited . . . orientation of man's psyche was recognized in Scripture, and this condition was viewed precisely as the source of man's sinful activities."[79] Lust is one expression of that inherited sinful nature, and the Bible condemns lust of all types, whether heterosexual or homosexual. In the biblical outlook, a recognition of the fallen nature is not intended to provide man with an excuse for unlawful behavior, but to bring him to a recognition of his need for the redemptive grace of God, which can liberate him from moral and spiritual bondage. "For the law of the Spirit of life in Christ Jesus has set me free from the law of sin and death" (Rom. 8:2).

It has been suggested by some that the biblical revelation is so *conditioned by Jewish culture* that its strictures against homosexuality can no longer be considered normative for us today. Could it be that the biblical outlook is more reflective of idiosyncratic Jewish attitudes toward human sexuality than it is of God's unchanging intent?

There are some basic problems, however, with this appeal to the "cultural conditioning" of biblical revelation. In the first place, the biblical teaching in this area is based on *creation norms*, i.e., the original male-female distinction (Gen. 1:27). Such creation norms apply to all cultures and antedate the particular features of the Mosaic economy specific to theocratic Israel.

In the second place, the *uniformity of biblical teaching throughout the canon* should be noted. On certain matters, e.g., foods people are allowed to eat, or the role of women in public worship, there are variations in the biblical regulations, according to time, circumstance, and the progressive unfolding of the divine plan. In reference to homosexuality, however, the Scriptures throughout, in a variety of cultural and historical contexts spanning some 1,500 years, teach uniformly that homosexuality is contrary to the divine will. This uniformity reflects the abiding, transcultural significance of this ethical norm.

In the third place, we are reminded by Scripture itself of God's *sovereignty in revelation*. "My word . . . shall not return to me empty, but . . . shall accomplish that which I purpose, and prosper in the thing for which I sent it" (Isa. 55:11). The God of Scripture is the Lord of culture, not its passive victim; if God wishes to make his word and will plain, sinful human culture cannot ultimately frustrate the divine intent.

In the fourth place, we can also recall how studies in cross-cultural anthropology have confirmed the transcultural validity of the biblical norms. As noted earlier (p. 108), the studies of Ford and Beach, based on data from 77 cultures, found that no known cultures permitted preferential homosexuality for most adults for the predominant portion of the life cycle. The studies of J. D. Unwin showed that a society's economic, military, and artistic vitality was closely associated with maintenance of heterosexual, monogamous marriage as a societal norm. The history of the rise and fall of cultures confirms the wisdom and truth of the ethical principles God has revealed in Scripture.

In light of the foregoing discussion, how should the church respond pastorally to the problem of homosexuality? It would seem that a properly balanced response on the part of the church would require at least two key elements: firm biblical teaching and meaningful personal support for the homosexual who seeks to overcome such an orientation. As John Batteau has observed, homosexuals "must not be left with a stern word of condemnation from a distant and repulsed body of people called the Church; instead they must be faced with a Church, with Christians, with a God who reaches out to bless even through condemnation."[80]

The church cannot compromise the fundamental biblical teaching: homosexuality is contrary to the divine will for human sexuality. To compromise at this point abdicates the fundamental responsibility of the church, namely, to sound forth to the society a clear word from God, which transcends the shifting currents of human opinion and fashion. For the church merely to echo the contemporary voices of human opinion in the last analysis is a real disservice to the homosexual, for such a stance on the part of the church may only help such people to rationalize their way of life, rather than challenging them to seek personal transformation through the power of God's Word and Spirit.[81]

At the same time, Christian congregations must honestly examine themselves in terms of their own attitudes toward the struggling homosexual. The Bible nowhere teaches that homosexuality is the unforgivable sin; churches must reject the sin but be willing and ready to be used of God in the reclamation of the sinner. That means the existence of Christian fellowships that can support people in various kinds of personal brokenness, including this one, as the Spirit of God seeks to transform the old behavior patterns. Such transformation generally does not occur in a vacuum, but requires the social reinforcement of a group of loving people who offer support along the way.

The Christian church also needs to sound forth clearly a message of the *power of divine grace* to transform sinful attitudes. The grace of God not only forgives the sins of the past, but is also available to transform the old sinful attitudes and dispositions that remain subsequent to conversion. After cataloging a variety of sexual sins of which the Corinthians had been guilty prior to their conversions (I Cor. 6:9, 10), Paul went on to write, "And such were some of you. But you were *washed,* you were *sanctified,* you were justified in the name of the Lord Jesus Christ and in the Spirit of our God" (v. 11, emphasis added). Some who were previously involved in homosexual practices were given a brand new start in the eyes of God, and the old nature was being transformed through faith in Jesus Christ and the work of the Holy Spirit in the depths of their personalities.

There is no reason that the Christian church should be guilty of the heresy of "powerless grace." If Masters and Johnson can achieve a 66 percent success rate in dealing with homosexuals with purely secular techniques, can we really believe that with the power of God's Holy Spirit even more dramatic rates of transformation are possible? Such a biblically based hope is one that Christian congregations should be in a position to hold forth as a tangible possibility for those who find themselves caught up in this sin.

Regarding ordination of homosexuals to church offices, a matter that has been vigorously debated in American denominations of late, it must be said that the Scriptures give very clear guidelines. No denomination seeking to place itself under the authority of Scripture can consistently ordain avowed and practicing homosexuals to positions of leadership within the church. If the unrepentant practice of sexual sin bars one from the kingdom of God (I Cor. 6:9), surely it bars one from leadership in the church, the visible kingdom of God. Those who have teaching responsibilities in the church will be judged with special strictness by God (James 3:1). The church leader is to set an example to the flock in love, in faith, and in purity (I Tim. 4:12).

On the other hand, there appear to be no biblical barriers to the ordination of one who has repented of such practices and whose life is transformed by the presence and power of God's grace and Spirit. "If anyone is in Christ, he is a new creation" (II Cor. 5:17). Saul of Tarsus, even though a persecutor of the church and a blasphemer (I Tim. 1:13), received mercy from God and was transformed into the great minister and apostle of Jesus Christ to the Gentiles. Such transformation and subsequent usefulness in the ministry of Christ is possible for the homosexual, as it is to persons caught up in other types of sin. This hope is part of the "good news" that the gospel brings to man.

HOMOSEXUALITY AND THE LAW

In Western civilization homosexual behavior has been treated in ways ranging from rigorous to severe in ecclesiastical and civil law. The Christian emperor Theodosius called for convicted homosexuals to be burned alive, while Justinian only required confession, amendment of life, and penance under supervision of the church.[82] The Eastern Church imposed penalties similar to those for adultery, requiring seven years of public penance, after which the offender could be reinstated as a communicant.[83] A church council held in Elvira, Spain during the years A.D. 305-6 refused even deathbed communion to a confessed homosexual.[84] During the Middle Ages Anselm of Canterbury (d. 1109) urged that the ecclesiastical penalties be moderated somewhat, in that "this sin has been so public that hardly anyone has blushed for it, and many, therefore, have plunged into it without realizing its gravity "[85]

A commentary on English law published in 1290 states that "those who commit bestiality, and sodomists are to be buried alive."[86] The term "buried alive" in this case evidently meant drowning in a swamp. It is not clear, however, how often if ever such capital penalties were actually inflicted. Penalties for homosexual activity continued to be severe in English law, however, well into the modern period. It was not until 1861 that the penalty for sodomy was reduced from life imprisonment to ten years.[87] The Criminal Law Amendment Act of 1885 reduced private homosexual acts between consenting adults to the category of misdemeanor.[88] This act remained the law of the land until 1967, when the Sexual Offenses Act completely decriminalized private homosexual behavior among consenting adults.[89]

In the United States the law and public policy in recent years have reflected the turbulence in the society as a whole generated by the growing visibility and militance of the homosexual subculture. In May of 1979 the California Supreme Court, for the first time in American legal history, extended to homosexuals protection against discrimination in employment.[90] In May of 1980 the Carter administration's Office of Personnel Management issued new policy guidelines that stated that "applicants and employees are to be protected against inquiries into, or actions based upon, non-job-related conduct, such as religious, community, or social affiliations or sexual orientation."[91] As of 1980, 21 American states had decriminalized private homosexual acts between consenting adults.[92] The political impact of homosexual lobbying groups was reflected in that, as of 1983, almost 46 percent of the total income of homosexual nonprofit organizations was derived from local, state, and federal tax funding.[93]

Some have argued that churches should support the drive to ensure "civil rights" for homosexuals. That would presumably discourage discrimination in such areas as employment, housing, and education. There are serious objections, however, to such proposals. Homosexual behavior, unlike one's race or gender, is not a truly involuntary condition. The analogy that some homosexual activists have attempted to draw with the civil rights movement is a specious one. Unless the homosexual insists on *societal acceptance of the public declaration* of his or her lifestyle, discrimination need not become an issue. At its heart, then, the drive for "civil rights" is in fact a drive for society's stamp of approval on a form of behavior that historically has been considered deviant.

Christians cannot consistently support making a civil *right* of that which the Scriptures teach to be morally *wrong*. On biblical grounds, it would make as little sense to argue that society should endorse basic "civil rights" to commit adultery, to operate houses of prostitution, or to commit child abuse. A moral *wrong* can never become the basis of a civil *right*. True civil rights, e.g., freedom of speech and assembly, are based on the fundamental dignity of the human person as created in the image of God. Homosexuality, however, does not represent such a fundamental human good, but rather a sinful disordering of human nature as originally intended by God.

Endorsing homosexual behavior as a legally protected "civil right" could also lead to serious abuse of "affirmative action" philosophies legislated by the courts. Such policies could deprive Christians of the right to shun contact with persons whose behaviors they consider morally perverse.[94] "Affirmative action" policies could give homosexuals unfair advantages in the job market, for employers might fear "discrimination" lawsuits if homosexual applicants were not hired.[95] "Civil rights" for homosexuals could be extended to the right to adopt children, to have equal time for homosexuality and lesbianism in sex-education classes, and equal representation in the literature of public libraries.[96]

The denial of legal sanction and societal approval for homosexual behavior does not imply that Christians should condone or encourage the deliberate entrapment, harrassment, or persecution of practicing homosexuals. "In a lawful and fair society even those accused of criminal activity do not forfeit all civil rights," notes Bahnsen. "The Christian should insist on that, just as much as he maintains that homosexual acts are not to be sanctioned by civil law."[97] The homosexual, like every other citizen, has rights of due process, but these legitimate rights do not extend to the societal legitimation of any and every form of sexual behavior. The proper role of the Christian church is not to support confused notions of "civil rights" in this area, but rather to hold forth the clear teachings of biblical revelation, whose wisdom has been confirmed by history, and to offer the homosexual the hope and promise of new life through the gospel of Jesus Christ and the transforming power of the Holy Spirit.

CHAPTER 6

Abortion

If we compare a severely defective human infant with a non-human animal, a dog or a pig, for example, we will often find the nonhuman to have superior capacities, both actual and potential, for rationality, self-consciousness, communication and anything else that can plausibly be considered morally significant. . . . Humans who bestow superior value on the lives of all human beings, solely because they are members of our own species, are judging along lines strikingly similar to those used by white racists who bestow superior value on the lives of other whites, merely because they are members of their own race.

Peter Singer
Professor of Philosophy
Monash University
Victoria, Australia

So God created man in his own image, in the image of God he created him; male and female he created them.

Genesis 1:27

"Two-and-a-half years ago I did have an abortion," said "Bonnie." "I would never do it again. I still feel like I killed someone. I feel guilty and I don't feel that I've righted it by having the baby this time. . . . In the short run, abortion is the easiest way out. But in the long run it's hell. I know because I had one. If I get pregnant again I would be tempted to have an abortion, but I wouldn't. I couldn't do it again. I would hate the nine months of carrying the baby, the labor, the stretch marks and getting cut open. But I would go through it all again rather than have another abortion."[1]

"Bonnie," 20 years old, had been living with her baby's father for eight months when she became pregnant. She left her midwestern hometown rather than let her parents know. Bonnie's testimony is a vivid reminder that abortion in America today is not just a mass of statistics or a massive social problem, but an intensely personal reality that profoundly affects the lives of countless individuals. And as the quotations that opened this chapter remind us, abortion also raises the most profound questions about the value of human life itself: Are human beings uniquely valuable as bearers of the divine image, or is the value of a human life to be assessed on some sliding scale of social utility? The debate is not a theoretical one, but is daily being played out in abortion clinics, intensive care units, and legislative halls across the nation.

According to the Alan Guttmacher Institute, there are some 1.6 million abortions each year in the United States. Of women having abortions, three-fourths say that having a baby would interfere with work or school or other responsibilities; two-thirds say they cannot afford another child; one-half say they do not want to be a single parent or have problems in their relationship with their husband or partner. Only 2 percent say that they are seeking an abortion because of rape, incest, or anticipated birth defects.[2]

Abortion represents a $700-million-a-year industry in this country.[3] The United States leads the world in teenage abortions, with over 500,000 every year. Some 150,000 abortions are performed in the second trimester of pregnancy, "the most grisly of all," notes Dr. Matthew J. Bulfin, "the ones that some hardened abortionists refuse to do because the killing is so real and unmistakable."[4]

These figures mean that each day an average of 4,257 unborn human beings are aborted in the United States. In Washington, D.C., the nation's capital, abortions now outnumber live births.[5]

HISTORICAL AND LEGAL BACKGROUND

Abortion was a common practice in the ancient world. The earliest reference to any form of fertility control appears to be a prescription for an oral abortifacient written by the Chinese Emperor Shen Nung in the period 2737-2696 B.C.[6] Abortion was not uncommon in ancient Greece and Rome. In his *Republic* Plato wrote that ill-conceived embryos should not be brought to birth, and if the children were born, the parents should dispose of them.[7] Aristotle was also of the opinion that deformed children should be exposed and left to die.[8]

Approval or tolerance of abortion in the ancient world was not universal, however. Hippocrates included the following statement in his oath for physicians: "I will not give a woman a pessary to cause abortion."[9] The Code of Hammurabi, promulgated about 1728 B.C., contained prohibitions against abortion.[10] The laws of Tiglath-Pileser I, king of Assyria in the twelfth century B.C., also contained prohibitions against the practice.[11] The first-century Jewish philosopher Philo of Alexandria condemned abortion, together with the practices of infanticide and child abandonment.[12]

Early Christianity resolutely opposed abortion, which was common in the Roman world. The *Didache* or "Teaching of the Twelve Apostles," a manual of Christian morals and church affairs from the first or second century, stated, "Thou shalt do no murder . . . thou shalt not procure abortion, nor commit infanticide" (2.2). Very similarly, the *Epistle of Barnabas* stated, "Thou shalt not procure abortion, thou shalt not commit infanticide" (19.5).[13]

In the second century the Christian apologist Athenagoras wrote, "How can we kill a man when we are those who say that all who use abortifacients are homicides and will account to God for their abortions as for the killing of men. For the fetus in the womb is not an animal, and it is God's providence that he exists."[14]

Tertullian, an attorney from Carthage converted to Christianity around the close of the second century, rebutted pagan charges that Christians practiced infanticide. Such charges were absurd, noted Tertullian. "For us, indeed, as homicide is forbidden, it is not lawful to destroy what is in the womb while the blood is still being formed into a man. To prevent being born is to accelerate homicide, nor does it make a difference whether you snatch away a soul which is born or destroy one being born. He who is man-to-be is man, as all fruit is now in the seed."[15]

By the fourth century, Christian condemnation of abortion was reflected in canon law. At the Council of Ancyra in 314 a gathering of Eastern bishops from Syria and Asia Minor denounced women who "slay what is generated and work to destroy it with abortifacients."[16]

Augustine, the most influential of the church fathers in the West, condemned abortion in no uncertain terms. Speaking of the married who avoided having children, he noted, "Sometimes this lustful cruelty or cruel lust comes to this, that they even procure poisons of sterility, and if these do not work, they extinguish and destroy the fetus in some way in the womb, preferring that their offspring die before it lives, or if it was already alive in the womb, to kill it before it was born."[17]

In Anglo-Saxon law prohibitions against abortion date back to the Middle Ages. In the middle of the thirteenth century Henry De Bracton, Chancellor of Exeter Cathedral and a Justicer of the Court, stated, "If there be anyone who strikes a pregnant woman or gives her a poison whereby he causes an abortion, if the foetus be already formed or animated, and especially if it be animated, he commits homicide."[18] De Bracton's statement reflects the commonly accepted Aristotelean embryology of the day, according to which the "rational soul" was infused after forty days of gestation in the male and after eighty days of gestation in the female.

In 1803, as part of a general revision of the British criminal law, abortion was made illegal before as well as after "quickening," the time when the mother is first able to feel movement in the womb. The British reform became the model for similar legislation in the United States during the nineteenth century.[19] From 1859 until the end of the century the American Medical Association campaigned vigorously to outlaw abortion except in cases where the mother's life would be endangered by a continuation of the pregnancy.[20] The concern to limit abortion was spurred by new scientific discoveries in human embryology, which clearly established that a new human being was in existence from the time of conception.

Until 1967 abortion was illegal in most states except in cases where the mother's health was threatened. Between 1967 and 1969, eleven states extended the conditions for "therapeutic" abortion to include various social circumstances such as number of children and financial need.[21]

The Supreme Court ruling in *Roe v. Wade*, handed down on January 22, 1973, dramatically altered the legal situation and effectively gave the United States abortion on demand. In this decision the Justices, by a 7-2 majority, held that during the first trimester of pregnancy the state could not regulate abortion, but must leave such decisions to the woman and her physician; that during the second trimester of pregnancy, the state might choose to regulate abortion, but only in ways that were reasonably related to protecting the woman's health; and that during the third trimester, in the interest of protecting potential human life, the state might choose to regulate or even prohibit abortion, except in cases where it might be necessary to preserve the woman's health or life.[22] By adopting a very broad definition of "health," which includes social and psychological, as well as purely medical conditions, the Court in effect allowed abortion up to the very moment of birth—if the woman desired it, and the physician was agreeable.

On July 1, 1976 the Court went a step further, ruling in *Planned Parenthood of Missouri v. Danforth* that a state cannot in cases of abortion impose a requirement for consent by a third party. Parents are not allowed to "veto" the abortion decisions of their minor daughters, nor are fathers allowed to exercise veto power over the abortion of the children they have helped to conceive. The Court held that in such cases of conflict, the wishes of the woman must prevail. This decision, like *Roe v. Wade* before it, provoked a great deal of criticism. Pro-life and pro-family groups charged the Court with subverting the authority of parents over their children, and of ignoring the rights of fathers to protect the lives of their own unborn offspring.

On June 30, 1980, by a 5-4 majority, the Court held in *Harris v. McRae* that Congress and the states may cut off funds for "medically necessary" abortions. In September of 1976 Congress passed the "Hyde Amendment," which in its various versions restricted the federal funding of abortion. The Court upheld the constitutionality of the Hyde Amendment, holding that it did not contravene the due process or equal protection provisions of the Constitution. The Court also ruled that the Hyde Amendment did not constitute an "establishment of religion." Critics had alleged that the amendment represented a particular religious viewpoint, that of the Roman Catholic Church. The Court responded by noting, "That the Judeo-Christian religions oppose stealing does not mean that a State or the Federal Government may not, consistent with the Establishment clause, enact laws prohibiting larceny." The Court also noted that the Hyde Amendment was consistent with the "legitimate government objective" of protecting the potential life of the unborn child.[23]

On June 15, 1983 the Court struck down an array of local ordinances designed to place restrictions on abortion. The Justices, in a 6-3 decision in *City of Akron v. Akron Center for Reproductive Health, Inc.*, held that it was unconstitutional for the city of Akron to require a 24-hour waiting period for abortions, to require that second-trimester abortions be performed in a hospital, or to require a doctor to tell the woman that the fetus "is a human life from the moment of conception" and that abortion can have dire physical and emotional consequences. The majority in the *Akron* case emphatically endorsed the virtually unrestricted abortion policy enunciated ten years earlier in *Roe v. Wade*.

In a very incisive dissent, however, Justice Sandra O'Connor noted fundamental flaws in the legal reasoning of the *Roe* decision, which provided the rationale for the *Akron* case. "In *Roe*, the Court held that although the State had an important and legitimate interest in protecting potential life," O'Connor observed, "that interest could not become compelling until the point at which the fetus was viable. The difficulty with this analysis is clear: *potential* life is no less potential in the first weeks of pregnancy than it is at viability or afterward."

In 1992 the Supreme Court in *Planned Parenthood v. Casey* upheld provisions of a Pennsylvania law requiring informed consent, a 24-hour waiting period, and parental consent for minors. Pro-lifers were disappointed, however, that in the 5-4 decision the Court left a central premise of *Roe v. Wade* intact, stating that there is a consititutional "right of a woman to choose to have an abortion before viability and to obtain it without undue interference from the state."[24]

MEDICAL ASPECTS

In the United States commonly used methods of abortion include vacuum curettage, dilation and curettage (D&C), dilation and evacuation, hysterotomy, prostaglandins, and hypertonic saline.[25] Since 1967 vacuum curettage has become a very common method for first-trimester abortions. In this technique the cervix is first dilated, and then a vacuum device is introduced into the uterus, which tears apart and suctions out the various bodily parts of the unborn child. The doctor or nurse then uses a magnifying glass or microscope to examine the bodily parts and verify the complete removal of the contents of the uterus.

In dilation and curettage (D&C), a traditional gynecological technique, the body of the developing child is cut to pieces with a sharp curette, and the uterine wall is scraped. This method is usually more painful than a vacuum abortion, requires larger dilation of the cervix, and causes a larger loss of blood.

Dilation and evacuation (D&E) combines elements of the traditional D&C and vacuum techniques. It is used for abortions in the thirteenth to sixteenth weeks of gestation, though some proponents have used it up through 20 or more weeks of gestation. During the second trimester of pregnancy the skeleton and skull of the unborn child are more developed, and as a consequence, the physician who is performing the abortion must use special instruments to crush the bones and skull of the child before removing them with the suction apparatus.

A hysterotomy is a small C-section. An incision is made in the abdominal wall, the unborn child is removed and, if still living, the child is left to die. "The overall morbidity and mortality of this procedure," observes Dr. Robert Hatcher of the Emory University School of Medicine, "have severely limited its use."[26]

Chemical substances known as prostaglandins are sometimes used in second-trimester abortions. These chemicals are infused into the amniotic sac through a long needle, and labor is prematurely induced. Prostaglandin abortions have the disadvantages of a higher incidence of gastrointestinal disturbances and associated cervical lacerations. This technique has also led to the "embarrassment" of the delivery of a live baby, rather than the dead one desired.

Second-trimester abortions can also be performed by infusing the amniotic sac with a salt solution ("salt-poisoning" abortion). The baby breathes in the saline solution and is poisoned by it. The outer layer of skin is burned off and brain hemorrhages may result. The woman goes into labor and about a day later delivers a dead, shriveled baby. Some observers have compared this method to the effect of napalm on war victims.[27]

The vast majority of abortions performed in the United States are done not for medical reasons—to preserve the life or health of the mother—but primarily for social reasons: pregnancy outside of marriage, contraceptive failure, economic considerations, questions of personal convenience and lifestyle, and so forth. Even before the 1973 Supreme Court abortion decisions, abortion on strictly medical grounds was becoming increasingly rare. Dr. Louis Hellman and Dr. Jack Pritchard, authors of a widely used medical textbook, *Williams Obstetrics*, noted that as a result of a "sharp and continuing decline in traditional indications (heart disease, hypertension, pulmonary tuberculosis, and hyperemesis [excessive vomiting], for example), the number of operations performed on these grounds has fallen dramatically over the past two decades, with the result that the interruption of pregnancy on physical indications is becoming rare."[28] Conditions such as heart disease and tuberculosis, which in an earlier day might have made continuation of the pregnancy dangerous, can now generally be managed so as to protect both the life of the mother and that of the developing child.

No discussion of the medical aspects of abortion should ignore the facts of prenatal development. Advances in medical knowledge are making it increasingly clear that human life of a very special order is being destroyed every time an abortion takes place. Eighteen to twenty-five days after conception, the baby's heart is already beating.[29] At eight weeks, brain waves can be detected and fingerprints have already formed. By the ninth and tenth weeks, the thyroid and adrenal glands are functioning, and the child can squint, swallow, and move the tongue. By the twelfth and thirteenth weeks, the child can suck his thumb and recoil from pain if pricked with a needle. By the fourth month the unborn child is eight to ten inches in height. All these changes occur before the fifth month, when the mother usually is first able to detect movements within the womb. The moment of "quickening," however, does not signal the first presence of life; a living human being has been present from the time of conception.

As early as 1970, in the midst of growing debate over abortion, the editors of the journal *California Medicine* noticed the "curious avoidance of the scientific fact, which everyone really knows, that human life begins at conception and is continuous whether intra- or extrauterine until death."[30] The proponents of changes in the then-restrictive abortion laws were usually not eager to discuss the physiological evidence concerning the humanity of the unborn.

Recent studies in the emerging fields of fetology and prenatal psychology have sharpened the medical community's perception of the unborn child as a patient in his own right. According to Susan M. Ludington, an Assistant Professor of Nursing at UCLA, numerous studies have shown that the unborn can respond to different colors of light directed toward the mother's belly, and to different types of music. (Vivaldi, apparently, is calming, while hard rock is not.) "We now know that from about 17 to 24 weeks, gestational age, all the systems are operational. The baby does respond, and early learning can occur," stated Ludington.[31]

In an article published in the February 17, 1983 issue of the *New England Journal of Medicine*, Drs. John Fletcher and Mark Evans reported that women who had seen ultrasound pictures of their unborn children during the first trimester or early second trimester of pregnancy experienced significant emotional bonding with the children as a result. Prior to their study, Fletcher and Evans believed that such emotional bonding occurred only during the relatively late stages of pregnancy, after "quickening" had occurred. The new ultrasound techniques, however, which make the body and movements of the unborn child visible to the parents and the physician, are likely to have great impact on the way in which the unborn child is perceived—a "humanizing" and "personalizing" effect, to be specific. Fletcher and Evans suggest that as a result of the ultrasound technology, ". . . a new stage of human existence, 'prenatality,' previously only mirrored in poets' and mothers' dreams about the fetus, will be as real to our descendants as childhood is to us."[32]

The "unborn child as patient" has been an emerging medical reality during recent years with the development of various forms of intrauterine surgery. Young Paul Bennett, born in January of 1982, was previously diagnosed as being hydrocephalic during the fifth month inside his mother's womb. Surgeons at the University of Colorado Health Sciences Center performed a delicate intrauterine operation that saved Paul from a life of severe retardation by placing a tiny shunt in his skull while he was still in the womb.[33] Such operations demonstrate dramatically that when physicians deal with a pregnant woman, two patients rather than one are involved. The simultaneity of heroic efforts to repair birth defects of some unborn children and the abortion of other children with similar defects, sometimes in the same hospital, points to the deep moral and legal schizophrenia surrounding abortion in the United States today.

There has been considerable controversy within the medical community concerning the safety of abortion. A study published in the *Journal of the American Medical Association*, based on an analysis of abortions performed in the period 1972-78, concluded that women were seven times more likely to die from childbirth than from legal abortion. The study claimed that the risk of death from legal abortion was about 1/100,000.[34] Such studies are quoted to support the claim that "abortion is seven times safer than childbearing."

Other researchers, however, have questioned the validity of these claims for the safety of legal abortion. Dr. Thomas W. Hilgers of the Creighton University School of Medicine has argued that the statistics comparing mortality from childbirth and from abortion are not really based on comparable quantities. Abortion mortality is defined in terms of maternal deaths per 100,000 cases of induced abortion. Maternal mortality, on the other hand, notes Hilgers, "includes deaths related to (a) the entire course of pregnancy, (b) childbirth and (c) the post partum period of up to three to six months."[35] Most abortions are performed in the first thirteen weeks of pregnancy; statistics on maternal mortality from "childbirth" include the entire term of pregnancy and even the period beyond. Consequently, the figures usually cited are skewed in favor of the relative safety of abortion. When truly comparable conditions and time periods are taken into account, argues Dr. Hilgers, natural pregnancy is actually found to be safer than abortion in both the first and second twenty weeks of pregnancy.[36]

There has also been considerable debate concerning nonfatal complications of abortion. Such complications would include immediate problems such as infection, bleeding, blood clots, laceration of the cervix, accidental perforation of the uterus, and long-term adverse effects on childbearing capacity.

It is generally claimed that short-term complications appear in about 3-6 percent of the cases of legal abortion.[37] Since most abortion clinics do not keep follow-up records on their clients, it is likely that the true incidence of serious abortion complications is underreported.

Pamela Zekman and Pamela Warrick, two investigative reporters for the Chicago *Sun-Times,* conducted a five-month probe of Chicago's abortion clinics in 1978. They discovered that some of the abortion clinics were assembly-line operations more concerned with making money than with the health and safety of the clients. Some abortions were performed on women who were not even pregnant. One doctor at the Water Tower Reproductive Center went from one abortion to another without washing his hands or using sterile gloves. Other doctors perforated the uterus or vagina; record keeping was shoddy; lab tests were lost or scrambled. Concluded Zekman: "In 1973 the Supreme Court legalized abortion. As it turns out, what they legalized in some clinics in Chicago is the highly profitable and very dangerous back-room abortion."[38]

One of the most dreaded immediate "complications," from the perspective of the abortionist, is live birth: a baby that manages to survive the abortion procedure. Such live births are most common in second-trimester abortions, especially in those performed with prostaglandin infusion. Prostaglandins were initially welcomed by doctors as a safer alternative to saline poisoning, but subsequently they have been found to cause, in many instances, diarrhea and vomiting. Prostaglandin abortions have resulted in seven to nine live births per 100 abortions, a rate 30 times higher than with saline.[39]

In 1977 Dr. William B. Waddill performed a salt-poisoning abortion on an 18-year-old girl in Orange County, California. The baby was born alive, and according to later testimony, Dr. Waddill ordered the staff to do nothing and to let the baby die. Dr. Waddill went to the hospital, and a pediatrician testified that he saw Waddill choke the 2.5

pound baby girl. "I saw him put his hand on this baby's neck and push down," testified Dr. Ronald Cornelson in court. Cornelson also claimed that Waddill suggested injecting the baby with potassium chloride or filling a sink and drowning her. In two separate murder trials Waddill denied Cornelson's story, and the jury deadlocked on both occasions.[40]

In recent years considerable attention has been devoted within the medical establishment to the long-term effects of abortion, especially its impact upon subsequent childbearing capability. Contradictory results have appeared in the medical journals. A Swedish study, based on women having abortions in the period 1970-75, found no significant association between women having vacuum abortions and unfavorable outcomes of subsequent pregnancies.[41] A study of women in Hawaii who had abortions during the years 1970-74 found no significant increase in the numbers of miscarriages or tubal pregnancies during subsequent pregnancies.[42] A 1979 study published in the *New England Journal of Medicine* concluded that the risks of having a miscarriage in a pregnancy subsequent to abortion had diminished since 1973.[43]

Other research, however, done both in the United States and in foreign countries has reported significant adverse effects of legal abortion on subsequent pregnancies. A 1981 study published in the *American Journal of Obstetrics and Gynecology* found that women with a previous history of abortion showed slight but significant increases in subsequent pregnancy failures: tubal pregnancies, miscarriages, and fetal or neonatal deaths.[44] Professor Erik B. Obel, reporting on a Danish study, noted that "bleeding before 28 weeks of gestation and retention of placenta or placental tissue occurred more frequently after legal abortion than in a control group matched for age, parity [number of children previously born], and socio-economic status."[45]

Professor Knut Dalaker and his associates, studying the effects of legal abortions in Norway on subsequent pregnancy outcomes, did find a higher rate of complications such as miscarriage, cervical incompetence, prematurity, and tubal pregnancies. "Amongst those not having been pregnant previously, the complication rate was 25.5% compared to 13.2% in the controls."[46] This study would seem to indicate that teenage girls who have an abortion before having a live birth are especially subject to risks in future pregnancies.

Researchers at the University of Athens Medical School concluded that abortion significantly increased the risks of secondary infertility, and that about 45 percent of the cases of secondary infertility in Greece may be attributed to previous induced abortions.[47] Another Greek study, performed at the Alexandra Maternity Hospital in Athens, including 13,242 women admitted for delivery over a two-year period, found that the percentage of stillbirths and premature births among women with previous abortions, spontaneous or induced, was double that of the control group.[48]

One Israeli study involved 11,057 women in Jerusalem who were interviewed during their pregnancies. The researchers found that the 752 women who reported one or more induced abortions were more likely to report bleeding in the first three months of subsequent pregnancies, were more likely to experience complications of labor, and were more likely to require manual removal of the placenta. There were also significant increases in the incidence of low birth weights and birth defects.[49]

Some proponents of the safety of abortion have suggested that figures from foreign countries are not reliable, since medical standards may be lower in those countries. That argument is unconvincing, especially with regard to Scandinavian and Israeli medical practices. Furthermore, these same problems in pregnancy subsequent to abortion have been reported in American studies.

Research performed by Boston medical scientists found that women who had had two or more abortions experienced a twofold to threefold increased risk of miscarriage during the first trimester of a subsequent pregnancy. The increased risks were found to be present for women who had had abortions since 1973, and the method of abortion appeared to make no difference.[50]

Dr. Jeffrey Barrett and his associates at the Vanderbilt University Hospital in Nashville studied women who had obtained abortions during the periods 1972-74 and 1979-80. Those who had undergone first-trimester abortions experienced a seven- to fifteen-fold increase in a subsequent complication known as *placenta previa*, in which the placenta implants on an abnormal site in the uterus. "Given the large number of first-trimester abortions performed yearly in the United States," stated Barrett, "the potential ramifications of such an association are obvious."[51] Dr. Barrett suggested that the vigorous scraping of the uterus performed during an abortion, which can cause significant scarring of the endometrium (the mucous membrane lining the uterus), together with the process of suctioning, may make more likely the implantation of the placenta on an abnormal site.

Dr. M. C. Pike and his associates studied the possible links between abortion and breast cancer in young women. Their research was based on the experience of 163 young women in Los Angeles County, 33 years of age or younger, who had developed breast cancer. There was evidence that a first-trimester abortion before a first full-term pregnancy significantly increased the risk of breast cancer. The nature of the connection was not clear, but the existence of such a possible link appeared to be indicated by the data.[52]

The debate on the long-term complications of abortion is likely to continue for years to come. Given the large numbers of women who have abortions each year in the United States, if only a small number of women experience such complications, the total number of such adverse outcomes represents a major medical problem. A significant body of scientific research from foreign countries, as well as the United States, indicates that women who seek abortions may well be damaging their future ability to experience a successful pregnancy.

THE PSYCHOLOGICAL DIMENSION

An event like abortion, which touches human sexuality and procreation at an intimate and profound level, is bound to have significant psychological repercussions. Although "hard data" are difficult to obtain because of the highly subjective nature of the reporting and the emotionally charged nature of the subject, nevertheless there is evidence that guilt, depression, and other forms of psychological conflict plague many women who have had abortions.

Some studies have maintained that abortion has few if any serious psychological side effects. In a 1963 study Kramer surveyed 32 psychiatrists in the Los Angeles area and found that during an average of 12 years of practice, 75 percent of the physicians had not observed a serious psychological complication stemming from abortion.[53] In 1973 Ewing and Rouse surveyed 126 women and concluded that "women without gross psychiatric illness can usually take the procedure in stride."[54]

The validity of such conclusions has been questioned, however. In a critical study Drs. Richard Maddock and Ray Sexton pointed out that surveys and questionnaires are not suitable for uncovering repressed emotional conflicts. "Defenses in these patients are especially strong because the event is of such an intimate and emotionally charged nature," they noted. In their clinical experience Maddock and Sexton have observed symptoms directly related to abortion surfacing as late as 37 years after the event.[55]

Workers at the Pregnancy Aftermath Helpline in Milwaukee, a 24-hour telephone counseling service, received 95 post-abortion calls between November 1976 and October of 1978. Fifty-eight of the women expressed a direct relationship between their abortion and their symptoms of distress. Feelings of guilt, anxiety, depression, sense of loss, remorse, and deterioration of self-image were reported by this group. Guilt was the most common reaction. Some stated that they had "murdered a baby," or "didn't do what a good mother would have done." One caller expressed a sense of guilt over an abortion that she had undergone 25 years previously. One woman had wanted to get pregnant immediately after her abortion, but said, "I should never have a child because I can't undo this abortion."[56]

The husbands or boyfriends of the women who have abortions are also affected, though their reactions are generally overlooked in discussions of the subject. Dr. Arthur Shostak, Professor of Sociology at Drexel University, has interviewed hundreds of men who have been involved in some way in the abortion procedure. "They don't think of it just as an operation that their wives or girlfriends are having," stated Shostak. "They think of it—even if they don't always describe it this way—as a loss of fatherhood." During one interview Shostak mentioned the word "fetus," and the man's eyes filled up with tears. "It's not a fetus we're talking about. It's my son. He would be three years old now."[57]

Abortion also takes its psychological toll on doctors and nurses. The killing of human life in abortions produces tremendous tension with the medical profession's stated ideals of healing and preserving life. The impact can be felt both by the doctors who perform the abortions and by the nurses who frequently have the grisly task of inspecting the dismembered parts of the baby's body to make sure that no parts have been left in the uterus after the abortion.

Dr. Bernard Nathanson, who was once the director of an abortion clinic in New York City that performed as many as a hundred abortions a day, later changed his pro-abortion position when the medical evidence convinced him of the humanity of the unborn. He had personally observed the psychological impact of the routine killing on his clinic staff. Doctors began "losing their nerve in the operating room," he recalled. "I remember one sweating profusely, shaking badly, nipping drinks between procedures." Some nurses were plagued by depression, and one doctor's wife complained to Nathanson at a party that her husband was dreaming continually of blood. "I was seeing personality structures dissolve in front of me on a scale I had never seen before in a medical situation," he said. "Very few members of the staff seemed to remain fully intact through their experiences."[58]

Not all reports concerning the psychological impact of abortion are as vivid as Nathanson's, of course. Nevertheless, it seems quite evident that the continuing practice of abortion in the United States is building a tremendous load of guilt in millions of lives, the consequences of which will be felt in various ways for years, if not decades, to come.

BIBLICAL, THEOLOGICAL, AND ETHICAL CONSIDERATIONS

Analyses of the morality of abortion tend to cluster around three major positions: abortion on demand, abortion on "indications," and abortion only to preserve the life of the mother. The abortion-on-demand position sees abortion as morally acceptable under almost all circumstances. The abortion-on-"indications" position assigns value to the life of the unborn child, but argues that the greater value of the mother's life relative to that of the developing child would justify abortion when the mother's medical, social, emotional, or economic well-being would be threatened by the continuation of the pregnancy. The "life of the mother" position holds that only in those rare cases (e.g., a tubal pregnancy or a cancerous uterus) when continuation of the pregnancy would endanger the mother's life is abortion morally justified. Within Christian circles, the real debate is between the proponents of the "indications" and "life of the mother" positions.

The abortion-on-demand position reflects a secular outlook on the value of human life. A prominent representative of this position is Joseph Fletcher, perhaps best known for his 1966 book, *Situation Ethics: The New Morality*. In a later work, written in 1974, *The Ethics of Genetic Control*, Fletcher articulates his case for abortion. According to Fletcher, the key issue in the whole debate is "whether a fetus is a person or not."[59] In Fletcher's pragmatic and situational approach to ethics, determinations of right and wrong are based on calculations of costs and benefits of various lines of action for the persons involved. If the unborn child does not represent a person in the moral sense of the term, then there will obviously be many circumstances when the cost-benefit analysis will justify abortion in terms of the woman's interest.

Fletcher identifies personhood with a minimum degree of human consciousness and intelligence—roughly a minimum score of 20 on the Binet I.Q. scale. "Obviously," he notes, "a fetus cannot meet this test, no matter what its stage of growth."[60] In Fletcher's view, the most sensible position is to hold that the unborn child becomes a person at the moment of birth, when the umbilical cord is cut. Prior to this point, the unborn child is a nonperson, and abortion would always be justifiable except in those cases where undesirable consequences *for the woman* would outweigh desirable ones. In short, the basic ethical principle for Fletcher is that "pregnancy when wanted is a healthy process, pregnancy when not wanted is a disease—in fact, a venereal disease. The truly ethical question is not whether we can justify abortion but whether we can justify compulsory pregnancy."[61]

It is clear that biblical ideas such as the creation of man in the image and likeness of God (Gen. 1:26-28) play no role in Fletcher's analysis: The life of the unborn child is assigned little or no value in and of itself, and abortion is justified in almost all cases in which the woman desires it.

While few if any conservative Protestants would identify themselves with the abortion-on-demand position, some would argue for abortion on "indications." Professor D. Gareth Jones has articulated such a position in his book, *Brave New People: Ethical Issues at the Commencement of Life.*[62] Jones addresses the issue of therapeutic abortion, with particular reference to the questions of physical and genetic defects in the unborn child. "Is it right to inflict upon the fetus the consequence of a particular disability, whether it be Down's syndrome or Tay-Sachs disease?" asks Jones. "In this instance, it has to be decided whether abortion will benefit the fetus, the parents, society, or none of them."[63]

Professor Jones notes that the issue of the *status of the fetus* is the critical point upon which the question of therapeutic abortion will be resolved. According to the *potentiality principle,* a potential person is "an existing being which, while not yet a person, will become an actual person during the normal course of its development."[64]

This principle of potentiality recognizes that though the developing embryo is a member of *Homo sapiens,* there are nevertheless profound differences between a 6-day-old embryo and a 6-month-old fetus. While the 6-day-old embryo is to be treated with respect, it is nevertheless much further from manifesting the "full qualities of human personhood."[65]

"I believe that the potentiality principle is an option for Christians," states Jones. "Its high view of the status of the fetus means, that in practical terms the fetus will be protected under all normal circumstances."[66]

In discussing the biblical material, Jones notes that no biblical text explicitly forbids procuring an abortion. He concedes, however, that little stress should be placed on arguments from silence. While texts such as Psalm 139:13-16 underscore God's involvement with the unborn child, they should not be used to conclude that the fetus is to be equated with a living person. The fetus is in the process of being built into the image and likeness of God, but that process is not yet complete prior to birth.[67]

Jones then discusses specific conditions that might justify abortion. He argues that Down's syndrome does not rob the fetus of potentially human qualities, and abortion would not be justified in such cases. On the other hand, the condition of anencephaly, where the major brain centers are lacking, means that, in Jones's view, "there is no prospect of anything remotely resembling human life." Cases such as Tay-Sachs disease, which involve deterioration of vision and motor skills, and usually death within 2-4 years, would fall somewhere in between. In making a decision in such cases, a balance needs to be struck between the human potential of the deformed child and the impact that having such a child would have on the family unit. Some families are not able to cope with such challenges, and a reluctant compromise must be adopted, in Jones's view, to terminate the pregnancy.[68]

"In practical terms," writes Professor Jones, "the position I am advocating probably differs little from a strong anti-abortionist stance." However, the realities of our fallen humanity may mean that some of these "appalling dilemmas may be resolvable only by therapeutic abortion."[69]

The third major position on the morality of abortion, the life-of-the-mother position, is widely held in conservative Protestant circles. It is also represented in the official pronouncements of Roman Catholic, Eastern Orthodox, and Orthodox Jewish religious leaders. In this understanding, only in those rare cases where continuation of the pregnancy would present a threat to the mother's life would abortion be morally justified. In a tubal pregnancy, for example, continuation of the pregnancy could lead to a rupture of the Fallopian tube and the danger of a fatal hemorrhage. Surgical intervention would be justified as an effort to salvage the life that has some real prospect of survival under the circumstances, i.e., the mother's. Given the present state of medical technology, it is not possible to save the human embryo developing outside the normal uterine location. Rather than letting two lives perish, surgical intervention is indicated in order to save the life that can be saved. The intervention is not made on the assumption that the embryonic life is without value; the intervention merely reflects the condition that with existing medical technology, the mother's life is salvageable, and the unborn child's is not.

This third position is represented in *Death Before Birth* by Professor Harold O. J. Brown, formerly of Trinity Evangelical Divinity School. Professor Brown was instrumental in the formation of the Christian Action Council, the nation's largest Protestant evangelical pro-life organization.

In developing his life-of-the-mother position, Brown utilized key biblical texts together with scientific data from human embryology. Brown acknowledges that the Bible does not explicitly condemn abortion. He observes, however, that neither does it explicitly condemn infanticide. The crucial question is whether or not in the biblical outlook the fetus is considered a human life. "If the developing fetus is shown to be a human being, then we do not need a specific commandment against feticide any more than we need something specific against uxoricide (wife killing). The general command against killing covers both."[70]

Brown argues that in the abortion debate, the burden of proof is on the advocates of a permissive position to show that the unborn child is not human. If a hunter were to see a movement behind a bush and shoot at it, without being sure that the movement was not caused by a human being rather than by an animal, such an action would be morally irresponsible. Regarding abortion, any doubts concerning the humanity of the unborn child should be resolved in favor of developing human life.[71]

While the Bible nowhere offers a technical definition of personhood that might satisfy a philosopher, the Scriptures do assume a fundamental continuity between prenatal and postnatal human life. The Hebrew word *yeled*, used of children generally, is also used of the unborn child in Exodus 21:22. The Greek word *brephos*, used in Acts 7:19 to refer to the children killed at Pharaoh's command, is used in Luke 1:41, 44 to refer to John the Baptist while he was still in his mother's womb.[72]

The biblical teaching of the creation of man in the image and likeness of God (Gen. 1:27) is the foundation of the dignity and sacredness of human life. Because man is made in the divine image, the shedding of innocent blood pollutes the land and cries out to God for judgment (Num. 35:33). "If a nation permits the slaughter of the innocent," warns the author, "it will surely bring God's judgment upon itself."[73]

But is the image of God present in the unborn human being? Brown cites Psalm 139:13, 14; Jeremiah 1:5; Luke 1:44; and Psalm 51:5

as evidence that God relates in a personal way to the unborn human. God's involvement in the creation, preservation, moral evaluation, and setting apart of his people for future service is evident in these passages. Brown concludes that such passages imply that "God clearly says the unborn child is already a human being, made in the image of God and deserving the protection of law."[74]

Brown also points to the known facts of human embryology to support his position. When the sperm and egg unite, a genetically unique human being comes into being. While the developing child is dependent on the mother's body for nourishment and oxygen, physiologically the unborn child is not simply a part or extension of the mother's body. The unborn child is an individual in his or her own right, with a separate and distinct life trajectory. The case of identical twins shows that absolute individuality in the conceptus may not be present at the moment of conception, but by the time of implantation on the uterine wall, either *one* or *two* distinct lives are in existence. "Admittedly, there may be some dispute as to precisely *when* fetal life is 'fully human,' but everyone *knows* it is a long time before birth, and the Supreme Court permits abortions right up to the moment of birth," notes Brown.[75]

According to Brown, then, both the biblical data on the sacredness of human life made in God's image—the evidence that God relates to the unborn in a personal way—and the scientific facts of human development lead one to the "life-of-the-mother" position. Evangelical Protestants, he urges, should oppose the present abortion-on-demand situation in the United States and work for the restoration of the legal rights of the unborn.

Of the three approaches surveyed, the "life-of-the-mother" position would appear to have the most support from Scripture. As Brown and others have pointed out, the biblical texts assume a basic continuity between prenatal and postnatal life, and God's love and concern for the unborn is not limited to the advanced stages of pregnancy, after some point of "viability" has been attained. In Psalm 139:16, David used the term *golem*, "unformed substance," to refer to God's care for him during the embryonic state—the first eight weeks after conception, long before the mother can feel life in the womb. "Although the Bible makes no claim to be a textbook of embryology," notes John Stott, "here is a plain affirmation that the growth of the fetus is neither haphazard nor automatic but a divine work of creative skill."[76] Texts such as Job 10:8-13 and 31:13, 15 also make the point that God, and not some blind biological process, is responsible for the creation of human life in the womb.

In the New Testament, the incarnation of Jesus Christ is a profound testimony to God's affirmation of the sanctity of prenatal life.[77] In theory it might have been possible in the eternal plan of God for the Savior to come to earth as a grown man, but in the wisdom of God, Jesus Christ recapitulated the full span of human existence—from conception through death—in order to fulfill the purposes of God. The personal history of the Son of God on earth begins not when he was "born of the Virgin Mary," but when he was "conceived by the Holy Spirit." His human history, like ours, began at *conception*. His conception was, of course, a supernatural one, but the significant point is that God chose to begin the process of incarnation there, rather than at some other point, thus affirming the significance of that starting point for human life. As the writer of Hebrews says, he had to be "made like his brothers in every respect" (2:17), in order to be a merciful and sympathetic high priest on their behalf.

In today's world, a young, unmarried woman like Mary with a "problem pregnancy" would be tempted to end it all with an abortion. But in Mary's case, abortion would have meant the death of the Son of God, who was already present within her womb.

It is also of interest to note that among the sins of the flesh listed by Paul in Galatians 5:20 there appears the term *pharmakeia*, usually translated as "sorcery," but more adequately translated as "medicine" in the sense in which a North American Indian medicine man makes "medicine." The term refers to the use of drugs with occult properties for a variety of purposes, including sorcery, but also including abortion. "Paul's usage here cannot be restricted to abortion, but the term he chose is comprehensive enough to include the use of abortifacient drugs," notes Professor John T. Noonan, Jr.[78] The term *pharmakeia* is specifically used of abortifacient drugs in a second-century A.D. text of Soranus of Ephesus, an early Greek gynecologist.[79]

Some have argued for a more permissive view of abortion on the basis of Exodus 21:22-25.[80] According to one interpretation of this passage, the text states that if a man causes a pregnant woman to have a miscarriage, but no further harm comes to the woman, then capital punishment is not required for the loss of the life of the unborn child, no matter how advanced the pregnancy. According to this interpretation, Old Testament law does not consider the unborn child a soul or human life, thus implying a clear distinction between the value of the life of the unborn child and that of the mother.

The linguistic evidence of the text itself does not support the "miscarriage" translation, however. The verb *yatza* when used alone, as it is here, refers to a live birth, not a miscarriage (Gen. 25:25, 26; 38:28-30; Jer. 1:5; 20:18). *Yatza* is used of a stillbirth only when accompanied by some form of *muth*, "to die," as in Numbers 12:12 and Job 3:11. The term used in Exodus 21:22, *yeled*, means "child," including the newborn child, whereas for "embryo" or "unformed fetus" there is the word *golem*, which is not used in the text. There is a specific Hebrew word for "miscarriage," *shakol* (Exod. 23:26; Hos. 9:14), and this word is not used in Exodus 21:22-25. Consequently, the better translation of the passage takes it to refer to a *premature live birth*, not a miscarriage. The text actually treats the life of the mother and that of the unborn child as equally valuable and thus renders strong support to the "life-of-the-mother" position.[81]

It has also been suggested that the biblical association between human life and *ruah*, "breath" (e.g., Gen. 6:17; Job 34:14-15; Hab. 2:19; Zech. 12:1; Ps. 104:29-30) points to a more permissive view of abortion, especially during the first trimester.[82] Since independent breathing is generally not possible before the twentieth week of gestation, it is suggested that a human life is not yet present, given the biblical association between "life" and "breath." Yet in order to safeguard developing human life, abortion should be prohibited after the first trimester.

There are a number of serious difficulties with that view. In the first place, it places a value on "independent" human existence that the Bible itself does not appear to stress. The fundamental fact in Scripture is that human beings are *creatures* at every stage of their development, both prior to and subsequent to birth, and always dependent on the sustaining mercy of God for their life. "In him we live and move and have our being" (Acts 17:28). God is the only totally "viable" and self-sustaining being in the universe; all other creatures, including adult human beings, are constantly dependent upon his gracious will for their continuing life and existence. It is the constant temptation of us creatures, however, to forget this condition of dependence, and act as though, like God, we had the power of life in ourselves.

These considerations show the difficulty of pointing to "viability" as a criterion for assessing the value of a human life. David was valuable in God's sight, the object of his love and concern, in the first eight weeks of gestation (Ps. 139:13-16)—long before he was capable of independent breathing. A diabetic may be totally dependent on insulin, but we do not rightly conclude that such a dependence diminishes the value of the person.

There is a further difficulty in that this "life-and-breath" approach takes texts (Gen. 6:17, etc.) that speak of common manifestations of *postnatal* life—such as breathing—and applies such texts to *prenatal* life, of which they are not meant to speak; and it then makes a *value judgment* on the basis of this questionable inference. The writers of these Old Testament texts hardly intended to make "scientific" judgments about the moment of viability or the time at which independent breathing could occur; to use them in this fashion is to take them out of their proper context and impute to them a meaning the original author never intended. If the question is raised, "What is God's valuation of and relation to unborn human beings," then there are texts that speak clearly and directly to that issue (Ps. 139:13-16; Jer. 1:5; the Incarnation). They are the ones on which to focus when one seeks answers concerning the *value* of prenatal life.

It is also difficult to apply the life-and-breath position with consistency. If it is argued that the association between "life" and "breath" should be applied in a literalistic fashion to make judgments about prenatal life, then one must also allow that there is a literal association in the Old Testament between *blood* and life—e.g., in Genesis 9:4: "You shall not eat flesh with its life, that is, its blood." By applying a literalistic hermeneutic, the Jehovah's Witnesses have concluded that blood transfusions are prohibited by the Bible, because they would cause a mingling of the souls or lives that are contained in the blood. If a literalistic use of the texts in that case is improper, it is also improper in the case of "life" and "breath," for the two usages are parallel.

For these reasons, the "life-and-breath" approach does not provide a sound exegetical or hermeneutical basis for a permissive view of abortion. The witness of Scripture is that God values the life of the unborn child at every stage of development, not just during the advanced stages of pregnancy.

Proponents of the abortion-on-demand and abortion-on-indications positions generally take the fetus to be less than a full "person" or "human being" because of the lack of fully developed consciousness. It is dangerous, however, to equate the *fact* of personhood with certain *psychological states*. Personhood is a metaphysical reality out of which arise, during the normal course of human development, the psychological manifestations of the person.[83] A newborn baby does not possess the adult's powers of speech or thought, but in due course the baby will develop these powers, because they are inherent in the child's nature. The same argument that justifies abortion because of the lack of consciousness in the unborn could also justify infanticide after birth.[84] The equation of personhood with certain states of consciousness could also be extended to argue for the killing of the comatose, the senile, and the mentally retarded. As has been seen in reference to Psalm 139:13-16, God values human life long before the emergence of human consciousness; God loved David well before David became conscious of that love. A "person" in the proper sense exists from the earliest moments of human existence. Personhood denotes not merely conscious, postnatal humans, but all members of the human species, those who are genetically distinct human entities with their own unique life trajectory and developmental futures. Rather than saying that the unborn represent "potential human life," it is more accurate to say that the unborn represent *actual* human life with *great potential*. The problem with the "potential-actual" distinction as it has frequently been used in the abortion debate is that this same distinction applies just as much after birth as it does before. No adult can say that he or she has "fully actualized" his or her human possibilities. God is the only "fully actualized" person in the universe.

A more adequate approach to understanding "personhood" defines it not in terms of the human being in isolation, or merely in terms of qualities immanent within the individual, but in terms of relationship to God. A "person" is a being to which God relates in a personal way; it is God's initiative in relationships that "personalizes" the creature. This definition includes our common usage, but is also broad enough to include texts such as Jeremiah 1:5 and Psalm 139:13-16, which speak of unborn human life.

The problem of rape is often discussed in relation to the ethics of abortion. If a woman becomes pregnant as a result of rape, is abortion a morally legitimate option? During the late 1960s this issue was often raised in arguments to liberalize the then-existing laws, which generally reflected the life-of-the-mother position. In a sexually chaotic society, where rape unfortunately appears to be on the rise, the question is one of continuing relevance and concern.

Rape is without question a physically and emotionally traumatic event for the woman involved, and society and the churches should offer whatever support and assistance to the woman they can reasonably offer. Even in such cases, however, it should not be assumed without further analysis that abortion is justified. Several factors need to be taken into consideration in forming a moral judgment.

Pregnancy due to confirmed cases of rape is relatively rare. Several careful studies have documented the actual incidence of rape-related pregnancies. The findings have ranged from 0 to 2.2 percent of the victims involved.[85] The largest of these studies, conducted by Dr. Charles Hayman and involving 2,190 women concluded that the probability of either becoming pregnant or contracting some sexually transmitted disease is "small, very roughly, from 1 in 200 to 1 in 50."[86]

A number of physiological factors make pregnancy unlikely as a result of rape. Even under normal circumstances, a woman is able to conceive on only two or three days of each monthly menstrual cycle. One study concluded that even a woman raped on the very day of ovulation had only a one in ten chance of becoming pregnant.[87] Other studies have indicated that a relatively high percentage of rapists have some type of sexual dysfunction, e.g., failure to ejaculate. Rape does not necessarily involve a completed act of intercourse. Some rape victims are taking oral contraceptives, or are infertile for other reasons. All these factors contribute to the rarity of pregnancy as a result of rape.

But what of those cases in which pregnancy does result? General statistics provide little comfort to the woman who does get pregnant. There are, admittedly, such hard cases. Even in such an event, it could be argued that it is right and in the woman's best *long-term* interests not to have an abortion.

As a matter of simple justice, it is the rapist who should be punished, not the innocent child conceived as a result of the rape. In the Mosaic law it was commanded, "The fathers shall not be put to death for the children, nor shall the children be put to death for the fathers; every man shall be put to death for his own sin" (Deut. 24:16). What this text emphasizes is the principle of personal responsibility and personal accountability. The rapist has committed a crime, not the child who may be conceived as a result. It is true that the woman has suffered an injustice; but abortion would represent a further injustice, this time against the unborn child. "Two wrongs do not make a right."

By not having an abortion in such a case, the woman avoids the psychological and spiritual problems arising from the guilt involved in the taking of innocent human life; she also avoids the risks of endangering her future reproductive capacity. Those individuals and organizations that counsel the victims of rape should be prepared to offer the concrete emotional, spiritual, and financial support that can help to make such "heroic" decisions a viable option for the women involved.

Anticipated birth defects are frequently mentioned as an "indication" for abortion. Amniocentesis and other techniques of prenatal diagnosis now allow the detection of a growing list of genetically related conditions. The scriptural outlook, however, gives no justification for a "search and destroy" ethic, or for a mentality that would allow only the physically and intellectually superior to live.

Even birth defects can play a part in the sovereign plan of God. Moses, called by God to lead the children of Israel out of slavery in Egypt, complained that he was not an eloquent speaker. God replied, "Who has made man's mouth? Who makes him dumb, or deaf, or seeing, or blind? Is it not I, the Lord?" (Exod. 4:11). God is able to use such human weaknesses to demonstrate his own divine power, which is in fact perfected in man's weakness (II Cor. 12:9).

When Jesus Christ demonstrated the perfect compassion and justice of God, he did not destroy the sick and the blind and the lame, but healed them. "He will not break a bruised reed or quench a smoldering wick" (Matt. 12:20; Isa. 42:3). Christ's ethic was not "search and destroy," but "to seek and to save."

In the incident of the healing of the man born blind (John 9), Jesus' disciples asked whether it was the man's own sin or the sin of his parents that was the cause of the blindness. Jesus replied that neither supposition was correct; in the mystery of God's providence, the condition had been permitted that the glory of God might be manifested through a miracle of healing (v. 3).

It has been suggested that the abortion of the defective prior to birth is really the "humane" course of action, since it can spare these individuals the agony of "lives devoid of quality and meaning." It is more to the point, however, to allow the handicapped the opportunity to speak for and decide for themselves. A striking testimony of this sort appeared some years ago in the London *Daily Telegraph* in the wake of the Thalidomide tragedy, when abortion was being suggested as a solution to the problem of defective babies:[88]

> Trowbridge
> Kent
> December 8, 1962

Sirs:

> We were disabled from causes other than Thalidomide, the first of us having two useless arms and hands; the second, two useless legs; and the third, the use of neither arms nor legs.
>
> We were fortunate . . . in having been allowed to live and we want to say with strong conviction how thankful we are that none took it upon themselves to destroy us as helpless cripples.

Here at the Delarue school of spastics, one of the schools of the National Spastic Society, we have found worthwhile and happy lives and we face our future with confidence. Despite our disability, life still has much to offer and we are more than anxious, if only metaphorically, to reach out toward the future.

This, we hope, will give comfort and hope to the parents of the Thalidomide babies, and at the same time serve to condemn those who would contemplate the destruction of even a limbless baby.

Yours faithfully,

Elane Duckett
Glynn Verdon
Caryl Hodges

Although those with serious handicaps experience obvious limitations, that does not mean that their lives are devoid of meaning. Only a "master-race" ethic would hold that only the physically and intellectually elite have a right to live.

The biblical ethic upholds the dignity and worth of every human being, regardless of the state of development or physical dependency, from the moment of conception until natural death. The life-of-the-mother position is consistent with this position. The Christian community should endorse such a position both in personal practice and in public policy, and back it up with tangible spiritual, emotional, and financial help for women who are facing difficult pregnancies.

CHAPTER 7

Infanticide and Euthanasia

INFANTICIDE

The child "is at this very moment at Bloomington Hospital starving to death," prosecutor Larry Brodeur told the Indiana Supreme Court during an emergency hearing on the case of "Infant Doe" on April 14, 1982. The infant has "a constitutionally guaranteed right to live," stated Brodeur.[1]

Infant Doe was born in Bloomington, Indiana with Down's syndrome and a misformed esophagus, which prevented normal feeding. The parents of the child, who remained anonymous throughout the controversy, had refused permission for corrective surgery on the child and had ordered the doctors to withhold all nourishment. Even though ten different couples had expressed interest in adopting the child, the parents refused to give up custody.

At an emergency hearing, the justices of the Indiana Supreme Court voted 3-1 to support the wishes of the parents. The court was, in effect, allowing the parents to starve their deformed infant to death. Infant Doe died on April 15, 1982.

One person who had offered to adopt Infant Doe was Mike Lorentay, who teaches the printing trade to the retarded in Edmonton, Canada. "I believe that every person, no matter who or what their ages, has a right to live," Lorentay stated. "I'm not well off, but I'd pay for it [the operation] and bring the baby back to Canada."[2] Lorentay's generous offer was foreclosed by the parents' refusal and Infant Doe's death by starvation.

The attorney who had represented Infant Doe's parents had coined the euphemism "treatment to do nothing" in reference to the parents' decision. Columnist George Will, himself the father of a happy Down's syndrome boy, noted, "It is an old story: Language must be mutilated when a perfumed rationalization of an act is incompatible with a straightforward description of the act. . . . the broader message of the case is that being an unwanted baby is a capital offense."[3]

HISTORICAL BACKGROUND

The case of Infant Doe in Bloomington, Indiana is not, unfortunately, an isolated one in recent American medical practice. In 1972 a storm of controversy was created in a similar case involving a Down's syndrome child born in the Johns Hopkins University Hospital. The child was born with duodenal atresia (intestinal blockage), and the parents, a middle-income couple in their twenties, refused permission for the relatively simple operation to remove the obstruction. All food and fluids were withheld, and the child died 15 days later from starvation and dehydration.[4]

In 1973 Doctors Raymond S. Duff and A. G. M. Campbell, in a widely discussed article published in the *New England Journal of Medicine,* documented 43 cases of withholding care from handicapped infants at the Yale-New Haven Hospital, thereby breaking what they termed the "public and professional silence on a major social taboo."[5]

In 1974 there was a major conference in Sonoma, California, which focused on ethical issues in pediatrics. Seventeen of the twenty participants agreed that the doctor could take direct action to end the life of a self-sustaining infant.[6]

In July of 1983 the editors of *Pediatrics,* the learned journal of the American Academy of Pediatrics, printed an article by philosopher Peter Singer of Monash University in Australia, which provided a rationale for infanticide in the case of the severely handicapped newborn. "We can no longer base our ethics on the idea that human beings are a special form of creation, made in the image of God," stated Singer, "singled out from all other animals, and alone possessing an immortal soul." We should recognize, argued Singer, that in some cases the life of a dog or a pig could be more morally significant than that of the defective infant, because the dog or pig might possess superior powers of rationality and self-consciousness. Mere membership in the species *Homo sapiens* is not necessarily morally significant. "Humans who bestow superior value on the lives of all human beings," wrote Singer, "solely because they are members of our own species, are judging along lines strikingly similar to those used by white racists who bestow superior value on the lives of other whites, merely because they are members of their own race."[7]

Such sentiments, which repudiate the Judeo-Christian teaching of the sanctity of each human life made in the image of God, are not uncommon in recent American history. It is alarming, however, to see such repudiations given wide visibility in the most prestigious journal of the American Academy of Pediatrics—an organization presumably dedicated to the interests of all children, handicapped or not.

Recent expressions of disregard for the lives of handicapped infants by both the courts and members of the medical profession prompted Dr. C. Everett Koop to observe that such acts of infanticide are being practiced by a "segment of the medical profession from which we have traditionally expected more— pediatricians and pediatric surgeons—and it is being ignored by a segment of our society from whom the victim has a right to expect more—namely, the law."[8]

Infanticide is hardly the invention of modern American medicine. The disposal of unwanted children has been a widespread practice in pagan cultures around the world. In ancient Greece, the abandonment of weak and deformed infants was not uncommon and in Sparta was even required by law. In the *Republic*, Plato's design for the ideal state, the philosopher recommends that infants with defective limbs be buried in some obscure place.[9] Aristotle urged that "nothing imperfect or maimed" should be brought up, and that the state should regulate the number of children permitted to each married couple. Pregnancies beyond the permitted number would be ended by abortion.[10] In ancient Rome, the Twelve Tables forbade the rearing of deformed children. Among the Australian aborigines, who at one time practiced infanticide, women who killed their own children occasionally ate them.[11] In preindustrial Japan infanticide was so common that it was referred to as *mabiki*, which means "thinning," as in rice seedlings.[12]

It was the spreading influence of the Christian faith that eventually brought to a halt such life-destroying practices of the Roman Empire as infanticide and gladiatorial combat. The care for human life in its humblest forms, "the slave, the gladiator, the savage, or the infant, was indeed wholly foreign to the genius of Paganism," observed the historian William Lecky. Such concern for human life was produced by the

Christian doctrine of the "inestimable value of each immortal soul. It is the distinguishing and transcendent characteristic of every society into which the spirit of Christianity has passed."[13] In the year 305 the church decreed excommunication for life as the punishment for women guilty of the double crime of adultery and subsequent infanticide.[14] Constantine, the first Christian emperor, enacted laws against infanticide, declaring that "the killing of a child by its father, which the Pompeian law left unpunished, is one of the greatest of crimes."[15] The reappearance of infanticide in the recent American scene is a manifestation of a repudiation of Christian ethical standards and a reversion to the practices of the pagan world.

THE LEGAL SITUATION

Even though infanticide by neglect has apparently become common in American hospitals, such withholding of lifesaving medical care from handicapped newborn children runs afoul of existing law in a number of respects. In a comprehensive analysis published in the *Stanford Law Review*, Professor John A. Robertson concluded that such acts of willful neglect may constitute crimes ranging from murder and involuntary manslaughter to conspiracy and child abuse or neglect.[16] Under existing law, a parent's decision to refuse consent for a medical or surgical procedure necessary to maintain the life of a handicapped newborn child falls within the bounds of homicide by omission.[17] The attending physicians, nurses, and even members of the hospital staff who acquiesce in or promote such decisions not to treat may be guilty of crimes including homicide and failure to conform to child-abuse reporting laws.[18] In addition to possible criminal liability under homicide laws, the physician may also be guilty of a conspiracy with the parents and other members of the hospital staff to kill the handicapped child through the deliberate omission of lifesaving care.[19]

In the wake of the death of Infant Doe in April of 1982, it also became evident that the action of the parents, physicians, and hospital staff in this case was in violation of federal law. William Bradford Williams, Assistant Attorney General of the United States, Civil Rights Division, pointed out that Section 504 of the Rehabilitation Act of 1973 prohibits discrimination solely on the basis of handicap in federally assisted programs.[20] In the case of Infant Doe, the decision not to provide life-sustaining treatment was clearly based on the child's having Down's syndrome.

Much of the medical and media discussion of the Infant Doe and similar cases has tended to overlook the issues of criminal liability for such actions. As Robertson has pointed out, "A custom among physicians to violate a criminal law does not in and of itself modify the law."[21]

Before June of 1981, no parents or doctors were prosecuted under American law for decisions to withhold food or medical treatment from a handicapped newborn infant. In May of that year, in Danville, Illinois, Siamese twins were born, joined at the waist with three legs. The attending obstetrician allegedly said, "Don't resuscitate, let's just cover the babies." An order that the twins be given no food or water—"Do not feed in accordance with parents' wishes"—was written on the medical chart, and the infants were taken to the newborn nursery to die by starvation and dehydration.[22]

On May 13 an anonymous call to the Illinois Department of Children and Family Services reported that Siamese twins at Lakeview Medical Center in Danville were being deliberately neglected. A social worker investigated, and on June 11 the county district attorney filed charges against the parents and the attending physician for conspiracy to commit murder and endangering the life and health of children. At a preliminary hearing none of the nurses was able or willing to directly link the parents or physicians with the orders to withhold food and water, and the charges were dropped.[23] The notoriety created by this and other cases, however, may make it more likely that in the future criminal charges will be brought in similar cases of decisions to withhold life-saving care.

The growing practice of infanticide by neglect also runs counter to developments in twentieth-century law that have increasingly ascribed legal rights such as the right to inherit property and the right to sue for bodily damages even to the unborn. A century ago it was a common legal dictum that the unborn child "has no existence as a human being separate from its mother; therefore it may not recover for the wrongful conduct of another."[24] Advancing medical knowledge made this position untenable, and American courts increasingly began to recognize the legal claims of the unborn child. In the 1959 case of *Puhl v. Milwaukee Auto Ins. Co.* the court held that damages could be recovered on behalf of the unborn child, and that "viability" or lack of it was not a crucial concern, given the biological continuity of prenatal life.[25] In 1964, in the case of *Raleigh Fitkin-Paul Morgan Memorial Hospital v. Anderson,* the court ordered that a blood transfusion be given to a pregnant woman in order to prevent fatal hemorrhaging, in spite of the woman's religious objections based on her Jehovah's Witness conviction.

The court held that the preservation of the child's life took precedence over the mother's First Amendment right of freedom of religion.[26]

These developments in American law, which extend legal rights to the *unborn*, should apply with even greater force to the *already born*, despite their handicaps. Today's practice of infanticide by neglect is contrary to both existing statute law and a growing number of court decisions that have attempted to enlarge the legal rights of those not yet born.

MEDICAL AND PSYCHOLOGICAL DIMENSIONS

It is frequently suggested that the agonizing ethical dilemmas surrounding the birth of handicapped infants have been "created" or at least exacerbated by recent progress in medical technology. While medical advances in salvaging newborn infants that would have been considered "hopeless" ten years ago have contributed to such dilemmas, it would nevertheless be hasty to conclude that technological factors are the sole or even the leading contributors to the incidence of infanticide by neglect in America today. The changing climate of moral values would appear to be the real culprit. Without the widespread practice of abortion since 1973, with its attendant erosion of the respect for the sanctity of life, it is doubtful that infanticide would now be considered a thinkable "treatment option" in medical circles.

There has been dramatic progress in the field of neonatology, the medical specialty dealing with the human infant during the first month subsequent to birth. A dozen years ago the survival cut-off point for a premature infant was 1,500 grams, a little more than three pounds. Now survival for infants above 1,000 grams (2.2 lbs.) is routine, and prognosis can be favorable down to 800 grams.[27]

A 1978 study released by the Congressional Office of Technology Assessment showed that of premature babies released from neonatal intensive care units, "the overwhelming majority of survivors are normal, a small number have minor handicaps, and an even smaller number are severely handicapped."[28]

Mortality rates in the United States for the first week of life have steadily declined since 1950, when there were 20.5 neonatal deaths for every 1,000 live births. By 1970 the figure was down to 15.1, and by 1978 to 9.5.[29] Newer techniques such as ultrasound scans are able to spot problems such as intracranial hemorrhaging during the first few hours following birth, in many cases averting fatal damage.[30]

With the advent of fetal surgery, the infant is emerging as a separate patient in his or her own right even while still in the womb. Multidisciplinary medical teams in Colorado and elsewhere have implanted shunts into the skulls of children with hydrocephalic conditions while these infants were still *in utero*. As of June 1983, there were 38 recorded cases of prenatal surgery on the bladder. As one medical writer observed, "While the 1970's was the decade of prenatal diagnosis, the 1980's may well be the decade of prenatal surgery."[31] Lifesaving technology is rapidly becoming available to deal with handicaps even prior to birth; the key question concerns whether the moral climate will be such as to make such therapies available to handicapped children in a consistent and nondiscriminatory fashion.

Two relatively common birth defects that have been the subject of "nontreatment" decisions are spina bifida ("divided spine") and Down's syndrome ("mongolism"). Satisfactory moral analysis presupposes accurate medical knowledge of the nature of and prognosis for such handicapping conditions.

Spina bifida is a congenital cleft of the vertebral column, with a protrusion of the membranes enveloping the spinal cord. Spina bifida may involve urinary tract deficiencies, hydrocephaly, and paralysis of the lower extremities.[32]

In the 1950s most children born with spina bifida were left to die. In the 1960s, however, physicians began to treat spina bifida vigorously, and recent studies have shown that between 80 and 95 percent of such children who are aggressively treated from the start survive.[33] "The fact is that spina bifida is a medically arrestable problem at birth," notes Howard Burrell, vice president of the Spina Bifida/Hydrocephalus Association of Western Pennsylvania.[34]

With early treatment, virtually all spina bifida children are able to stand in braces and platforms by one to two years of age.[35] Although 70-90 percent of such children will develop hydrocephalus, the development of new shunt technology allows most of these patients to grow up into adulthood with normal intelligence. Most of these children are able to attend regular schools.[36]

According to Drs. Claire Leonard and John Freeman of the Johns Hopkins Hospital, recent medical advances have changed the outlook for children born with spina bifida from one of "hopelessness, myriad hospitalizations, enormous expense, and a future of dependency and despair to one in which most children will grow to be productive, participating adults."[37]

The "quality of life" for such children can be quite satisfactory, and in any case, determinations of "quality of life" should be left for the handicapped themselves. "Quality of life is a matter of individual taste," notes Howard Burrell. "I do not want my doctor, my parents, my church, or a committee of all three deciding what my life quality or that of a newborn should be."[38]

Down's syndrome ("mongolism") is one of the more common birth defects, occurring approximately once in every 1,000 births.[39] Down's syndrome is caused by the presence of 47 rather than 46 chromosomes in the patient's cells, and it is characterized by moderate to severe retardation, by slanting eyes, a broad, short skull, and by broad hands with short fingers.[40]

This condition was first described clinically in 1866, but not until 1959 did the French scientists Lejeune and Turpin discover that it was caused by *trisomy* ("three chromosomes") for chromosome 21.[41]

Since Down's syndrome children who are afflicted with other handicaps (e.g., a surgically removable intestinal blockage) have sometimes been left to die, it is important to note that these children typically fall into the category of the trainable mentally handicapped and can be expected to fit into settings where they can be taught socialization and self-help skills. In Zurich, Switzerland, for example, persons with Down's syndrome have been employed to repair telephone equipment.[42]

According to Dr. Eugene F. Diamond, most Down's syndrome children do better at home and only a small percentage should ever be institutionalized. And yet if all 5,000 such children born in a typical year had to be institutionalized at an average cost of $12,000 per child per year (1980 estimates), the cost of such care would still be only about one-tenth "of what we spend as a nation on dogfood," noted Diamond.[43]

Programs stressing early intervention and therapy are improving the prognosis for Down's syndrome patients. According to Dr. Allen Crocker of the Children's Hospital in Boston, a program begun a few weeks after birth designed to give special stimulation to the senses and to develop motor and learning skills has helped to raise the I.Q. of patients an average of some seven points. The early intervention program combines specialists in a number of disciplines, including speech and physical therapy, nutrition, rehabilitation, and special education. "It's such a contrast to a decade ago," noted Crocker. "Now we're making the child with Down's syndrome and the parents feel part of the human family."[44]

Raising any handicapped child creates special burdens, but many parents of Down's syndrome children have actually been enriched by the experience. In a letter to the editor of the *New York Times*, Elizabeth Villani of Yonkers stated that their own Down's syndrome child was at home, flourishing in the family environment, and attending special education classes in the public school. "He is active and responsive, with a love of life hard to match. . . . He has filled all our lives with joy."[45] Mrs. Villani's experience could be matched by that of many other parents as well.

Accurate medical information concerning the exact nature and prognosis of the handicapping condition is absolutely essential if the ethical decision making process is to have integrity. All too often nontreatment decisions have been made without accurate medical knowledge and under circumstances of intense emotional stress.

A mother who is given the news that her newborn child has a serious handicap is denied the normal tension relief from the stresses of pregnancy, and both parents may feel a crushing blow to their sense of self-esteem and self-confidence.[46] In a very short time the parents experience grief for the loss of the normal child expected, anger at fate, numbness, and feelings of helplessness and disbelief. They may blame themselves or their spouses for the outcome, and they fear that their social position and mobility may be permanently endangered.[47] Decisions made in the immediacy of such emotional stresses are unlikely to be objective and may easily be prejudicial to the interests of the handicapped newborn child, who is not being represented by a neutral party.

In the case of the Siamese twins born in Danville, Illinois, where the parents and doctors allegedly agreed that the twins would be left to starve to death, at the moment of birth neither the parents nor the physicians had information available to them beyond a visual impression of the infants' condition.[48] The parents apparently had no information concerning the care and development of the twins, adoption, institutional alternatives, and state assistance for cost of care.[49] In commenting on this case, Professor John Robertson noted that a physician "who made life-and-death decisions knowing that more information was needed would not be practicing good medicine, just as a judge who sentenced merely on a defendant's appearance would not be dispensing justice."[50]

As Dr. Rosalyn B. Darling, a medical sociologist, has pointed out, often "the deck is stacked against treatment of the defective newborn." Not only do parents bring into such situations a cultural background that values physical attractiveness and mental prowess, but the physicians themselves also bring a professional background in which perfection and dramatic curing are valued, rather than remedial care.[51] Both factors can be contrary to the interests of the handicapped newborn child. Older physicians, who were trained when institutionalization of the handicapped was the norm, may have little awareness of the satisfaction that such a child can bring to parents who are able to provide care in the home. The lives of the handicapped may never be perfect, but their lives can be made immeasurably more productive and fulfilling by doctors and parents "who have learned how to create success out of failure with love and aggressive treatment," notes Darling.[52]

Parents are at times intimidated by the imposing medical surroundings of the hospital, and the scientific knowledge of the physicians. It should be realized, however, that medical prognoses are always probabilistic, and that physicians frequently disagree among themselves about therapeutic decisions. Medical expertise does not guarantee that medical decisions will be morally sound ones.

Such life-and-death decisions, if left in the hands of parents and physicians, can lack some essential checks and balances. As Robertson has pointed out, in nearly all the cases in which infanticide-by-neglect decisions are made, "neither the parents nor physicians are required to justify their choice, nor is the decision reviewed by a disinterested party. . . . We thus have a situation in which interests other than the infant's can dominate, and in which arbitrary and unjustified killings can and have occurred."[53]

Physicians who deal with the handicapped newborn should recognize that the vast majority of disabled infants are within the realm of treatment. Dr. C. Everett Koop, a noted pediatric surgeon and Surgeon General of the United States, in testimony before the House Select Committee on Education and Welfare, stated that "we should not let anyone's emphasis on the most difficult cases distract our attention from the basic principle that we must not discriminate against handicapped infants."[54] The one "bottom line" in all such cases, said Koop, is that "you feed the patient— either orally or intravenously."[55] Starvation is never a legitimate "treatment option." Koop was speaking out of a 35-year history of personal involvement in the treatment of the handicapped newborn.

Physicians need to be extremely cautious in making guesses as to the "quality of life" that any handicapped infant will ultimately enjoy or find personally acceptable. Dr. Stephen P. Coburn, after 16 years of experience on the staff of the Fort Wayne State Hospital and Training Center, an institution for the mentally retarded, noted that he had not once encountered a patient who complained to the doctors, "Why did you let me live?" Coburn concluded that "an attitude of regretting one's existence is so rare that it should not be a factor in the decision to end a baby's life."[56] It is simply not fair to impose our own standards of happiness on those whose experience of life is so different from our own. As Dr. Koop has observed, the physician's proper task is to do "whatever possible so that the patient can enjoy to the fullest whatever *he or she* determines is 'quality.'"[57]

MORAL CONSIDERATIONS

The debate on the ethics of infanticide has been posed in terms of a "sanctity of life" versus a "quality of life" perspective. The traditional Western reverence for each life, irrespective of age, social class, or condition of health, reflects the Judeo-Christian doctrine of the creation of man as the image of God—a being of unique worth as a direct creation of the Almighty. In recent years, this "sanctity of life" ethic has been under widespread attack. The first major blow came with the legalization of abortion by the U.S. Supreme Court in its 1973 decisions in *Roe v. Wade* and *Doe v. Bolton*. More recently, a second major blow was struck, when it became a matter of public knowledge that it was not an uncommon practice in American hospitals to choose infanticide by neglect as the course of "treatment" for certain handicapped newborns. Infants who in the judgment of parents and physicians could not expect a certain "quality of life" were presumably better off dead.

Even more recently, certain philosophers and ethicists have begun to provide theoretical rationalizations for a social practice—infanticide—that heretofore was only practiced covertly without public legitimation. An example is the article by Professor Peter Singer in *Pediatrics*, the official journal of the American Academy of Pediatrics, in which he attempted to provide such a rationalization for infanticide. That the academy would even print such a piece in its journal is in itself a telling comment on the recent directions in American medicine.

As we noted earlier, Professor Singer contends that we can no longer base "our ethics on the idea that human beings are a special form of creation, made in the image of God, singled out from all other animals, and alone possessing an immortal soul."[58] If one strips away the "religious mumbo-jumbo" surrounding the term "human," believes Singer, "we will not regard as sacrosanct the life of each and every member of our species, no matter how limited its capacity for intelligent or even conscious life may be."[59] Intelligence and self-consciousness are the real criteria for moral value; thus Singer concludes that the life of a dog or a pig may have more value than that of a severely defective human infant.[60]

In similar fashion, another philosopher, Michael Tooley, builds an argument for infanticide by using consciousness or brain function as the key criterion of moral worth. Since the newborn infant "is not capable of possessing the concept of a continuing self, is not capable of envisaging a future for itself, and is not capable of self-consciousness, it is reasonable to conclude that an infant does not possess a serious right to life at that time, and hence that infanticide is morally permissible in most cases when it is otherwise desirable."[61] To alleviate practical problems such as determining the exact level of the infant's developing consciousness, some period, such as a week after birth, could be chosen as the interval within which infanticide would be permitted.[62]

The choice, then, between the "sanctity of life" ethic based on the idea of the image of God, and the "quality of life" ethic based on brain function, is a choice between an ethic that protects all human beings in principle, and an ethic with a sliding scale of human worth based on estimates of intelligence and mental function. The "quality of life" approach throws open the doors to all kinds of arbitrariness and abuse; those selected for nontreatment have no say in such "quality of life" decisions. In practice, this leaves the weak and the powerless subject to the arbitrary will of the strong and the powerful. The "sanctity of life" ethic is in principle nondiscriminatory and is most consistent with the principle of equal justice under law for all human subjects, irrespective of handicap, social class, or state of health. The "quality of life" philosophy, based on degree of brain function, endangers the lives not only of the handicapped newborn, but also of the mentally retarded, the comatose, and the senile. Their lives, too, may be considered burdensome and inconvenient. The argument for infanticide on "quality of life" grounds quickly becomes an argument for the active euthanasia of other classes of unwanted human beings.

Decisions not to treat the handicapped newborn are sometimes rationalized not only on the basis of "quality of life" considerations, but also on the basis of "cost-benefit" calculations. Infanticide by neglect is justified as a more cost-effective option for both the parents and society.

There is no question that specialized medical treatment for the handicapped newborn can be expensive. In 1978, for example, the cost of providing neonatal intensive care for 5 percent of the nation's 3.3

million newborns was estimated at more than $1.5 billion.[63] It has been suggested that some of these expenditures on "marginal" patients could more profitably have been diverted to other forms of medical treatment for patients whose "quality of life" suggests a more viable future.

As John Robertson has pointed out, however, when compared with the approximately 7 percent of the GNP spent on health, the money spent on defense, or tax revenues in general, "the public resources required to keep defective newborns alive seems marginal, and arguably worth the commitment to life that such expenditures reinforce."[64] It was noted earlier that the costs of providing institutional care for the 5,000 Down's syndrome children born in a typical year would amount to only about one tenth of what Americans spend on dog food.[65]

Down's syndrome children suffering from other congenital handicaps have been discriminated against on the basis of their mental retardation and presumed lack of future social and economic utility. As Professor James Gustafson of the University of Chicago has pointed out, "Not all intelligent persons are socially commendable. . . . Also, many persons of limited intelligence do things that are socially commendable, if only minimally providing the occasion for the expression of profound human affection and sympathy."[66]

It should also be pointed out that the *morally* handicapped— e.g., habitual criminals—constitute a far more serious economic liability in our nation's life than do the physically and mentally handicapped. A recent study involving the personal histories of 243 heroin addicts in Baltimore found that these individuals admitted to committing some 500,000 crimes over an 11-year period, an average of 187 crimes per addict per year. And one out of every five U.S. prison inmates serving time for robbery was a heroin addict at the time of the commission of the crime.[67] In the light of such comparative figures, the cost-benefit approach to the handicapped newborn reflects not so much a shortage of financial and medical resources as misplaced national priorities and a shortage of caring and compassion for handicapped human beings.

The language of "cost-benefit" analysis and "quality of life" considerations provides echoes of the earlier debate in this country on the morality of abortion. When the U.S. Supreme Court in its 1973 *Roe v. Wade* decision ruled that states could not prohibit abortion prior to the stage of fetal viability, it did so on the basis of the opinion that prior to this stage, the child was not capable of "meaningful life" outside the mother's womb.[68] Critics of the Court's decision astutely pointed out that the "meaningful life" criterion could be used to justify not only abortion, but infanticide and euthanasia for the terminally ill, comatose, and senile as well.

Even prior to *Roe v. Wade*, as early as 1970, Professor Paul Ramsey of Princeton had pointed to the similarity in the logic of the arguments for abortion and for infanticide. The same arguments that justified the one also provided a rationalization for the other. Human life is a biological continuum from conception through birth until natural death. If the killing of an innocent human being can be rationalized before birth, then why should the transition of the birth process make any crucial moral difference? As Ramsey noted, "It would seem to be only the oddity of our current mores that could prevent there being stronger reason for killing gravely defective children immediately after birth . . . than for killing both the damaged and the undamaged *in utero*."[69]

The parallel between the logic of abortion and that of infanticide has been explicitly recognized by philosophers such as Michael Tooley, who advocates both.[70] The logic of the arguments has worked itself out in American practice: legalization of abortion in the 1970s gave rise to infanticide in the 1980s.

A consistent Christian ethic will oppose both abortion and infanticide. As Dr. Eugene Diamond has said, if the legal rights of unborn children are to be restored, "we cannot concede the logical extension of the abortion mentality into the nursery."[71] The sanctity-of-life ethic must be affirmed both prior to and subsequent to birth. This Judeo-Christian ethic, "which now spreads its tattered mantle of protection over newborn defective infants must be upheld," stated Diamond. "It is really protecting us all."[72]

The "bottom line" in such treatment decisions is that parents and physicians must not discriminate against the handicapped newborn.[73] Surgery or other forms of treatment that would be prescribed for a normal infant must not be denied to Down's syndrome children or the other handicapped newborn.

At times the common ethical distinction between "ordinary" and "extraordinary" means has been misused to justify nontreatment decisions. "Extraordinary" means have been defined as "all medicines, treatments, and operations, which can't be obtained or used without excessive expense, pain, or other inconvenience, or which, if used, would not offer a reasonable hope or benefit."[74] Such distinctions have legitimacy with respect to competent adults and persons who are *already* in the *dying process*. It is altogether another matter, however, to deny a handicapped child life-saving surgery or even food and water simply because of his mental retardation or some other handicap. Surgery that can save the life of a Down's syndrome child with an intestinal blockage is not "extraordinary" but *ordinary* treatment and is morally obligatory.[75]

There is, however, no moral obligation to provide useless treatment to a genuinely terminal patient. In such cases, the patient will die whether or not the treatment is provided. There is no moral necessity to extend an irreversible process of dying.

In certain cases of the handicapped newborn, no known medical intervention can reverse a genuinely hopeless prognosis. As C. Everett Koop has noted, there are no known medical solutions in the cases of anencephaly (a child born with virtually no functioning brain) or cephalodymy (a one-headed twin). "In these cases the prognosis is an early and merciful death by natural causes."[76] Such cases are, however, quite infrequent, and should not be used as a rationalization for the deliberate neglect and abandonment of handicapped children whose lives could be saved by available medical interventions.

The proper practice of medicine should be guided by a life-affirming ethic in all cases, even when the physician can only provide care and comfort to a patient—young or old—who is already in an irreversible process of dying. A medical practice informed by the spirit of Christ and love for the neighbor will see as its goal never to harm or choose death as a primary end, to cure whenever possible, and always to provide care and comfort to all patients, both in their living and in their dying. There is indeed a time to die, just as there is a time to be born (Eccles. 3:2), and modern medicine must acknowledge its limitations. But the basic thrust of medicine should always be to choose life (cf. Deut. 30:19), because all human life is sacred to God who made it.

DEATH, DYING, AND EUTHANASIA

The moral issues surrounding death and dying pertain to the very old, as well as the very young. Advances in medical technology that allow the sustaining of biological life in terminal cases also bring in their wake ethical dilemmas that were not so acute in an earlier age. The very definition of death has been a matter of moral and medical dispute. Fears of prolonged overtreatment have raised the public's interest in the so-called "living will." Some have proposed voluntary euthanasia as a legal and moral option for the terminally ill, thereby raising a host of complex issues for society, the medical profession, and for the dying individual and his family.

At the beginning of the twentieth century, two-thirds of the people in the United States died before the age of 50, and most died at home in their beds, in the presence of family and friends. Today most deaths occur in an older population, and two-thirds die in medical institutions and nursing homes.[77] In a changing demographic situation, with the American population having an increasing percentage of elderly people, the ethical dilemmas surrounding death in institutional settings will become more rather than less acute.

In 1929 the United States spent 3.5 percent of its gross national product on medical care; by 1982, the figure had increased to 10.3 percent.[78] The public's seemingly insatiable demand for health care, including highly expensive forms of therapy such as cardiac transplantations and kidney dialysis, make the issues of the "rationing of life and death" more than purely academic and speculative concerns. Pressing issues of death and dying will inescapably face Americans for the rest of the foreseeable future.

WHAT IS DEATH?

Advances in modern medical technology have raised new questions about the very definition of death. Prior to the 1960s, a mortally ill patient who stopped breathing and continued in such a state was pronounced dead.[79] With the advent of artificial respirators, however, the traditional criteria for defining death in terms of irreversible cessation of spontaneous respiration and circulatory functions became blurred. Artificial respiration could in many cases be maintained indefinitely, raising questions as to whether the patient was truly "alive" or "dead." The following cases, recounted by Dr. W. P. Williamson, are not unusual:

> I have seen patients with brain stem failure, with dilated, fixed pupils, decerebrate rigidity, and cessation of spontaneous respiration, who have had tracheostomy and were assisted with a mechanical respirator. With fluids, electrolytes, and good nursing care, the essentially isolated heart in such a patient can sometimes be kept beating for a week. I have never seen such a patient begin to breathe spontaneously and survive, and autopsy always shows advanced liquefaction necrosis of the brain, for it "died" several days before the heart did.[80]

The older definition of death centering on respiratory and circulatory function was never a legislated definition; death was, in effect, what the doctor identified as such.[81] Technological advances have brought courts, lawyers, and legislatures into the picture as the definition of death has become a question of social and political significance.

The issues were further complicated by the development of organ transplant technology. Some saw in newer brain-death definitions a way of gaining access to organs for transplantation before they had suffered significant deterioration. The prospect of programs for "harvesting the dead" raised its own set of moral problems. As Dr. Willard Gaylin observed, "While it is one thing to define death in order to ease the agony of the dying family or the individual, it is quite another thing to define death because of an eagerness to get spare parts, even for humanitarian ends."[82]

In 1968 the Harvard Medical School's Ad Hoc Committee to Examine the Definition of Brain Death developed a definition that involved the following criteria: (1) "unreceptivity and unresponsivity" to "externally applied stimuli and inner need"; (2) absence of spontaneous muscular movements and spontaneous respiration; and (3) no elicitable reflexes. Additionally, a flat electroencephalogram was said to be "of great confirmatory value" for the clinical diagnosis.[83]

In 1981 the President's Commission for the Study of Ethical Problems in Medicine and Biomedical and Behavioral Research drafted a Uniform Determination of Death Act, which was subsequently adopted as a legal definition of death in many states. According to this definition, death now means either (1) irreversible cessation of circulatory and respiratory functions, or (2) irreversible cessation of all functions of the entire brain, including the brain stem.[84]

This latter part of the definition makes it clear that "brain death" means not merely cessation of the cerebral or cortical functions, but cessation of all functions of the *entire* brain. This guards against hasty pronouncements of death for those in a state of coma or with damage to only part of the brain. This definition in terms of the entire brain is morally acceptable, and actually provides a check against euthanasia, inappropriate and premature "harvesting of the dead," and other forms of unethical experimentation upon the sick and dying.

TERMINAL ILLNESSES AND TERMINATION OF TREATMENT

Questions of when, if ever, it is morally justifiable to terminate medical treatment for dying persons are likely to become more pressing for the balance of the twentieth century. Demographic trends alone make this virtually certain. The proportion of the U.S. population 75 years of age and older increased more than 37 percent during the 1970s and continues to be one of the fastest-growing segments of the population.[85] These trends caused Nicholas Rango, a geriatric specialist, to observe that "human society has never before faced the issue of so many people living for so long with such severe impairment."[86]

There are no specific cures for many of the chronic diseases that afflict today's elderly patients: rheumatic disease, osteoporosis, arteriosclerosis, stroke, senile dementia, and advanced cancer. In an earlier generation, death often came in the form of pneumonia—once referred to as the "old man's friend"—but modern pacemakers, antibiotics, and respirators have changed the situation. These devices, notes Dr. Alexander Leaf of Harvard Medical School, "often resolve the immediate problem and return the patient again to a nursing home."[87] In some cases "heroic" intervention may be genuinely therapeutic and life-extending; in other cases, the technology may simply prolong the process of dying.

Twentieth-century medicine has tended to become less personal and more technological in nature. As Dr. Willard Gaylin has noted, when a patient is dying today, "he may be cared for by four or more physicians, none of whom he knew as a child, and most will have no opportunity to talk with the family."[88] Still, decisions concerning forms of treatment and its possible termination must be made, but the growing institutionalization and impersonality of modern medicine can make those decisions more difficult.

The problem of termination of treatment has become not only a medical and moral issue, but a legal one as well. In the well-known case of Karen Ann Quinlan, the father of this young girl who had become comatose petitioned the court for permission to discontinue all extraordinary means for sustaining her life, there being no apparent hope of recovery. A lower court denied the request, but this decision was reversed by the New Jersey Supreme Court (In re Quinlan, 355 A2d 647 NJ 1976). The court held that the patient's constitutionally protected "right to privacy" included the right to decline medical treatment under certain circumstances. The court attempted to balance a number of competing interests: the patient's right to decline treatment (in this case presumably exercised on her behalf through the "substituted judgment" of a legal guardian); the state's interest in the preservation of life; protection of any third parties; the maintenance of the ethical integrity of the medical profession. In this case, the court held that the state's interests must yield to those of the patient, especially since the treatment being administered was "highly invasive" and offered no reasonable prospect of curing or improving the patient's condition.[89] Karen Ann was taken off the respirator and continued to live in a comatose state until her death on June 11, 1985.

In a case heard before the Appeals Court of Massachusetts in 1978, *In the Matter of Dinnerstein*, the issue was whether prior judicial approval was necessary in every case before medical treatment could be discontinued on terminally ill, incompetent patients. In this instance, the patient was an incompetent 67-year-old widow in the advanced stages of Alzheimer's disease, with a predicted life expectancy of approximately one year. The patient's family and attending physician petitioned the court for a declaratory judgment that a "do not resuscitate" order (DNR) could be entered on her medical record without prior judicial approval. In its ruling the court held that the validity of a DNR order did not depend on prior judicial approval, nor did the law "prohibit a course of medical treatment which excludes attempts at resuscitation in the event of cardiac or respiratory arrest" (380 NE2d, at 139). According to the court, the decision whether to resuscitate is one that falls within the competence of the medical profession to decide what measures are appropriate "to ease the imminent passing of an irreversibly, terminally ill patient in light of the patient's history and condition and the wishes of [the] family."[90]

In the case of *Eichner v. Dillon* 420 NE2d 64 (1981), the Court of Appeals of New York determined that prior judicial approval is not necessary under some circumstances to discontinue the use of a respirator. The case involved "Brother Fox," an 83-year-old member of a Catholic religious order who was being maintained on a respirator in a permanent comatose state. Father Philip Eichner, the head of the religious order, with the support of the surviving relatives, petitioned the court to direct the removal of the respirator after the patient's attending physicians and two consulting neurosurgeons concluded that there was no reasonable chance of recovery. The court pointed out that there was "clear and convincing" evidence that Brother Fox, while competent, had carefully reflected on the subject, and had made known his desire not to have his life artificially prolonged under such circumstances. The petition to disconnect the respirator was granted.[91]

According to Suber and Tabor, the cases of *Quinlan*, *Dinnerstein* and *Eichner*, when taken together, suggest that "substantial decision-making-authority is to be vested in the patient's family or guardian and attending physicians, where the circumstances surrounding the patient's background, condition, and prognosis support the valid exercise of 'substituted judgment' on his behalf."[92]

In a review of cases of termination of treatment, the President's Commission for the Study of Ethical Problems in Medicine and Biomedical and Behavioral Research did not find any instances in which criminal or civil liability had been imposed upon physicians or family members for acquiescing to a patient's refusal of life-sustaining treatment, or for discontinuing life-sustaining treatment for an incompetent patient or one who was in imminent danger of death.[93] There have been, however, instances of prosecution or attempted prosecution in such cases. In 1982 a prosecutor in Los Angeles brought charges of murder against two physicians, Neil Barber and Robert Nejdl, who, at the request of the family, had removed a respirator from 55-year-old Clarence Herbert, who had been in a coma for three days. Two days later, the doctors removed Herbert's intravenous feeding tubes. In October of 1983, a California appellate court vacated the murder charges, holding that "although there may be a duty to provide life-sustaining machinery in the *immediate* [emphasis original] aftermath of a cardio-respiratory arrest, there is no duty to continue its use once it has become futile in the opinion of qualified medical personnel."[94]

In discussions of treatment of the terminally ill, questions of *terminology* play a crucial role. Perhaps even more so than in the abortion debate, fine distinctions can have significant moral consequences.

One of the most prominent and common distinctions in this issue is the distinction between *ordinary* and *extraordinary* means. In a 1958 address to an international congress of Roman Catholic anesthesiologists, Pope Pius XII articulated a position that has been very frequently quoted since: "Normally one is held to use only ordinary means—according to circumstances of persons, places, times, and culture—that is to say, means that do not involve any grave burden for oneself or another. . . . On the other hand, one is not forbidden to take more than the strictly necessary steps to preserve life and health, as long as he does not fail in some more serious duty."[95]

Prior to this, Gerald Kelly, a Roman Catholic ethicist, had in a widely quoted journal article, stated this distinction in the following rather precise fashion:

> *Ordinary means* are all those medicines, treatments, and operations, which offer a reasonable hope of benefit and which can be obtained and used without excessive expense, pain, or other inconvenience.

Extraordinary means are all medicines, treatments, and operations, which cannot be obtained or used without excessive pain,
or other inconvenience, or which, if used, would not offer a reasonable hope of benefit.[96]

As thus defined, it was generally understood that "ordinary means"
were morally obligatory, while "extraordinary" ones were not.

Such terminology has a long history in Roman Catholic moral theology, dating back at least to Francisco Vitoria (d. 1546), who discussed
cases of terminal illness. Those who followed in this tradition, such as
Alphonsus Liguori (d. 1789), used as an example of an "extraordinary"
means the amputation of a leg. Before the discovery of anesthetics, such
an operation was extraordinarily painful, and it was not until the second half of the nineteenth century that the survival rate for such operations rose above 50 percent.[97] The moralists in this tradition were able
to incorporate advances in medical insight into the basic distinction first
articulated by Vitoria in the sixteenth century.

It has been suggested at times that the rapid progress of medical
science in the twentieth century has rendered obsolete the distinction
between "ordinary" and "extraordinary" means. Respirators, kidney dialysis, and other new forms of medical technology, it is said, are now so
commonly available as to be "ordinary" means; consequently, the distinction is no longer meaningful. This criticism overlooks, however, the
original meaning of the distinction. The terminology was never limited
to medical technology per se, but took into view the total circumstances
of the patient. A respirator might be "ordinary" under some circumstances, and "extraordinary" in others. Whatever progress might occur
on the technological front, it will always be necessary to consider the
total circumstances of the patient and the family when making decisions concerning the possible termination of treatment. The classical
distinction still has value in that it reminds the decision makers of the
need to take all factors into account, not merely the medical ones.

In discussions of death and dying reference is occasionally made to
the "principle of double effect." This principle, long discussed in the tradition of Roman Catholic moral theology, recognizes that under some
circumstances a given human action will produce two effects, one desirable, and one undesirable. Is it morally permissible, for example, to
administer to a dying patient a drug that will alleviate pain, but at the
same time deprive the patient of sense and reason? Four criteria have
been suggested in order to evaluate such actions: (1) the action must

be in itself a morally good action, or at least morally indifferent; (2) the good effect must precede the evil effect or at least be simultaneous with it; (3) the motive prompting the action must be directed toward the good effect, and not the evil; (4) the good effect must be at least equivalent to the evil effect.[98] In applying these criteria to the case in question, Charles J. MacFadden, a conservative Roman Catholic ethicist, concludes that it is not euthanasia "to give a dying person sedatives merely for the alleviation of pain, even to the extent of depriving the patient of the use of sense and reason, when this extreme measure is judged necessary."[99] Such sedatives should not be given, however, to patients who are not spiritually prepared for death, or to those patients who are willing and able to endure pain for spiritual motives.

Distinctions are sometimes drawn between acts of "commission" and acts of "omission." As generally understood, under certain circumstances it would be morally permissible to omit heroic forms of treatment (e.g., cardiopulmonary resuscitation in certain hopeless cases), whereas certain acts of *commission* (e.g., administering a poisonous drug to a dying patient experiencing considerable pain) would amount to an act of euthanasia or homicide and would be morally illicit. This distinction is sometimes expressed as the difference between *killing* and *letting die*.

In a 1975 article in the *New England Journal of Medicine*, James Rachels questioned the validity of this distinction. "The doctrine that says a baby may be allowed to dehydrate and wither, but may not be given an injection that would end its life without suffering seems so patently cruel as to require no further refutation."[100] Rachels contended that "active euthanasia" was not in fact worse than "passive euthanasia."[101] Rachels' outlook assumes, of course, that there are cases when it would be right to leave a child to die by starvation—an assumption that must be unequivocally rejected.

Robert Veatch and others have argued in favor of maintaining the important distinction between "killing" and "letting die," however fine that distinction might seem in cases of incurable terminal illnesses. Veatch points out that the actual cause of death is different in the two cases—"letting nature take its course" versus actively inducing or hastening death—and that active killing is inconsistent with the physician's historic role of curing and caring. The collapse of the distinction between killing and letting die could also open the door to the deliberate killing of other categories of persons: the senile, the comatose, and the economically burdensome.[102] Veatch wisely concludes that "although the differences between commission and omission are much more subtle than some traditions would indicate, the wisdom of the common judgment is sound."[103]

There is also the important distinction between "sustaining life" and "prolonging dying," or as Paul Ramsey states it, between "saving life by prolonging the living of it and only prolonging a patient's dying."[104] There is no moral obligation to prolong artificially a truly terminal patient's irreversible and imminent process of dying. This is sometimes called employing "useless means" of treatment. The point of any form of medical treatment is to cure the patient, or if curing is not possible, at least to contribute to a reasonable expectation of life and level of comfort. A form of treatment with no reasonable expectation of accomplishing these ends is not therapy in any meaningful sense of the word, but may in fact represent an inappropriate imposition upon the dying patient.

BIBLICAL PERSPECTIVES AND GUIDELINES

According to the Bible, death is *unnatural, inevitable,* and for the Christian, *not final.* Death is an unnatural intrusion into God's good universe. It is a direct consequence of man's sin (Gen. 2:17, "On the day you eat of it, you will surely die"; Rom. 6:23, "for the wages of sin is death"). Death is the "last enemy," an enemy of man that will be finally overcome at the time of Christ's return and the final resurrection (I Cor. 15:26, 56). Because death is unnatural, the Christian will reject humanistic philosophies that see death and dying as only a "natural" transition to either oblivion or to some higher stage of existence. According to the Bible, for the unbeliever death is in fact a prelude to final judgment in the presence of God (Heb. 9:27).

Because of the influence of the Judeo-Christian tradition in Western culture, death has been seen as unnatural, as an evil to be opposed, and this value system has influenced the medical profession in its death-resisting efforts. The unnaturalness of death and the biblical warnings of judgment also point to the crucial necessity of preparing the patient spiritually, insofar as this is humanly possible, before irreversible decisions regarding termination of treatment are made.

At the same time, the Bible teaches that death, under the present conditions, is inevitable. There is a time to be born, and a time to die (Eccles. 3:2). Barring the immediate return of Christ, each individual must experience death. Given this inevitability, there comes a point when heroic medical measures may simply prolong the patient's dying agony. Medicine's death-resisting instincts must be tempered by ones that are in some sense death-accepting. Both in medicine and in morals it is the delicate balance between hope and resignation for the dying patient that must be sought. For the Christian, of course, death is not final, and it holds no ultimate terrors; it is the doorway to eternal life. "Death is swallowed up in victory. . . . Thanks be to God, who gives us the victory through our Lord Jesus Christ" (I Cor. 15:55, 57).

With these principles in mind, the following general guidelines for termination of treatment may be considered. When a disease has advanced to the point where no known therapy exists and death is imminent despite the means used, then forms of treatment that would secure "only a precarious and burdensome prolongation of life" may be discontinued or not instituted.[105] In such truly terminal cases, the use of certain means would not be therapeutic, but would only prolong an irreversible process of dying. Only palliative care is indicated. By "terminal illness" is meant an incurable, irreversible, and hopeless illness for which further interventions are expected only to delay the moment of death. "Imminent death" is taken to mean a circumstance in which apart from intensive medical support, death would probably occur within two weeks. "Palliative care" means therapeutic measures designed to increase the patient's comfort and control pain, to provide food and water and normal nursing care, and to minimize stress for the dying patient and the family.[106]

To say that in certain cases palliative care alone is indicated is not to abandon the patient. An anencephalic newborn with other handicaps may have a life expectancy of only a few days or weeks. But even in such an extreme case, customary hygiene, normal feeding, clearing of nasal passages, providing warmth, and so on, would be morally mandatory.[107] The obligations of neighbor love still apply in such cases; abandonment is always illicit. One has a constant obligation to show neighbor love to the patient in his dying, as well as in his living and hoped-for recovery, even when that obligation can only be expressed through measures designed to provide care and comfort rather than to cure.

THE LIVING WILL

By 1991 more than 40 states had enacted living-will statutes.[108] These documents typically stipulate that extraordinary means not be used to keep the patient alive should hope of recovery be gone and the person be physically or mentally incompetent to make his or her wishes known.

The desire to enter such legal arrangements stems from the fear of "overtreatment" under such circumstances. According to A. J. Levinson, executive director of Concern for Dying, a New York group, such "living wills" presumably ensure that "the rights that exist for competent patients can be preserved when they become incompetent."[109] Critics of such legislation, the first example of which was California's "Natural Death Act" of 1976, claim that living wills are at best unnecessary, given existing laws concerning patients' rights, and at worst, a dangerous step toward euthanasia.

Drafters of living will legislation have not succeeded in removing the inherent ambiguity in such terms as "terminal illness." Circumstances of terminal illness reflect multitudes of specific factors that are only precisely known in the doctor-patient relationship, and that are very difficult, if not impossible, to specify adequately in the abstractions of legal language. Phrases such as "reasonable hope of recovery," "artificial means," and "extraordinary measures" are in fact quite fluid, given the dynamic nature of medical advances and the complexities of a specific patient's case. Such semantic difficulties, when reflected in the law, are likely to lead to further litigation, confusion in application of the law, and other unsuccessful legislation, rather than giving substantial help in an already-difficult area of medicine and morals.[110]

The widespread adoption of living-will legislation would also have an unhealthy "chilling" effect on the doctor-patient relationship. Rather than focusing exclusively on the interests of the patient, the doctor may fear legal penalties resulting from such legislation and thus be biased toward forms of treatment least likely to provoke a malpractice suit. As Richard McCormick and Andre Hellegers of the Kennedy Institute have pointed out, such legal penalties will contribute to a situation in which those with living wills are needlessly underresuscitated, and those without living wills overresuscitated.[111] Fear of malpractice suits, rather than best medical judgments, could become weighty motivations for physicians in such terminal cases, given the penalties of the laws. As Kenneth Vaux has observed, the patient-physician relationship "will be further eroded by invasive public policy. The adversary relations will replace the covenant and contractual relations."[112]

An alternative to the living will, which avoids its legal difficulties and detrimental effects on the patient-physician relationship, is the concept of a "durable power of attorney," recognized in 41 states. The "durable power of attorney" allows a person to designate an individual who would act on his behalf should he become physically or mentally unable to make such decisions.[113] Such an arrangement meets the fears of "overtreatment," without reducing the physician's flexibility to provide the optimal medical care given the specifics of a particular terminal illness. In a society prone to see legislation and litigation as the solutions to personal and social problems, the "durable power of attorney" concept is much to be preferred to the "living will." The "durable power of attorney" places the emphasis on a relationship of trust and understanding between patient, family, and physician, and such a climate is crucial for preserving the proper interests of both the patient and the medical profession.

EUTHANASIA

Euthanasia may be defined for the purposes of this discussion as "the deliberate killing of a person suffering an illness believed to be terminal, ostensibly out of 'mercy.'" This definition reflects the popular terminology of "mercy killing." Unfortunately, much semantic confusion surrounds the subject. Some writers point out that the word *euthanasia* derives from the Greek (*eu* + *thanatos*) and literally means "good death." This etymology, however, does not contribute to the ethical analysis and, if anything, merely fosters confusion. Similarly, distinctions are sometimes drawn between "active" and "passive" euthanasia, where the latter term is taken to refer to cessation of useless means in truly terminal cases. This distinction is not really helpful, however, since it has the effect of suggesting that *some* types of euthanasia are morally acceptable. For the sake of clarity, it is best to avoid this distinction altogether and simply to speak of euthanasia as defined above.[114] Cessation of useless means in truly terminal cases should in no way be confused with euthanasia, which involves an act of killing and the deliberate choice of death as a moral end.

In the Western nations the question of euthanasia broke into the public's consciousness with the publication of two essays by laymen in the 1870s. S. D. Williams argued that when patients suffering from incurable and painful illnesses requested that their lives should be ended, the physician should have a legal right to assist them. A similar essay by Lionel Tollemache supported this point of view, stressing the suffering and burden experienced by the dying patient. These arguments for "assisted suicide" did not produce any modifications in the then-prevailing medical ethics or laws, but did raise issues that were to surface even more persistently in the twentieth century.[115]

At present the pro-euthanasia perspective has its own organized lobbying group. Hemlock identifies itself as a "society supporting active voluntary euthanasia for the terminally ill."[116] Derek Humphry, the executive director of the organization, in March of 1975 gave his dying wife, suffering from cancer, a cup of coffee with lethal drugs that speeded up the process. Humphry's book *Let Me Die Before I Wake* is described as "a guide to self-deliverance for the dying." It discusses various ways of committing suicide, including fatal doses of drugs. Hemlock claimed some 7,000 members as of the end of 1982, and Humphry's manual on suicide had sold some 10,000 copies.[117]

In recent times ethicist Joseph Fletcher has been one of the more prominent advocates for the legalization of euthanasia. Back in 1954 Fletcher set forth a number of arguments for "voluntary" euthanasia in his book *Morals and Medicine*. Central to his approach was a "personalistic" and pragmatic approach to ethics, which gave little weight to traditional religious prohibitions and stressed the "personal" rather than the merely "biological" dimensions of human life. According to Fletcher, "personality is supreme over mere life. To prolong life uselessly, while the personal qualities of freedom, knowledge, self-possession and control, and responsibility are sacrificed is to attack the moral status of the person."[118] He further argued that euthanasia is consistent with the biblical virtue of mercy; that since it does not involve malice, it is not the moral equivalent of murder; that the moral legitimacy of martyrdom implies a similar legitimacy for euthanasia; that mercy should be shown to dying humans, as well as to dying animals; that suffering is not an inherent good; and that many physicians were already covertly engaging in the practice.[119]

As of 1979, 25 years after the publication of *Morals and Medicine*, Fletcher's thinking on euthanasia had evolved from the position that the practice could be morally *permissible* in some circumstances to the view that it was sometimes morally *obligatory*. "If we are *morally obliged* [emphasis added] to put an end to a pregnancy when amniocentesis reveals a terribly defective fetus, we are *equally obliged* [emphasis added] to put an end to a patient's hopeless misery," writes Fletcher, "when a brain scan reveals that a patient with cancer has advanced brain metastes."[120] Fletcher even goes so far as to say that in some cases *involuntary* euthanasia could be morally right, as, for example, "when an incorrigible human vegetable, whether spontaneously functioning or artificially supported, is progressively degraded while constantly eating up private or public financial resources in violation of the distributive justice owed to others."[121] Such a patient would be in no position to give consent to the "mercy killing," and so the act would clearly be a case of involuntary euthanasia, recognized by the law as an act of murder. Fletcher's language is reminiscent of references to the "useless eaters" of Hitler's Third Reich, the victims of the Nazi euthanasia program.

Fletcher's argument for euthanasia is hardly convincing. While motivation is an important component of any moral evaluation of human action, a "merciful" motive does not justify an objectively immoral act. Stealing money from a bank in order to show "mercy" to the poor is stealing just the same; likewise, motives of mercy do not make euthanasia something other than the deliberate killing of an innocent person. While human life is more than biological existence, respect for man's bodily life is the essential presupposition for respect for his life as a whole. The problem with assessing the value of a human being's life in terms of brain states is that the same arguments that justify euthanasia (for the comatose, for example) justify abortion and even infanticide. Justifying the killing of innocent persons in some cases justifies the killing of other humans whose states of consciousness happen to differ from our own. Newborn children have less developed mental states than do adults; this does not, however, provide moral justification for killing infants should that be deemed expedient by parents, physicians, or society at large.

The argument from martyrdom is not appropriate. The martyr gives up his or her life for a cause or set of principles external to the self, not merely to avoid personal pain or discomfort. The early Christian martyrs, for example, were willing to suffer extreme pain and even bodily dismemberment for the sake of what they held to be of transcendent worth—faith in Jesus Christ. A very "undignified death" was in fact a death filled with great purpose and meaning.

"Showing mercy" to a dog or to a horse suffering great pain is likewise not a good argument for euthanasia. Although the secular humanist sees both the dog and the human being as ceasing to exist at death, the Christian view of man's immortal soul precludes any consideration of man's death that leaves out the question of his eternal destiny.

While the Bible never explicitly condemns suicide, every instance of suicide in the Bible is directly associated with the person's spiritual collapse, from Saul to Judas (I Sam. 31:4; II Sam. 17:23; I Kings 16:18-20; Matt. 27:5; Acts 1:18).[122] The biblical attitude toward human life is so affirmative that an explicit condemnation of suicide is unnecessary; its evil is self-evident.

Neither is the claim that many physicians covertly practice euthanasia a moral justification for the practice. Christian ethics is a normative discipline, concerned not primarily with what individuals in a fallen world do in practice, but rather with what moral agents ought to do, based on divine standards of righteousness. For Christian ethics the will of God, not the Gallup poll, is the crucial arbiter of right and wrong.

Arguments for euthanasia usually appeal to cases of incurable suffering, where the level of pain is presumably intolerable and beyond the range of medical relief. Contrary to some popular opinion, however, even in cases of terminal cancer pain can be managed in an acceptable manner. By the proper use of modern analgesics such as phenothiazines, hydroxazine hydrochloride, methylphenidate hydrochloride, or dextroamphetamine sulfate, pain can usually be relieved without too much sedation or other undesirable side effects.[123] There is some clinical evidence that those whose pain is relieved may outlive others whose nutrition and rest are disturbed by persistent pain.[124] In addition to analgesics, other treatment options are available to the physician for pain control: chemotherapy, nerve-blocking, and biofeedback.[125] These modern medical techniques refute the argument for euthanasia on the basis of pain in terminal illnesses.

In a widely read article that first appeared in 1958, Professor Yale Kamisar pointed to a number of serious nonreligious objections to euthanasia. Kamisar's article was a response to the work of writers such as Joseph Fletcher and Glanville Williams, who had argued for its practice. Kamisar pointed to the contradiction in some proposed legislation for the legalization of "voluntary" euthanasia, which simultaneously supposed that the patient was "crazed by pain" and yet rational enough to make a clear-headed choice for his own death.[126] The legalization of euthanasia would put pressure on the terminally ill to "do away with themselves" in order to spare their families further emotional burdens and expense.[127] Diagnoses of "terminal" illness can be mistaken; in one study it was discovered that eleven patients admitted or transferred to Montefiore Hospital in New York City who were diagnosed as having "advanced cancer in its terminal stages" did not have cancer at all.[128] A spokesman for the Euthanasia Society of America, which proposed legislation for "voluntary" euthanasia in 1939, stated that the society "hoped eventually to legalize the putting to death of nonvolunteers beyond the help of medical science" when public opinion was ready to accept it.[129] Such a slide from voluntary to involuntary euthanasia actually occurred in Germany during the 1930s and 1940s. The euthanasia mentality was gaining ground in the German medical profession even before the Nazis seized control; it began with a change of attitude toward the nonrehabilitable sick, with the acceptance of the attitude that some lives were not worthy to be lived.[130]

As Germain Grisez has pointed out, there is an insidious dynamism to the humanist's argument for euthanasia. Critics of traditional Judeo-Christian morality begin by arguing that certain practices are permissible and then later argue that such actions are morally *obligatory* in many cases. Once it is agreed "that some individuals have a duty to consent to their own deaths, then it will be argued that those who fail to do their duty must be required by law to do it."[131] What begins as a permission can turn into an obligation, even an "obligation" coerced by the force of law.

The legalization of euthanasia would further endanger the lives of unwanted newborn infants with handicaps—a class of human beings whose right to life has already been eroded by the abortion mentality. As Grisez has observed, "There is no reason to suppose that the killing of infants with the sanction of law would be limited to the killing of some few suffering from the most serious defects."[132] This concern is given further credibility by the grim fact that in the United States unborn children have been killed by abortion simply for the reason that their gender was not that desired by the parents.

The legalization of euthanasia would also have a detrimental impact on the mentally disturbed. Those who had suicidal tendencies would find themselves in a situation where the historic restraints against suicide and euthanasia would be missing. The absence of such restraints would weaken one's resolve to face his personal difficulties and would increase the temptation to escape by taking one's own life.

The medical profession itself would be affected. Euthanasia as a legal option would seriously compromise the physician's historic commitment to healing and curing. The physician would assume the role of society's executioner, as well as its healer, and this would have the inevitable consequence of weakening the indispensable element of trust between doctor and patient. Would not the weak and the dying suspect that the doctor, acting on behalf of others or on the basis of some new utilitarian social ethic, comes to the bedside not to administer care and comfort, but to speed the ending of a "useless life"? The euthanasia mentality, which deliberately chooses death as a moral end, is totally incompatible with the historic life-affirming stance of medicine.

From the perspective of the Judeo-Christian tradition, euthanasia violates the commandment "You shall not murder" (Exod. 20:13). The taking of human life—for whatever motives—is strictly forbidden in Scripture, except in those very narrowly defined circumstances such as justifiable war, self-defense, and capital punishment. Societies that have gone beyond these narrow exceptions have opened the door to unintended but tragic levels of bloodshed and violence.

Human life is sacred because God made man in his own image and likeness (Gen. 1:26, 28). This canopy of sacredness extends throughout man's life, and is not simply limited to those times and circumstances when man happens to be strong, independent, healthy, and fully conscious of his relationships to others. God is actively at work in the womb, for example (Ps. 139:13-16; Job 10:8-13), long before the human being can exercise the mental functions that secular humanists tend to see as the key criteria of value for human personality. The same God who lovingly is present in the womb can be present in the dying and comatose patient, for whom conscious human relationships are broken. The body of the dying can still be a temple of the Holy Spirit (cf. I Cor. 6:19), and hence sacred to God.[133]

The euthanasia mentality sees man as the lord of his own life; the Christian sees human life as a gift from God, to be held in trusteeship throughout man's life on earth. "You are not your own; you were bought with a price. So glorify God in your body" (I Cor. 6:19b, 20). Determining the moment of death is God's prerogative, not man's (Job 14:5). Man does not choose his own death, but acquiesces in the will of the heavenly Father, knowing that for the believer, death is both the last enemy, and the doorway to eternal life. Because man bears the image of God, his life is sacred in every state of its existence, in sickness or in health, in the womb, in infancy, in adolescence, in maturity, in old age, or even in the process of dying itself. Among a society all too often characterized by the choosing of death and violence, Christians are to be shining lights to a world of darkness, who choose life for themselves and for others—offering to the dying not deadly poisons, but rather neighbor love and the hope of life eternal.

CHAPTER 8

Capital Punishment

The electric chair at the state prison in Grady, Arkansas, with its thick leather straps and cables that can crank out 2,500 volts, is bolted to the floor on a black rubber mat and sits silently under the glare of fluorescent lights. Warden Willis H. Sargent, in charge of the prison since 1980, says, "I don't want to take a life or be involved in taking a life, but I have to look at the other side of the fence—at the victims and the victims' families."[1] Sargent's comments reflect the ambivalence that many Americans feel about one of the most controversial issues of the day: capital punishment.

Fourteen states have no death penalty. Of the 36 states that do, 19 have not executed anyone since the penalty was reinstated by the U.S. Supreme Court in 1976. Eleven of the 36 states with the death penalty have life-without-parole statutes, and six others require a minimum time served.[2]

Capital punishment may be defined as "the execution of a criminal under death sentence imposed by competent public authority."[3] The term "capital" derives from the Latin *caput*, used by the Romans to refer variously to the head, the life, or the civil rights of an individual. "Capital" punishment thus implies the idea of "chief," "principal," or "extreme" penalty.[4]

Can capital punishment be fairly administered in imperfect societies tainted with racism and class consciousness? Does the use of such penalties actually deter potential murderers? Is capital punishment inherently "cruel and unusual," being based on outmoded notions of revenge? Is such a practice consistent with a biblical ethic of love and forgiveness? These are only a few of the significant questions facing the thoughtful participant in the modern debate on the morality of capital punishment.

HISTORY AND THE LAW

Capital punishment has been practiced since the beginning of recorded history.[5] The Code of Hammurabi (c. 1750 B.C.) applied the death penalty to some 25 different offenses, including corruption by government officials, theft, and various sexual offenses. In the Old Testament, the law of Moses imposed the capital penalty for murder, blasphemy, adultery, homosexual and bestial intercourse, sorcery and witchcraft, cursing a parent, and eleven other crimes. Death was a specified penalty in the Assyrian laws (c. 1500 B.C.), but mutilation appears to have been a more common penalty. The legal code of the Hittites (c. 1400 B.C.) specified the death penalty for a variety of offenses. The records from ancient Egypt indicate that criminals were sentenced to death as early as 1500 B.C.

In ancient Athens murder, defacing coins, certain cases of theft, kidnapping, and pickpocketing were considered capital crimes.[6] In the early period of Roman history capital punishment was imposed primarily for crimes among the military. Later, during the time of the empire, capital punishment became more common. The Romans considered the death penalty to be a deterrent and publicly executed criminals by crucifixion, decapitation, and burning. Under Nero, victims were at times impaled and often suffered death in the arena.[7]

Among the church fathers, attitudes were mixed. Lactantius opposed capital punishment, while Augustine spoke cautiously of the state's right to impose it. During the Middle Ages the number of capital crimes increased, and the methods of execution were often cruel. Pope Leo I (fifth century) and Pope Nicholas I (ninth century) spoke against the involvement of the church in capital punishment. The Council of Toledo (675) and the Fourth Lateran Council (1215) forbade the clergy to participate in capital judicial trials.[8]

Thomas Aquinas, the greatest theologian of the Middle Ages, argued for the right of the state to inflict capital punishment for certain crimes.[9] Martin Luther wrote that "even heathen rulers have the right and power to punish," alluding to Romans 13:4 and the power of the sword.[10] Calvin also supported the practice, stating that the law of God "forbids killing; but, that murderers may not go unpunished, the law-giver himself [God] puts into the hands of his ministers [government officials] a sword to be drawn against all murderers."[11]

In late medieval and early modern England capital punishment became increasingly common. Some 72,000 people were executed during the 36-year reign of Henry VIII. Elizabeth I ordered executions on an average of 800 per year.[12] By 1769 the number of crimes for which the capital penalty could be imposed had grown to 160. Drowning was used as a method of execution until 1697, and burning at the stake was in use until 1790. Beheading as a method of execution was abolished in 1747.

In 1814, three English boys, aged eight to eleven, were executed for stealing a pair of shoes. In 1833, a boy aged nine was hanged for stealing a set of children's paints from a shop in London.[13] Excesses such as these tended to promote sympathy for movements toward the abolition of the death penalty in modern English history.

The work of Cesare Beccaria, *On Crimes and Punishments* (1764), was one of the earliest pleas for the abolition of the capital penalty. Beccaria's treatise was influential in the abolition of capital punishment in Tuscany (1786) and Austria (1787), and it had some influence in England, which eliminated some 190 crimes from the capital category in 1860. In the eighteenth and nineteenth centuries Voltaire, Rousseau, Karl Marx, David Hume, Jeremy Bentham, Benjamin Franklin, and Thomas Paine protested against capital punishment as it was then being practiced.[14]

In America, the first documented instance of capital punishment occurred in the colony of Virginia in 1622. Daniell Frank was hanged for stealing a calf and other chattels from Sir George Yerdley.[15] In 1630 in Plymouth, Massachusetts, John Billington became the first person in the colonies to be hanged for murder.[16] During the revolutionary period, most of the colonies considered murder, treason, piracy, arson, rape, robbery, burglary, and sodomy to be capital crimes. Hanging was the usual form of execution.[17]

The nineteenth century saw the rise of a growing abolitionist movement, marked by the founding of the American Society for the Abolition of Capital Punishment in 1845. In 1846 the territory of Michigan abolished the death penalty for all crimes except treason. Michigan's example was followed by Rhode Island in 1852 and by Wisconsin in 1853.[18] At one time or another, at least 23 states have abolished the capital penalty, and at least 12 have restored the penalty after having rescinded it.[19]

During the twentieth century the greatest number of executions in the United States occurred in the period 1930-49. During that span of time an average of 148 persons were executed each year.[20] By 1967, however, without any significant legislative action, the use of the death penalty came to a halt. Gary Gilmore's death in 1977 before a Utah firing squad ended a ten-year unofficial moratorium on capital punishment in the United States.[21]

The two most significant legal decisions of this century relating to capital punishment were handed down by the U.S. Supreme Court in the 1970s. On June 29, 1972, in *Furman v. Georgia*, the Court, in a split decision, held "that the imposition and carrying out of the death penalty in these cases [from Georgia and Texas] constitutes cruel and unusual punishment in violation of the Eighth and Fourteenth Amendments."[22] The Eighth Amendment forbids "cruel and unusual punishments"; the Fourteenth requires "equal protection of the laws" for all citizens. According to Justices Brennan and Marshall, capital punishment in all circumstances would violate these constitutional provisions. Justice Douglas, in dissent, held that only when the death penalty was imposed without proper guidelines would it in fact violate the equal protection clause. Because *Furman* did not establish any clear consensus on the constitutionality of capital punishment, it left state legislatures in considerable confusion. The ruling did, however, result in a number of sentences being set aside, and various legislatures did attempt to modify their statutes in light of the decision. Prior to the 1972 decision, 39 of the 50 states had retained the death penalty.[23]

The ambiguity and confusion created by the *Furman* case was essentially cleared up by the Court in *Gregg v. Georgia*, handed down on July 2, 1976. In this case the Court approved a new Georgia statute that set out in detail various aggravating and mitigating circumstances that would justify the imposition of the capital penalty. These circumstances included aircraft hijacking; treason; murder for hire; murder of a judicial officer, policeman, or fireman in line of duty; and murder by a person with a previous record of violent crime.[24] This decision made it clear that the justices did not consider the death penalty per se to be "cruel and unusual punishment" in the sense intended by the Constitution. Inasmuch as capital punishment was a fact of American life when the Eighth Amendment was adopted, unbiased historical and legal analysis could hardly have reached any other conclusion. Since 1976 the Georgia law has been used as a model by other states that have retained or reinstated the capital penalty.

THE TEACHINGS OF SCRIPTURE

One of the most important pronouncements in Scripture concerning capital punishment is found in Genesis 9:6: "Whoever sheds the blood of man, by man shall his blood be shed; for God made man in his own image." The reference to the image of God gives a rationale for the death penalty. As Charles C. Ryrie has observed, "When violence in the form of murder is done to a man, it is in effect an outrage against God."[25] Just as an act of desecration to a nation's flag represents an attack on the nation itself, so an attack on man represents an attack on the divine majesty. The act of killing "lays profane hands on that which is divine," H. C. Leupold has noted.[26]

The style in which this pronouncement is written is interesting. The verse displays chiastic parallelism, in that every word of the first member is repeated in reverse order in the second, as though reflecting the principle of measure for measure in the divine scheme of retributive justice.[27]

The question arises as to whether Genesis 9:6 is to be understood merely as a divine *prediction* of the future consequences of murder, or rather as a divine *command* concerning society's proper punishment of the murderer. Grammatically it is possible to construe the Hebrew verb translated "shall be shed" either way.[28] Several factors in the context of the verse, however, give strong indication that a divine command is intended. In the immediately preceding verse, 9:5, God states that he will *require* a reckoning for the lifeblood of man, whether that blood has been shed by man or beast. The language of requirement implies an imperative rather than a mere description. In the second place, a rationale for the action is given: the creation of man in the image of God. If a bare description had been intended, such an explanation would have been unnecessary. It should also be noted that later provisions of the Pentateuch such as Numbers 35:16-21 clearly require the murderer to be put to death. John Murray thus seems correct when he concludes that it would be contrary to the analogy of Scripture, as well as the natural sense of the passage, to understand Genesis 9:6 as "anything else than a charge given to man to execute the death penalty."[29]

In the Mosaic law the death penalty was prescribed for eighteen different offenses: murder (Exod. 21:12-14); causing the death of a pregnant woman, and possibly for causing the death of her child (Exod. 21:22-25); killing a person by a dangerous animal that had killed before, yet was not kept caged (Exod. 21:28-30); kidnapping (Exod. 21:16);

rape of a married woman (Deut. 22:25-29); fornication (Deut. 22:13-21); adultery (Lev. 20:10); incest (Lev. 20:11-12, 14); homosexuality (Lev. 20:13); sexual intercourse with an animal (Lev. 20:15, 16); striking a parent (Exod. 21:15); cursing a parent (Exod. 21:17); rebelling against parents (Deut. 21:18-21); sorcery and witchcraft (Exod. 22:18); cursing God (Lev. 24:10-16); attempting to lead people to worship other gods (Deut. 13:1-16); avenging a death despite acquittal by the law (Deut. 17:12); intentionally giving false testimony against someone in jeopardy of the death penalty.[30]

It should be noted that while the list of capital crimes in the Mosaic code is extensive, the standard of proof for conviction was very strict. Two or three eyewitnesses were required for conviction (Deut. 19:15). Circumstantial evidence alone would never be sufficient under these provisions.[31]

Questions of *interpretation* and contemporary *application* naturally arise at this point. Evangelicals, who look to the Scriptures as the highest authority for faith and practice, are faced with the issue of how the teachings of the Old Testament influence one's conclusions about the modern applicability of capital punishment. As Eric and Walter Hobbs have stated it, the question is, "How much, if anything, of ancient Israel's law is operative here, and what is set aside? On what authority?"[32] If the Old Testament is used as a justification for imposing the death penalty for murder, then why not for striking a parent or for cursing God?

The position taken here is that legitimate distinctions can be made between the legislation given to Israel as a theocratic state under Moses and the more universal revelation given to the human race through Noah. The abrogation of the specifics of the Mosaic covenant (e.g., circumcision, dietary laws, animal sacrifice) for the New Testament church does not necessarily affect the moral and legal principles given through Noah.[33] Noah stood at the head of a new human race after the flood, and stipulations of the Noahic covenant, such as the permission to eat meat and the promise of no further universal flood, applied not just to Noah and his family or to some limited ethnic group, but, in principle, to all mankind.[34]

Other continuing and universal features of the Noahic covenant include the promise of the continuation of the seasons (Gen. 8:22) and the dread of man by the animals (Gen. 9:2). Progressive revelation, notes William Baker, "has not altered the original mandate of Gen. 9:6."[35]

John Murray has also observed that there has been no abrogation of man's being in the image of God, the rationale given for the death penalty in Genesis 9: "it is as true today as it was in the days of Noah."[36] It follows that while the detailed provisions of the criminal code of Israel are no longer binding on the church, the mandate of Genesis 9:6 requiring the death penalty for murder remains one of continuing validity today.

Does the New Testament continue the Old Testament's affirmation of the legitimacy of the death penalty, or does it significantly modify or even rescind those provisions? Three of the most important texts on this question are John 7:53-8:11, Romans 13:1-7, and Acts 25:11.

It is sometimes argued that John 7:53-8:11, the account of the woman taken in adultery, shows that Jesus abrogated the death penalty, at least in cases of adultery. According to verses 10 and 11 of the text, Jesus said to the accused woman, "Has no one condemned you? . . . neither do I condemn; go, and do not sin again."

It should be noted that the evidence of the best Greek manuscripts indicates that this passage was not originally part of the text of John's Gospel. Professor Bruce Metzger and his associates conclude that the evidence "for the non-Johannine origin of the pericope of the adulteress is overwhelming."[37] Nevertheless, the text may well represent a bit of authentic oral tradition that preserves an actual incident in the ministry of Jesus and will be assumed to be such for the purposes of the present argument.

A key point in the proper interpretation of this passage is the meaning of *anamartetos* in 8:7, generally translated as "without sin." This is a rare word in biblical usage, appearing only once in the New Testament, and three times in the Septuagint, the Greek translation of the Old Testament (II Macc. 12:42; 8:4; Deut. 29:19). In secular Greek the term was used to mean "without fault" in a very general sense, as of the constitution of a city.[38]

To understand the implications of this rare word in the present passage, it is important to recall specific provisions of the Mosaic law that dealt with adultery.[39] According to Deuteronomy 22:22-24, both the man and the woman guilty of adultery were to be subject to the capital penalty, not just the woman alone. In John 7:53-8:11 there is no indication whatever that the scribes and Pharisees were also concerned to bring the guilty man to justice as well; their only concern was to use the woman as a tool to entrap Jesus. If he abrogated the death penalty, he would set himself against the law of Moses; if he gave sanction to the execution, he would run afoul of the authority of Rome, which at the time reserved the right of execution to itself.

In challenging the witnesses with the statement "Let him who is without sin among you be the first to throw a stone at her," Jesus was not using the term *anamartetos* in the sense of absolute sinlessness. If complete sinlessness were required of every witness, member of a jury, and judge, no criminal justice system would be possible at all, and this is clearly inconsistent with the New Testament's general affirmation of judicial sanctions as a demonstration of divine justice (cf. Rom. 13:1-7). The sense rather is that the scribes and Pharisees were not without fault as witnesses in such a judicial proceeding, because they themselves were guilty of violating the provisions of Deuteronomy 22:22-24. Stricken in conscience, the hypocritical witnesses left the scene, and Jesus dismissed the case when no one remained to press charges. Far from abrogating the provisions of the Mosaic law, Jesus demonstrated that he took their procedural guidelines for the protection of accused persons very seriously. This understanding of Jesus' action in this pericope is consistent with his statement in Matthew 5:17 that he did not come to abolish the law of Moses, but to fulfill it. Consequently, it cannot be established from this passage that Jesus intended to abolish the death penalty either in general or for the specific crime of adultery.[40] Arguments for the abolition of capital punishment must appeal to texts other than this one.

Romans 13:1-7 is important in any discussion of the New Testament and capital punishment. In verse 4 the apostle states that the civil magistrate "does not bear the sword in vain; he is the servant of God to execute his wrath on the wrongdoer." In his commentary on the book of Romans, F. Godet notes that the term "sword" (*machaira*) which Paul uses here is not the weapon the emperor carried as the symbol of the authority of his office, but rather the one worn in the provinces by the superior magistrates, who had the authority to inflict capital punishment.[41]

It has sometimes been suggested that Paul speaks here only of the *symbol* of capital punishment, rather than its actual infliction. This suggestion is not persuasive in the context, however, since, for example, the reference to taxes in verse 6 refers to an authority to tax that was not merely symbolic, but actually imposed. At the time Paul was writing the Epistle to the Romans, he was well aware that the Roman government inflicted the death penalty. (Cf. Acts 25:11, Paul before Festus, the Roman procurator of Judea: "If I have done anything for which I deserve to die, I do not seek to escape death.") Consequently, it is not legitimate to exclude the death penalty as one way the civil magistrate can rightfully execute God's wrath on the wrongdoer (13:4b). William

Baker has correctly observed that the sword "is not so much a symbol of capital punishment as it is the instrument of capital punishment."[42]

Many Christians have found it difficult to reconcile such mandates for the violent restraint of evil, spoken of here and elsewhere in the New Testament, with Jesus' teachings on love and nonviolence. But as A. R. Vidler has pointed out, the Bible clearly affirms that God is concerned both for the preservation of the world from evil and for the salvation of the sinner. The Bible affirms both the law "which worketh wrath" (Rom. 4:15) and the "faith which worketh by love" (Gal. 5:6)—both "Christ's strange work" and his "proper work."[43] God ordains the punishment in *time* of those whom he may in fact pardon in *eternity*. The Bible affirms the legitimacy of both "horizontal" (civic) and "vertical" (saving) righteousness. The two are not identical, and neither should displace the other.

Acts 25:11, already noted, is worthy of comment in another connection. Paul, imprisoned for the gospel and standing before Festus, stated that "if I have committed anything for which I *deserve* to die [emphasis added], I do not seek to escape death." Paul was saying that if he had in fact committed a capital crime he did not seek to escape the supreme penalty.[44] It is noteworthy that Paul clearly presupposed that some crimes are in fact *worthy of death*, a presupposition that runs counter to modern abolitionist thinking. In the mind of the apostle Paul, then, not only were some crimes intrinsically worthy of death (Acts 25:11), but the governing authorities actually had the divinely sanctioned authority to exercise capital punishment in such cases (Rom. 13:4).

The biblical evidence could thus be summed up concisely as follows: while the civil laws of Israel regarding capital punishment are no longer binding in the New Testament age, the mandate given through Noah (Gen. 9:6) is still valid and sanctions the capital penalty for the crime of murder. The New Testament, including the teaching of Jesus, does not overturn this basic mandate, but presupposes its continuing validity for nontheocratic societies.

PHILOSOPHICAL AND PRAGMATIC CONSIDERATIONS

Among Christians any discussion of the death penalty involves not only the interpretation and authority of Scripture, but also various pragmatic considerations. Perhaps even more importantly, the issue involves a debate about the very nature and purpose of the criminal justice system itself. Does the concept of *retribution* have a proper place in modern society? Or should it be the primary aim of the system to deter further criminal activity, or to rehabilitate the criminal? How one answers such questions can have great bearing on his view of capital punishment.

There are those who believe that retribution, i.e., the idea that crime inherently deserves punishment, is an outmoded and morally repugnant concept. L. Harold DeWolf, a liberal Methodist theologian, believes that retribution "is at best only a socialized and measured form of revenge."[45] As such, it is forbidden to the Christian in any form.

DeWolf appears to misunderstand the true intent of Scripture when he identifies retributive justice and revenge. Properly understood, retribution is a satisfaction of the requirements of justice, a restoration of a disturbed moral balance. Scripture clearly distinguishes between such a concept and feelings of personal hatred by forbidding such feelings and the actions that grow out of them, as William Baker has pointed out.[46] The Bible never calls for the torture of criminals; in fact it condemns excessive punishment. "The fact that a criminal is viewed as deserving his punishment," writes C. K. Poupko, "does not mean that he deserves inhumane treatment."[47]

One of the great merits of a retributive view of punishment, as opposed to other views, is, in the words of Robert Gerstein, that "it serves not only as a justification for punishment but also as a guide to the appropriate kind of punishment and a limit on the severity of punishment."[48] The punishment should fit the crime, reflecting its weight and severity—no more and no less. Such a balancing of crime and punishment is consonant with the basic moral instincts of mankind; it also protects the criminal in that the punishment has its limits. Criminals who are committed to psychiatric wards, conversely, are at the mercy of psychiatric elites who have the power to declare them "sick" or healthy, and their "treatment" can be extended indefinitely.

Norman Geisler is correct in pointing out that in a biblical perspective the main reason for capital punishment is that justice demands it. "A just order is disturbed by murder and only the death of the murderer can restore that justice."[49]

It should be noted that the plan of salvation itself is based on divine standards of retributive justice. According to the apostle Paul, in a very important statement concerning the necessity of Christ's atoning death on the cross, the death of Christ was a demonstration of God's justice, because God in his forbearance had left many previous sins unpunished. The cross proved God to be simultaneously just in punishing sin, and merciful in forgiving those who have faith in Jesus Christ (Rom. 3:25, 26).

The necessity of the death of Christ on the cross is grounded on the fundamental moral fact that in the sight of God certain actions (sin, crime) are *inherently worthy of punishment*. The moral scales of the universe must be righted. The concept of retributive justice is rooted in the very heart of God's character and the gospel itself. The good news is not that God has disregarded standards of justice, but that he himself has satisfied those standards for us and taken our rightful punishment upon himself in the person of his Son. Capital punishment is actually the application on the human plane of the principle of retributive justice demonstrated by God himself in the cross of Jesus Christ.[50]

The issue of *deterrence* inevitably arises in discussions of capital punishment. Both philosophical and pragmatic considerations are relevant in this regard.

Some scholars have argued that deterrence of further criminal activity, rather than retribution, is the only just basis for any penal system. Cesare Beccaria, in his influential work of 1764, *On Crimes and Punishments*, claimed that for any punishment to be just, "it should consist of only such gradations of intensity as suffice to *deter* [emphasis added] men from committing crimes."[51] Beccaria, an early proponent of the abolition of the death penalty, believed that capital punishment is inherently barbaric, representing the "war of a nation against a citizen whose destruction it judges to be necessary or useful."[52] A life sentence would be a greater deterrent for murder, Beccaria thought, since a single crime would "supply frequent and lasting examples."[53]

The fatal defect of any deterrence-only theory of criminal justice, however, has been shrewdly pointed out by C. S. Lewis. If the justification of the punishment of criminals is to be based solely on its efficacy in deterring others, rather than on intrinsic desert, then "it is not absolutely necessary that the man we punish should even have committed the crime."[54] On such a theory a teacher could arbitrarily punish an innocent student in order to give an "example" of the consequences of misbehavior to the class, but such action would be a grave travesty of justice, not its exemplification. True justice requires a real connection between the punishment meted out and personal responsibility for the crime committed.

Can sociological and historical studies demonstrate that capital punishment has a statistically significant deterrent effect? Scholars are divided on this issue. Abolitionists such as Harold DeWolf argue that states such as Michigan, Rhode Island, Wisconsin, and Maine, which abolished the death penalty in the nineteenth century, have had lower per capita homicide rates than such states as Georgia and Alabama, which have retained the penalty.[55] But Professor Isaac Ehrlich, on the basis of a careful statistical study of the period 1933-69, concluded that an additional execution per year in the United States may have resulted on the average in seven or eight fewer murders.[56] Stephen J. Knorr, in a 1979 review of literature in this area, concluded that statistical studies and tests "have not been satisfactorily conclusive either way."[57] Common sense suggests that capital punishment properly administered does have a deterrent effect, but the issue is likely to remain controversial for some time to come.

Proponents of the abolition of capital punishment argue that in practice the death penalty is applied in a discriminatory and arbitrary fashion. It is noted, for example, that the southern states are responsible for two of every three death sentences in the United States, and that Florida, Georgia, and Texas alone account for one-third of the national totals.[58] Black defendants, it is argued, are more likely to suffer the death penalty than whites, and murderers of white victims are more likely to be executed than murderers of nonwhite victims.[59] Abolitionists argue that in a society plagued with racism, capital punishment cannot be administered in a just and colorblind manner.

Those who defend the death penalty point out that it is an unhappy fact that blacks commit a disproportionate number of the known crimes in the United States, including capital crimes.[60] In 1974, for example, 57 percent of the people arrested for murder were blacks; at the same time, 50 percent of the homicide victims were also black.[61] According to Joseph Bishop, "Blacks are overrepresented on death row because, for a variety of reasons, they are overrepresented among murderers. Yet all of the five men executed in 1981 were white."[62] It should go without saying, of course, that most black people, like most white people, are not criminals, but decent, law-abiding people.[63]

Discrimination in any part of the criminal justice system is a matter of serious concern. At the same time, it is important not to exaggerate the problems in the system, and not to require perfection before the administration of criminal sanctions is possible. In any human society, the wealthy may be more capable of escaping the penalty of certain laws, but that is no argument for abolishing laws and prisons. If a given principle is valid—whether capital punishment or some other principle of criminal justice—then imperfections of administration are

justification not for the abolition of the principle, but rather for its reform and more evenhanded application.

Opponents of the death penalty point out that its use inherently
involves the risk of executing an innocent person—a miscarriage of justice that society can never reverse. Charles Bernstein was waiting in a
Washington, D.C. jail, minutes from execution. A messenger rushed in
with the news that his sentence had been commuted to life imprisonment. Two years later, the police found positive evidence of his inno-
cence. "In this instance truth finally won," wrote Jerry and Laura Gladson, "but what if the messenger had been detained in traffic?"[64]

There is another side of the story, however. Those who argue for
the retention of capital punishment point out that a sentence of life imprisonment does not protect the prison guards and inmates from the hardened murderer who may very well kill again. "Life" sentences are quite
frequently shortened by parole, and society may again be placed at risk.

In 1973 Henry Brisbon, Jr., forced a woman driver off Interstate
57 in Illinois at shotgun point. According to *Time* magazine, "As she
begged for her life, her assailant [Brisbon] thrust the shotgun into her
vagina and fired. After watching her agonize for several minutes he fin-
ished her off with a blast to the throat."[65] Brisbon was sentenced to a
term of 1,000 to 3,000 years, but that did not prevent him from murdering another inmate after being imprisoned.[66] Had Brisbon been executed, the inmate's life would have been spared.

There is no doubt that there are elements of risk in the administration of capital punishment. But proponents of abolition need to acknowledge the risks of life imprisonment as an alternative: the lives of
guards, inmates, and members of society at large that continue to be
endangered by hardened killers. Given the extensive appeals process
available to those convicted of capital crimes, and the need for society's protection, the balance of risks would still appear to be in favor of
retention.

Does not capital punishment foreclose the possibility that the criminal might repent and accept Christ as Savior? This question seems to
assume that each person has a right to determine the exact time when
he will make his final decision concerning his relationship to God and
eternity. The Bible speaks otherwise. Life is uncertain, and decisions
about our eternal destiny cannot be delayed at our own leisure. God said
to the rich and complacent fool, "Fool! This night your soul is required
of you" (Luke 14:20).

Rather than foreclosing the possibility of salvation, the reality of the death penalty forces the one convicted to think about his eternal destiny and consequently can even be seen as beneficial. Stanley Ellisen argues that God has "instituted the death penalty for the benefit of the murderer to shock him to repentance, if possible, by the immediate prospect of death and judgment."[67] The death penalty reminds the murderer, in a way that life imprisonment cannot, of the grim but inescapable truth that "it is appointed for men to die once, and after that comes judgment" (Heb. 9:27).

CONCLUSION

Capital punishment is a complex and controversial issue that raises profound questions concerning biblical interpretation, the nature of justice, and the meaning of life itself. On balance, the Bible favors the retention of capital punishment. The command given to Noah in reference to murder (Gen. 9:6) is still binding on all societies in the New Testament age. The proper administration of the death penalty is a display of divine justice and God's wrath on the wrongdoer (Rom. 13:4). The death penalty protects society from the hardened murderer and is an appropriate and fitting punishment for the most heinous of crimes. Because it underscores man's accountability for his actions it serves as a grim reminder of the need to make peace with God while that opportunity yet remains.

—

CHAPTER 9

Civil Disobedience and Revolution

"We are sorry that the laws of Nebraska and the orders of the Cass County District Court ran counter to our conscience. . . . We could not violate our conscience even if no one else in Nebraska shared the same conscience," stated Pastor Everett Sileven, who refused to obey a court order to close the Faith Christian School operated by his church in Louisville, Nebraska.[1] The court had ordered the church school closed until such time as the church agreed to hire state-certified teachers. Sileven had refused to close the school because he believed that to submit to state certification under such circumstances would have been equivalent to saying that "Jesus Christ is not my Lord or Lord of my church."[2]

CIVIL DISOBEDIENCE

The controversial decision of Pastor Sileven and his supporters to defy a court order is one of many examples in American history of conscientious resistance to the power of the state. Such an act of *civil disobedience* has been defined as "a public, nonviolent, and conscientious act contrary to law, usually done with the intent to bring about a change in the policies or laws of the government."[3] The *public* nature of such an act distinguishes it from other actions that are contrary to law, e.g., cheating on an income tax return. Its *nonviolent* nature distinguishes it from war, insurrection, and revolution. Civil disobedience is motivated by matters of conscientious conviction, rather than merely pragmatic or

189

prudential considerations. And in most cases, the act is undertaken in order to draw attention to a state of affairs considered unjust, to raise the moral consciousness of the citizenry, and to set in motion the dynamics of social change.

Under what conditions is civil disobedience a permissible option for the Christian, given the clear biblical mandates to be in subjection to legitimate governing authorities? Under what circumstances would civil disobedience become not merely permissible but morally *mandatory* for the believer? By what criteria is the responsible moral agent to decide when a contemplated act of civil disobedience is either permissible or mandatory? These are some of the fundamental questions on this subject, which call for careful analysis in the light of Scripture, history, and reason.

HISTORICAL EXAMPLES

"The only obligation which I have a right to assume, is to do at any time what I think is right," wrote Henry David Thoreau in his famous essay of 1849, "Civil Disobedience." "Under a government which imprisons any unjustly," he continued, "the true place for a just man is also prison."[4] Thoreau had gone to jail rather than pay a poll tax in support of the Mexican War.

Though perhaps the best known, Thoreau's act of civil disobedience was not the earliest example of such action in nineteenth-century America. During the years 1829-39 a handful of Presbyterian and Congregational missionaries to the Cherokee Indians refused to obey the law of the state of Georgia, which required them to support the removal of the Indians from their lands. These missionaries went to jail for their beliefs.[5]

In ancient Greece, Socrates, when offered his freedom on the condition that he give up his pursuit of truth and wisdom, is reputed to have said, "I shall obey God rather than you."[6]

The first mass protests as acts of civil disobedience were led by Mohandas K. Gandhi in the twentieth century, reflecting Gandhi's doctrines of *ahimsa* (nonviolence) and *satyagraha* ("truth force"). Gandhi became the spokesman for Indian grievances in South Africa under the government of Prime Minister Jan Smuts.[7] Beginning in 1930, Gandhi led mass protests against the British government in India. The first law broken was one making it illegal to take salt from the ocean or from any source other than the British salt monopoly.[8]

Gandhi's tactics were eventually instrumental in winning India's independence from British rule.

The example of Gandhi was influential in the life of Martin Luther King, Jr., who received the Nobel Peace Prize for his leadership in the American civil rights movement. King was vaulted into national prominence during the 1955 Montgomery, Alabama bus boycotts. Mrs. Rosa Parks had refused to move to the back of a Montgomery bus, and her arrest ignited the succeeding boycotts. "I had come to see early," King wrote, "that the Christian doctrine of love operating through the Gandhian method of nonviolence was one of the most potent weapons available to the Negro in his struggle for freedom."[9] In a nationally televised debate King stated in response to some of his critics that the individual "who discovers on the basis of conscience that a law is unjust and is willing in a very peaceful sense to disobey that unjust law and willingly and voluntarily suffers the consequences . . . is expressing the highest respect for law."[10]

In 1960 civil disobedience as a tactic in the civil rights movement reached a new plateau when four Greensboro, North Carolina black students sat down at a segregated lunch counter at a Woolworth's variety store and stayed when refused service. During the next year and a half, some 70,000 persons took similar action, and as a result over 100 southern communities desegregated one or more of their public eating places.

The nonviolent tactics practiced by Martin Luther King, Jr., provided models for draft protesters during the Vietnam War. In even more recent American history, Randall Terry and his followers in Operation Rescue have blockaded abortion clinics around the country. They have argued that Christians are morally justified in breaking trespass laws in order to save the lives of unborn children.[11]

BIBLICAL AND THEOLOGICAL PERSPECTIVES

There are clear precedents for civil disobedience in the Bible. In the first chapter of Exodus we are told that the Hebrew midwives refused to obey the order of the king of Egypt to kill the newborn male children of the Hebrew women (Exod. 1:15-22). The text specifically states that God approved the midwives' decision (vv. 20, 21). The king of Egypt evidently considered the high fertility rates of his Hebrew subjects (Exod. 1:7) a potential threat to his political power.

Norman Geisler has noted that the Egyptian king in this case clearly represented an oppressive government, which assumed the place *of* God rather than assuming its place *under* God.[12] The king had usurped the place of God by commanding the midwives to take innocent life, by forbidding Israel to worship in the way God had commanded (Exod. 4:23), by putting Israel into forced slavery (Exod. 1:11-14), and by refusing Israel permission to leave the country (Exod. 7:14, 22).[13] Under these circumstances God not only blessed the courageous act of disobedience of the midwives, but later brought judgment upon the oppressive government of Egypt and its false gods.

Prior to the fall of Jerusalem the prophet Jeremiah counseled the people to surrender to the Chaldeans rather than to resist and be destroyed in the impending invasion (Jer. 38:1-6). This advice, clearly contrary to the policies of King Zedekiah's advisors, was the cause of his being imprisoned in the miry cistern (v. 6). Jeremiah was not afraid to publicly defy, on God's authority, the policies of Zedekiah and his princes.

Daniel and his friends Shadrach, Meshach, and Abednego, refusing to comply with King Nebuchadnezzar's compulsory state religion, would not bow down to the golden image the king had erected on the plains of Dura in Babylon (Dan. 3:1). Unmoved by the threat of being thrown into the fiery furnace, the young men calmly replied, "If it be so, our God whom we serve is able to deliver us out of your hand, O king. But if not, be it known to you, O king, that we will not serve your gods or worship the golden image which you have set up" (vv. 17, 18).

When Peter and the other apostles were arrested and imprisoned by the Sanhedrin for refusing to obey the order not to preach in the name of Jesus, their defense was, "We must obey God rather than men" (Acts 5:29; cf. 4:19). As F. F. Bruce has commented, the "authority of the Sanhedrin was great, but greater still was the authority of Him who had commissioned them to make this good news known."[14]

Such heroic acts of resistance to overweening state authorities were repeated by the martyrs in the early church. In the year A.D. 165 Justin Martyr and his companions refused to yield to the command of the emperor and sacrifice to the pagan gods. "Do what you will. For we are Christians and offer no sacrifice to idols." Justin and his companions were beheaded for their faithfulness to the Savior.[15]

A Christian understanding of the authority of the state recognizes that no human authority is absolute. All authorities are ultimately subject to God, from whom their authority derives. If the commands of human rulers conflict with those of God, then God alone must be obeyed. As John Calvin observed, "The Lord . . . is King of Kings who . . . must alone be heard. . . . If they command anything against him, let it go unesteemed."[16]

The statement of Jesus recorded in Matthew 22:21, "Render unto Caesar the things that are Caesar's, and to God the things that are God's," was radical in the context of the ancient world's understanding of the power of the state. Far from acknowledging an unlimited authority of the state over the life of man, the words of Jesus relativize the power of human government by relating it to the more comprehensive and abiding claims of God. As the German New Testament scholar Gunther Bornkamm has noted, it is in fact the second half of the statement that has the real weight, and because of this the first half has its weight taken from it.[17] For indeed, "the reign of Caesar passes, but God's reign comes and does not pass away."[18]

The Pauline admonitions in Romans 13:1-7 concerning the believer's submission to state authority have at times been misconstrued in a one-sided way. Believers are indeed to be subject to duly constituted authority, but the passage also implies clear limitations upon the power of rulers. The ruler is *God's servant* and consequently is accountable to God for his conduct; he must rule in accordance with the divine standards of justice set forth in the law of God. This divine law, as Archie Jones has stated, "provides both an authoritative limitation on rulers and a duty of resistance to tyranny, as well as a basis for disobedience to ungodly laws promulgated by magistrates who fail to fulfill the high duties of their God-ordained ministry."[19]

All human authority is a derived authority; it is given to the ruler from above (John 19:11) as a sacred trust to be exercised justly on God's behalf. A government that persecutes the innocent in disregard of the laws of God and the dignity of man is no servant of God, but rather a beast and enemy of God (Rev. 13).

A theological consideration of the possibility of civil disobedience also involves an analysis of the nature and limitations of *law*. The Scriptures clearly recognize that not all human laws are just. Psalm 94 speaks of "wicked rulers . . . who frame mischief by statute" and who "condemn the innocent to death"(vv. 20, 21). Human laws, rather than reflecting divine righteousness and equity, can instead institutionalize and perpetuate human greed, violence, and oppression.

Thomas Aquinas, considering in his *Summa Theologica* the question "Whether Human Law Binds a Man in Conscience," recognized the crucial moral distinction between just and unjust laws. Laws that are unjust by virtue of opposing the divine good "must nowise be observed." Laws that are contrary to the commandments of God do not bind the conscience and should not be obeyed.[20]

John Calvin taught that the authority of human rulers was always subject to that of God. Obedience to human rulers should never lead away from obedience to God, "to whose will the desires of all kings ought to be subject, to whose decrees all their commands ought to yield, to whose majesty their scepters ought to be submitted."[21]

Article xvi of the Augsburg Confession, one of the most important confessional statements from the Lutheran wing of the Protestant Reformation, also recognizes the right of conscientious disobedience. Civil authorities ought to be obeyed in all that can be done without sin. "But when the commands of the civil authority cannot be obeyed without sin, we must obey God rather than men" (Acts 5:29).[22]

OBJECTIONS TO CIVIL DISOBEDIENCE

One of the more frequent objections raised against the concept of civil disobedience is that such activity promotes *anarchy and disrespect for law*. Former Senator Sam Ervin stated this outlook in no uncertain terms during the 1960s: "The right of clergymen and civil rights agitators to disobey laws they deem unjust is exactly the same as the right of the arsonist, the burglar, the murderer, the rapist and the thief to disobey the laws forbidding arson, burglary, murder, rape, and theft."[23]

The problem with the senator's statement is that it does not recognize the crucial distinction between just and unjust laws, which is precisely the distinction that civil disobedience is intended to dramatize. Unlike the thief or arsonist, the person engaging in civil disobedience does so out of *conscience* in a *public* fashion in order to dramatize the injustice of the existing order.

There is also the concern that civil disobedience might increase the incidence of crime. Former U.S. Supreme Court Justice Charles E. Whittaker wrote in 1966 that "it can hardly be denied that our current rash and rapid spread of lawlessness has derived from planned and organized mass disrespect for, and defiance of, the law and courts."[24]

While it is certainly important that those who contemplate acts of civil disobedience weigh carefully the possible negative impact of their example and not break the law for trivial reasons, nevertheless fundamental justice is not to be sacrificed to preserve the tranquility of the status quo. As John Rawls has argued, "If legitimate civil disobedience seems to threaten civil peace, the responsibility falls not so much on those who protest as upon those whose abuse of authority and power justifies such opposition."[25] The true "disturbers of the peace" are those who have perpetuated fundamental injustices, rather than those who attempt to call attention to them, even at the risk of losing their personal freedom.

In the biblical outlook, fundamental *justice* is a weightier value than the preservation of merely external order and peace. Because of their faith in God, the judges of Israel enforced justice and became mighty in war, putting foreign oppressors to flight (Heb. 11:33, 34). If authentic faith in God can lead one to engage in justifiable *war*, it is difficult to see how authentic faith could be inconsistent with a justifiable act of *civil disobedience*, which by definition is peaceful and nonviolent.

Other objections to civil disobedience may arise on the basis of a certain understanding of Romans 13, especially the admonition in verse 1, "Let every person be subject to the governing authorities." Subjection to governmental authority would appear to leave very little if any room for conscious resistance to the state.

Other features of the text, however, need to be carefully noted. Paul speaks not only of the believer's response to government, but of the proper nature and purpose of government as well. The ruler is to be a *servant of God* for the benefit of those who are ruled (v. 4). Consequently, as John Howard Yoder has observed, Romans 13 gives the citizen an important criterion for measuring whether government is fulfilling its God-ordained function. "We can judge," he notes, " . . . the extent to which a government is accomplishing its ministry, by asking namely whether it persistently . . . attends to the rewarding of good and evil according to their merits; to be a 'minister to you for good' is a criterion, not a description."[26]

It should also be noted that the apostle Paul appeals to *conscience* in his discussion of the Christian's relationship to the state. According to New Testament scholar Ernst Kasemann, this clearly implies that "Christian obedience is never blind; and, indeed, open-eyed obedience, directed by *suneidesis* [conscience], must even be critical."[27] And as Stephen Mott has noted, since conscience is to be a motivating factor in one's relationship to the state, "a basis may be inferred for disobeying government when its actions are not in conformity with the voice of informed conscience."[28] In other words, Paul's reference to *conscience* presupposes that for the Christian human power is not the final court of appeal or arbiter of human action; God alone is. If rulers command what is contrary to a biblically informed conscience, then "we must obey God rather than men" (Acts 5:29).

It should also be noted that Paul in Romans 13:1 chooses the term "be subject" rather than the term "obey." Generally speaking, being subject to authority means obeying the commands of that authority, but a government's decreeing an unjust law introduces new elements into the situation. One can be subject to the authority of the state in general, recognizing its overall legitimacy, but refuse to comply with a given requirement that is contrary to divine standards. The person engaging in civil disobedience who voluntarily accepts the penalty for such actions thereby acknowledges the general legitimacy of the state and "is being subordinate even though he is not obeying."[29] Even while consciously resisting the temporal authority at a given point, the conscientious objector still acknowledges in principle the legitimacy of the government, and this distinguishes his act from that of the terrorist, revolutionary, or anarchist.

Some scholars admit the theoretical legitimacy of certain acts of civil disobedience, but limit such acts within very narrowly defined boundaries. Charles Ryrie, for example, sees biblical justification for such action only in "spiritual" matters. To take the law into one's own hands "finds no support in the Scriptures. The only exception seems to be if the government forbids his worshipping God."[30]

This position, Stephen Mott has pointed out, reflects a narrowly defined doctrine of sin.[31] The will of God and the will of human authorities can conflict not merely in the areas of evangelism and worship, but in questions of social justice and basic human rights, as the cases of the Hebrew midwives (Exod. 1:15-21) and the modern civil rights movement in the United States demonstrate.

CRITERIA FOR JUSTIFIED ACTS OF CIVIL DISOBEDIENCE

Since under normal circumstances the believer has a duty to obey the law and to set a good example of citizenship, no act of civil disobedience should be undertaken lightly. Any contemplated act of civil disobedience should be evaluated in the light of basic principles derived from Scripture and common sense.

It should be recognized that there is an important distinction between circumstances that make civil disobedience *permissible* and those that make it *mandatory*. In general, the latter may be more easily recognizable. When the civil authority either *commands* the believer to do what is contrary to Scripture or *prohibits* the believer from doing what God has commanded, it is clear that the civil authority must be resisted, for "we must obey God rather than men." The case of the Hebrew midwives is an illustration of the first condition, and the prohibition to preach the gospel (Acts 4:18), an illustration of the second.

Other cases in which it may be *permissible* to engage in civil disobedience may not be so clear and require the application of a number of other criteria.[32]

First of all, *the law being resisted must be unjust and immoral, clearly contrary to the will of God*. Laws are not to be broken merely out of whim or for reasons of self-interest, but only when a scripturally informed conscience indicates such action. A given law may be inconvenient or burdensome, but respect for law and the good order of society will lead the Christian to suffer such burdens rather than engage in potentially disruptive actions.

Second, *legal means of changing the unjust situation should have been exhausted*. Civil disobedience should be seen as a method not of first resort, but rather of last resort, when legal channels have already been pursued. There may, of course, be situations in which the injustice is so grave and immediate that there is simply no time for lengthy legal appeals. In certain extreme circumstances, e.g., when Christians were required to cooperate in a program of the extermination of Jews in Nazi Germany, appeal to the existing legal system would be futile. Consequently, the significance of this particular criterion will vary according to the context of the action.

Third, *the act of disobedience must be public rather than clandestine*. A conscientious objector, unlike a criminal, does not seek to hide his actions from either the authorities or the public. As Mott has pointed out, "Openness is required not only for the sake of principle but also for the strategy of appeal to public opinion."[33] The intent of the conscientious objector is not only to act in accordance with his own conscience, but to arouse the conscience of the citizenry as well, and this requires public action.

Fourth, *there should be some likelihood of success*, particularly when the intent is to produce changes in laws and institutions. One must disobey for personal reasons when conscience demands it, of course, but when social change is also contemplated, then one must consider if civil disobedience as a *means* is effective in achieving specific moral *ends*.

The likelihood of success should be evaluated in light of the possible evil effects, such as social disruption, promotion of lawlessness, loss of personal freedom, responsibility to one's family and other ministry commitments, and so forth. A person considering withholding a portion of his income tax to protest a given war should recognize that such an act taken by itself will not prevent the spending of money for the war effort. Only by withholding all of one's tax could a person be sure that his tax money is not supporting the war effort. In such circumstances, the protester would do well to consider whether the possible litigation and even imprisonment is worth risking, or whether there might be more effective means of calling attention to an unjust war, including means that do not jeopardize existing responsibilities to family and other dependents.

Finally, *those who consider civil disobedience should be willing to accept the penalty for breaking the law.* Such an attitude demonstrates respect for the principle of rule by law and distinguishes legitimate civil disobedience from anarchy and insurrection. Acceptance of punishment under such circumstances is evidence of the ethical motivation of the person who has violated the law, and it can also serve to dramatize the situation and arouse the conscience of the public.

In the light of these criteria, then, one could conclude that an act of civil disobedience would be *permissible* even when the state did not require one *personally* to violate an explicit teaching of Scripture. A visitor in South Africa, for example, might participate in a protest against laws prohibiting the sale of certain lands to blacks, in order to demonstrate solidarity with an oppressed group, even though as a noncitizen he is not under the direct jurisdiction of the unjust law.

Civil disobedience, then, is an ethical challenge that can face the Christian because of the sinful character of the world and institutions within which man lives. Ordinarily, our clear moral obligation is to obey the existing authorities; but when the will of the state conflicts with that of God, "we must obey God rather than men."

REVOLUTION AND THE CHRISTIAN CONSCIENCE

"Revolts, revolutions, uprisings, rebellions, agitation, civil wars, *coups d'etat:* these are the very fabric of history," wrote Jacques Ellul.[34] The *fact* of violent revolution is an undebatable element in the history of mankind. The *value* question, however, namely, whether Christians should ever participate in violent revolution, is very much debated, and much harder to answer. What of the situation of oppressed Christians in certain parts of Latin America or the communist world? Could oppressive and unjust temporal conditions ever justify, in the light of biblical norms, participation in the violent overthrow of an existing government? And by what criteria should the Christian evaluate such "revolutionary" situations? Such questions may seem academic in our present American context, but they are very real for many Third World believers.

Revolution has been defined as an "attempt to make a radical change in the system of government," often involving "the infringement of prevailing constitutional arrangements and the use of force."[35] Unlike justified war, the "aggressor" is the existing government itself, rather than some external power; and unlike civil disobedience, the resistance to the existing government generally employs violent means, and the very legitimacy of the existing state is denied.

HISTORICAL PERSPECTIVES

While the history of rebellion and revolution is as old as the human race, a developed *theory* of the subject's right to resist the existing authorities is a relatively recent phenomenon in Western civilization. Until the Protestant Reformation, and later, the Enlightenment, men did not generally see themselves as having inalienable rights, which by their very existence limited the power of the state.[36] The Protestant Reformation asserted the authority of God in the Bible as superior to the authority of any human institution. It thus laid a theological foundation for a limited view of the powers of the state. Man, by virtue of his creation in the image and likeness of God, had a dignity and status as a free individual that was not created by the state, but that the state was bound to acknowledge by limiting its own powers. An emphasis on the unlimited sovereignty of God implied a limited sovereignty for human rulers and provided a check against absolutist concepts of the "divine right of kings."

John Locke's *Second Treatise of Government* (1690), which helped to give intellectual justification to the American Revolution, was an outgrowth of the limited view of government fostered by the Reformation. The basic purpose of government, according to Locke, is "the good of mankind." If a government does not actually serve this end, is it better, Locke asked, that the people be exposed to boundless tyranny, "or that the rulers should be sometimes liable to be opposed when they grow exorbitant in the use of their power and employ it for the destruction and not for the preservation of the properties of their people?"[37] Locke's treatise was written to argue the legitimacy of the English Revolution of 1688, which installed William of Orange as the new king of England, but his arguments had an influence far beyond the confines of that original context.

The philosophic justification of the right of revolution articulated by Locke was developed in various ways during the American and French Revolutions, and later radicalized by Karl Marx and his followers.[38] For Marx, given the class structure of bourgeois societies, class conflict and revolution were part of the very dynamic of history, an inescapable means of bringing the new classless utopia into existence. As Marx voiced this revolutionary outlook in the oft-quoted "Theses on Feuerbach," "The philosophers have only *interpreted* the world in various ways; the point is, to *change* it."[39]

The Marxist understanding of history and society has been influential in contemporary "theologies of liberation." Such theologies repudiate the spiritualization of salvation and the resigned acceptance of the status quo.[40] According to Latin American liberation theologian Gustavo Gutierrez, "By working, transforming the world, breaking out of servitude, building a just society, and assuming his destiny in history, man forges himself."[41] With liberation theologies, then, it seems that Christian reflection on revolution has itself been turned upside-down. In an earlier age, the gospel was thought to prohibit armed rebellion against the state; now, at least in the minds of some theologians, the fulfillment of salvation would seem in some cases to require it.

ARGUMENTS AGAINST REVOLUTION

Arguments against revolution can be made on both philosophical and biblical grounds. Philosophically, conservative thinkers such as Edmund Burke, author of *Reflections on the Revolution in France* (1790), have argued that political and social continuity are the essential prerequisites for any orderly society; revolutions, which tear the fabric of social continuity, cannot be in society's best interests.[42] Furthermore, according to Burke, revolutions are inherently destructive and tend to replace one despotism with another.[43] Not only the events of the French Revolution, with its overthrow of Louis XIV, followed by the Reign of Terror and the rise of Napoleon, but the bloody events of the Russian Revolution in this century would appear to give credence to Burke's analysis.

More recently, the French existentialist writer Albert Camus voiced skepticism concerning the justifiability of any revolution. However noble or lofty the stated goals of the revolutionary movement might be, in Camus' view "the means employed . . . represent so enormous a risk and are so disproportionate to the slender hopes of success, that, in all sober objectivity, we must refuse to run this risk."[44] Camus' reading of history evidently convinced him that the risks of revolutionary action will always outweigh the possible benefits.

Substantial arguments against revolution—or at least Christian participation in revolution—can be made on biblical grounds. One of the most obvious and perhaps one of the strongest lines of argument is drawn from Romans 13:2: "He who resists the authorities resists what God has appointed." As F. F. Bruce has commented, Paul states that civil rulers exercise their authority by delegation from God; "therefore, to disobey them is to disobey God."[45]

Similar admonitions are found in 1 Peter, written to Christians in Asia Minor who were suffering unjust persecution at the hands of the Roman authorities: "Be subject for the Lord's sake to every human institution" (2:13). The Christian is to follow the example of Christ, who patiently suffered at the hands of unjust authorities without reviling or threatening in return (2:21-23). J. N. D. Kelly notes that the writer is stressing that "the principle of the redeemed Christian life must not be self-assertion or mutual exploitation, but the voluntary subordination of oneself to others."[46] Given the admonitions both here and in Romans for Christians to be in subjection to civil authorities, even unjust ones, it would seem that the burden of proof would be upon those who would attempt to justify from Scriptures Christian participation in revolution.

ARGUMENTS FOR JUSTIFIABLE REVOLUTION

Despite the formidable arguments against the Christian's participation in revolution, justifications for such action have not been lacking in modern Western civilization. In a much-quoted sentence in the closing pages of the *Institutes of the Christian Religion,* John Calvin spoke of "magistrates of the people" whose lawful office was to restrain the tyranny of kings:

> For if there are now any magistrates of the people, appointed to restrain the willfulness of Kings (as in ancient times the ephors were set against the Spartan Kings, or the tribunes of the people against the Roman consuls, or the demarchs against the sen-

ate of the Athenians . . .), I am so far from forbidding them to withstand, in accordance with their duty, the fierce licentiousness of kings, that, if they wink at kings who violently fall upon and assault the lowly common folk, I declare that their dissimulation involves nefarious perfidy, because they dishonestly betray the freedom of the people, of which they know that they have been appointed protectors by God's ordinance.[47]

While not allowing for private revolutionary action, Calvin argued for the right of designated representatives of the people to resist the tyranny of kings. The influence of this important sentence can be seen in later writings on politics and revolution, such as the *Lex Rex* of Samuel Rutherford (1644), the *Politica methodice digesta* of Johannes Althusius (1603), and the Lutheran Magdeburg Confession of 1550, which affirmed the duty of armed resistance to a ruler who violated the law of God.[48]

In his commentary on Daniel 6:22, Calvin stated the right of resistance in even stronger language. Earthly rulers lay aside their power when they rise up against God, and they "are unworthy to be reckoned among the members of mankind. We ought rather utterly to defy them [lit., "to spit on their very heads"] than to obey them."[49] As John T. McNeill has commented, "This is rough language even for a fighting theologian."[50]

As noted earlier, John Locke, on the basis of a social contract theory of government and the assumption that the end of government is the welfare of the people, argued for the right of revolution when government no longer honors that end. Rulers should be opposed "when they grow exorbitant in the use of their power and employ it for the destruction and not the preservation of the properties of their people."[51]

The moral legitimacy of revolution can also be argued on biblical grounds. Scripture makes it clear that God's providential judgments in history can take the form of removing from power unjust civil authorities. The God of the Bible is the ultimate ruler of the nations, and he "looses the bonds of kings" and "overthrows the mighty . . . pours contempt on princes. . . . He makes nations great, and destroys them" (Job 12:18, 19, 21, 23). Daniel reminds the proud King Nebuchadnezzar that it is God who "removes kings and sets up kings" (Dan. 2:21). In the Magnificat the virgin Mary praises the God who "puts down the mighty from their thrones" (Luke 1:52).

Such judgments of God on unjust rulers are not exercised in a vacuum; God uses human instruments to accomplish his purposes. A clear biblical example of such action is found in the Book of Judges, where we are told that "the Lord raised up judges" to rescue his people from foreign oppressors (Judges 2:16). According to the writer of Hebrews, judges of Israel such as Gideon, Barak, and Samson demonstrated true faith in God by putting foreign armies to flight (Heb. 11:32-34). The key point in these passages is that in these instances God specifically willed the overthrow of the de facto governing authorities, and called the leaders of his people to use deadly force in the process of liberation. The passage from Judges shows that the de facto governing authority may not continue to be a *legitimate* authority in the sight of God.

While the people of God are to be "subject to the governing authorities" (Rom. 13:1), the key question in a potentially revolutionary situation is, "Who is the legitimate authority in the sight of God?" When the call of God came to Gideon (Judges 6), Gideon, rather than the Midianite rulers, became the legitimate authority for the people of Israel, and Gideon was called of God to forcibly overthrow the existing order. Although the example of the judges is taken from the history of theocratic Israel, the principle nevertheless is valid: God sometimes wills the overthrow of existing authority; he even calls his own people to be the instruments of that purpose. In general God wills the existence of the "powers that be," but Scripture clearly shows that God can also will to bring any existing government to an end and to replace it with another that is more in accordance with his standards of justice and righteousness.

CONDITIONS FOR A "JUST REVOLUTION"

It can be argued, then, that there is a biblical rationale for revolutionary action against existing governments under some circumstances. Given the moral gravity, however, of any course of action that involves resistance to authority and loss of human life, those who would contemplate such action should carefully and critically employ appropriate criteria before actually moving in such a direction.[52]

The *cause* for which the revolutionary group fights must be a *just* one, not merely a response to burdensome or inconvenient conditions, or merely a rationalization for narrow class or party interests. The demands of fundamental justice must outweigh the normal preference for social stability and nonviolence. The existing government in question should be one that persistently threatens or kills innocent human life and denies fundamental human rights such as freedom of worship, speech, and assembly. In such circumstances revolutionary action may then be comparable, notes Mott, "to repelling an international aggressor in the just war theory."[53] In this case, the "aggressor" is internal to the society, rather than external.

Revolutionary action should be a means of *last resort*. Given the very real possibility that violent means may escalate and go beyond the control of the leadership, peaceful means of achieving a more just situation should have been exhausted.

The call to revolutionary action should be issued by a *lawful authority*. This criterion, borrowed like the rest from just-war theory, may seem to be self-contradictory, given that revolution is a repudiation of the existing order. As was noted, however, in the cases of the judges of Israel (Judges 2:16), the *existing* (de facto) authority did not continue to be the *legitimate* authority in the sight of God. A revolutionary situation can call into question the moral legitimacy of the existing authority, and the people of God may be called to recognize a new leader or leaders raised up by God to restore a legitimate government.

Leaders of any just revolution must be able to claim wide support among the people, and such support would be forthcoming if their actions were manifestly more in accord with standards of fundamental justice than were the actions of the representatives of the status quo. The formation of a parallel government—one might think, for example, of the French Resistance government in exile led by Charles de Gaulle during the Second World War—would tend to give credibility to the emerging leadership.

The point here is that, in principle, the leaders of any just revolution are not engaging in private action, but intend to act with the best interest of the society as a whole in view. Their "calling" and "gifts," if truly valid, will be recognized by the people. This criterion of *lawful authority* is necessary to distinguish just revolution from vigilante action and anarchism.

For justifiable revolutionary action, there should be *reasonable hope of victory*. The costs of violent means, involving loss of life and civil disorder, are too grave to risk for frivolous causes or those that have little hope of succeeding. The existence of overwhelming military power supporting the oppressive regime, or the lack of popular support for the resistance movement would be contraindications for revolution. The situation of the Jews in the first century provides a case in point. The overwhelming military superiority of the occupying Roman forces in Palestine made revolutionary attempts foolish and futile, as the tragic events of A.D. 66-70 were to prove.

There should be a *due proportion* between the good to be achieved and the probable evil effects of employing violent means. As in the case of justifiable war, "the cure should not be worse than the disease." This condition implies the importance of wide popular support and the moral legitimacy of the cause, for apart from these elements, structural change can only come about through the use of excessive violence.

Finally, the revolutionary action must be *rightly conducted through the use of right means*. That is to say, even though violent means may be employed, some forms of violence are morally impermissible. Torture and mutilation of enemy soldiers or civilians, for example, can never be morally justified. As Mott has observed, "Torture is one of the surest indications of the denial of justice by a regime."[54] Any resistance movement that stoops to such reprehensible means thereby undercuts the same moral credibility it seeks to establish over against the existing regime. In any justifiable revolution, as in any justifiable war, the participants must make every attempt to limit the violence as much as humanly possible in order to maintain the justice of the cause.

THE LIMITS OF WHAT REVOLUTION CAN ACHIEVE

While revolution may at times become a tragic and justifiable course of action for a people, the Christian should have no illusions concerning its dangers and limitations. Secular revolutionists such as Karl Marx and his followers have had messianic expectations of revolutionary action, seeing in it the hope of heaven on earth. But as Martin Scharlemann has observed, such utopianism does not take evil seriously.[55] And, writes Brian Griffiths, "While revolution may create new social institutions and destroy old ones, it is powerless to change human nature."[56] The Christian may be driven by the compelling demands of fundamental justice to support or even be directly involved in a revolution, but at the same time the believer will never expect from any course of *political* or *military* action what only the Holy Spirit of God can accomplish: a renewed heart that seeks justice and works to realize it institutionally in the world. The Christian works for temporal justice, with the realization that perfect justice is not attainable under the present conditions, but will only be instituted when Christ returns and brings the kingdom of God in all its fullness.

CHAPTER 10

War and Peace

"Christians have to say that it is a sin not only to use, not only to threaten to use, but merely to build a nuclear weapon," stated William Sloan Coffin of New York's liberal Riverside Church, at an international meeting on nuclear disarmament in Amsterdam sponsored by the World Council of Churches.[1] Coffin's statement exemplifies the strong passions that have been aroused in the Christian community by the specter of nuclear war.

From the very beginning of the church's existence down to the present day the question of war has troubled the Christian conscience. The earliest Christians struggled with the question, Is service in the armed forces of the Roman Empire consistent with allegiance to Jesus Christ, the Prince of Peace?

Does the Bible give clear guidance in such matters? Do the Old and New Testaments have significantly different perspectives on the issues of war and peace? What ethical implications may be drawn from the cross of Jesus Christ in this issue? Have the realities of modern nuclear war made, for all intents and purposes, pacifism a moral obligation for the Christian? These are only some of the questions relating to war and peace that have become very urgent for the Christian church near the end of the twentieth century.

WAR IN HUMAN HISTORY

The history of warfare seems as old as the recorded history of the human race. Even the cave pictures seem to indicate that ancient man experienced warfare.[2] From a biblical perspective that is what one would expect, for war is ultimately a result of man's fallen, sinful nature. "What causes wars, and what causes fightings among you? Is it not your passions that are at war in your members?" (James 4:1). The ultimate causes of war are not to be found in the social and economic circumstances external to man, but within man himself.

War was a frequent part of ancient Israel's experience. By God's command, the Israelites invaded Canaan and engaged in holy war against its inhabitants. During the period of the judges, Israel fought mostly defensive wars against the Canaanites, Midianites, Moabites, Edomites, and Philistines. King David's army consisted entirely of infantry. Solomon introduced cavalry and the chariot corps (I Kings 4:26;10:26). During the Maccabean wars (c. 166-134 B.C.), the Jewish forces successfully used guerilla tactics against the powerful Greek cavalry and elephant corps (II Macc. 13:2, 15).[3]

In the fourth century B.C. Alexander the Great used the Macedonian phalanx formation, and siege engines conquered an empire that extended from the Indus River to Egypt and from Iran to Greece.[4]

The highly disciplined Roman infantry legions and cavalry in three centuries of warfare conquered an empire that encompassed the Mediterranean world and included some 150 million people at its height.[5]

During the medieval period the development of the institution of chivalry gradually evolved a set of rules for armed combat that represented a major advance over the anarchical combat that characterized the period following the fall of the Roman Empire.[6] Augustine formulated criteria for just wars, establishing a tradition in the Christian church that attempted to limit the destructiveness of armed combat. The church also attempted to develop practical policies to further these same ends. The Peace of God (A.D. 988) taught the sacredness of life and declared churches, the clergy, and the common people immune from attack. In the year 1095 Pope Urban II proclaimed the Truce of God, delimiting the seasons and days when military conflict could occur.[7]

Technological developments brought changes in the nature of medieval warfare. The invention of the English longbow, used with great effect at the battles of Crecy (1346) and Agincourt (1415), brought an end to the dominance of the feudal cavalry. The new longbow was capable of penetrating the armor of knights and their horses. The exploitation of gunpowder in weaponry led to the breaching of walls of cities that hitherto had been considered impregnable, and reduced the security of feudal lords in their castles. The use of gunpow-der in siege artillery in the successful attack of the Turks on Constan-tinople in 1453 is sometimes considered the beginning of the period of modern war.[8]

The widespread devastation in Europe caused by the Thirty Years' War, concluded in 1648, led to various attempts to develop interna-tional law to limit the scope and aims of warfare. During the seven-teenth and eighteenth centuries the nation-states of Europe developed well-disciplined professional armies, and as a result the great mass of the population was not often directly involved in the conflicts of this pe-riod. The rather primitive forms of communication, transportation, and industry also were factors that helped to make armed conflicts during this period somewhat limited in their effects.[9]

The Industrial Revolution and other technological developments during the nineteenth century altered the character of war and led to the mobilization of entire nations in the war effort. Modern means of transportation and communication made possible the deployment of massive armies over vast geographical areas.

The American Civil War marked the first major use of railroads to transport troops directly to the front, of the telegraph, of balloons for observation, and of armored steam warships. Artillery was becoming more powerful, and machine guns were introduced.[10]

The First World War marked the transition to modern total war, with the entire populations of the opposing nations pitted in the war effort against one another. This conflict cost some 9 million military and 30 million civilian lives.[11] The Second World War was even more deadly, costing 17 million military and 34 million civilian lives.[12] The world wars of the twentieth century were the largest in a long list of 278 wars recorded during the period 1484-1945.[13]

THE MORALITY OF WAR: THE PRE-ATOMIC ERA

THE PACIFIST TRADITION

From the beginning of the Christian era, there have been those who have believed that the use of deadly force is inconsistent with the ethics of Christ. Pacifism was a significant, though not dominant, presence in the early church. St. Hippolytus (c. 170-c. 236) condemned voluntary military service by Christians. Tertullian and Lactantius, going further, condemned military service outright.[14] Many converts, however, continued to serve in the Roman legions, and those who left the army seemed to have been motivated by a desire to avoid the idolatrous rites of the legions, rather than by a philosophical objection to warfare as such. After the conversion of Constantine, the problem of pagan religion in the armed forces was largely overcome.[15]

In the Middle Ages, the Waldenses, originating in the twelfth century, condemned all war and the taking of human life, but eventually fought in their own defense.[16]

During the Reformation, anabaptist groups such as the Swiss Brethren and the Mennonites advocated pacifist positions.[17] In the next century the Quaker movement, founded by George Fox in 1668 and brought to Pennsylvania by William Penn in 1682, also espoused the pacifist outlook.

In the modern period pacifism was advocated by the famous Russian novelist Leo Tolstoy and by the Indian reformer Gandhi. The ideals of peace and international law were formulated in international congresses leading up to the Hague Convention (1899), the Hague Court (1907), and the League of Nations Covenant (1920). The Kellogg-Briand Pact of 1928 attempted to outlaw war, obliging its 63 signatories to renounce war "as an instrument of national policy in their relations with one another."[18] Such agreements, while articulating the ideals of peace, were not successful in preventing either the First or the Second World War.

The biblical basis for the pacifist tradition is found preeminently in a certain understanding of the Sermon on the Mount. Texts such as Matthew 5:38-48 are central in the debate: "Do not resist one who is evil. . . . if anyone strikes you on the right cheek, turn to him the other also. . . . Love your enemies and pray for those who persecute you. . . . You, therefore, must be perfect, as your heavenly Father is perfect." These texts are taken to be not merely counsels concerning the Christian's *attitude* in the face of persecution and abuse, but rather literal prescriptions for Christian conduct. Thus the question, How can the stance of *nonresistance* be consistent with warfare, or *loving one's enemies* with the use of deadly force?

Christian pacifists recognize, of course, that the people of God engaged in warfare in the Old Testament. This could be seen, however, as a concession to "hardness of heart," after the analogy with God's permission of divorce (cf. Matt. 19:8). In the New Covenant, the believer's warfare is not carnal, but spiritual. The Christian's weapon is not the physical sword, but the sword of the Spirit (Eph. 6:17), which is the Word of God.

The ethical implications of the cross of Christ are central in the debate between the pacifist and the just-war traditions. For the pacifist, the death of Jesus as an innocent victim in the face of injustice is the pattern for the Christian. According to Ronald Sider and Richard Taylor, the ultimate ground "of biblical opposition to taking life is the nature of God revealed first in Jesus' teaching and life and most fully in his death."[19] In the pacifist understanding, if one finds oneself in a situation in which it seems impossible to preserve both the values of justice and of nonviolence, then one chooses nonviolence, even at the price of allowing great injustices to be perpetrated upon oneself and innocent third parties.

Other New Testament texts are said to support this interpretation of the cross. Believers are admonished to "repay no one with evil . . . but overcome evil with good" (Rom. 12:17, 21). "Love does no wrong to a neighbor; therefore love is the fulfilling of the law" (Rom. 13:10). "For this you have been called, because Christ also suffered for you, leaving you an example, that you should follow in his footsteps" (I Pet. 2:21). According to the pacifist understanding of these texts, Christians are precluded from serving in combat positions or from the office of civil magistrate, since these duties require from time to time the use of deadly force against the criminal or the aggressor. Such means are held to be inconsistent with the admonitions concerning nonviolence and nonresistance.

The pacifist tradition is based largely, as we have seen, on a literal interpretation of the sayings of Jesus in the Sermon on the Mount. Such a hermeneutical approach is difficult to maintain consistently, since it overlooks the hyperbolic mode of speech deliberately used in order to arrest the listener's attention and lodge the saying in the memory. Jesus also said that the lustful eye or hand was to be torn out or cut off (Matt. 5:29, 30), a forceful and memorable way of teaching the gravity of sin in the disciple's life. An insistence on a literalistic interpretation of the saying of Jesus in Luke 14:26 ("If anyone comes to me and does not hate his own father and mother and wife and children and brothers and sisters, yes, and even his own life, he cannot be my disciple") produces a grave contradiction of the clear teaching of another New Testament text, I Timothy 5:8 ("If anyone does not provide for his relatives, and especially for his own family, he has disowned the faith and is worse than an unbeliever"). It is clear from John 19:26, 27 that Jesus, just before his death on the cross, far from literally "hating" his mother, was concerned for her welfare and commended her into the care of John the beloved disciple. The point of the saying in Luke is that affection for one's family is not to usurp the place of supreme loyalty to God—not that one is literally to "hate" one's own family.

In John 18:22, 23 Jesus, after being arrested, was struck by one of the high priest's officers. Rather than literally turning the other cheek, Jesus challenged the injustice of the act: "If I have spoken wrongly, bear witness to the wrong; but if I have spoken rightly, why do you strike me?" In a similar situation the apostle Paul, standing trial before the Sanhedrin, was struck by one of the high priest's attendants. Like Jesus, Paul did not literally turn the other cheek, but challenged the injustice of the action (Acts 23:1-5). The actions of Jesus Christ himself and of the great apostle to the Gentiles clearly indicate that the sayings on turning the other cheek are meant to promote an attitude of nonrevenge, rather than the posture of a "doormat" for abuse in such situations.

A further difficulty with the pacifist hermeneutic is its understanding of the ethical implications of the cross. The cross of Christ is indeed a demonstration of patient suffering in the face of injustice, as I Peter 2:21-25 shows, but it is incorrect to see this as the only lesson to be drawn from the crucifixion. As Romans 3:25, 26 indicates, the cross is centrally a demonstration of the righteousness and justice of God— the God who both must punish sin to uphold his righteous moral universe, and yet justifies those who put their faith in Jesus. The New Testament understanding of the cross shows that the demonstration of God's mercy to the sinner cannot be separated from the vindication of the requirements of justice in the punishment of sin. In drawing ethical implications from the death of Jesus, the pacifist tradition focuses on an "exemplary" theory of the atonement (i.e., the life of Jesus seen as an example for believers), but overlooks the implications of the penal, substitutionary dimensions of the New Testament teachings. The result is an unbalanced view of the cross, one that gives too little weight to the requirements of divine justice.

There has also been the tendency in pacifist interpretation to concentrate on one set of ethical inferences drawn from the death of Jesus (nonresistance in the face of injustice), and to give insufficient weight to the connection in the New Testament between the cross and the resurrection. As David Hollenbach has observed, "Neither the crucifixion alone nor the resurrection alone adequately represents the content of Christian conviction. The death of Christ on the cross is one aspect of the coming kingdom. The Father's act of raising him from the dead and inaugurating the kingdom of justice is a second and equally significant aspect of the paschal event."[20] God's active vindication of justice in the resurrection is the divine balancing of the passive suffering of injustice on the cross.

It should also be observed that there are limits to the "exemplary" understanding of the life and death of Jesus, because such a theory overlooks the utterly *unique* vocation of Jesus to be a vicarious sin-bearer for his people—a calling that is shared by no other Christian. Jesus' death was unique and unrepeatable in its design and purpose; it was never intended to be the sole and comprehensive model for dealing with questions of civil justice in the temporal order.

A further difficulty with the pacifist interpretation of the New Testament texts is the confusion of private and public duties. As a private individual, considering only my own interests and standing before God, I may choose to literally turn the other cheek in the face of unjust aggression. When I stand in a relation of guardianship to third parties, as a civil magistrate, a parent, or a husband, however, then the responsibilities of Christian love have a different application. Because of my love for those under my care, and out of concern for their lives and welfare, I must resist unjust aggression against them. Love of my neighbor does not mean standing idly by when my wife is being brutally raped; it means using whatever force is necessary to protect her life and safety. My divine obligation to provide for the needs of my own family (I Tim. 5:8) certainly includes, as an irreducible minimum, protecting them from deadly assault.

The contention that Christians, in light of the passages on nonresistance, are barred from the office of magistrate, and consequently do not face such obligations for the armed defense of third parties, is not really tenable according to Hebrews 11:32-34. In this text, the judges of old are held up to the New Testament church as positive examples of *faith*. By this faith, these saints "conquered kingdoms, enforced justice . . . became mighty in war, put foreign armies to flight."

In spite of its hermeneutical weaknesses, the pacifist tradition does express the genuine biblical desire for a world of peace, and it challenges a world all too often given to the violent solution of its problems. There will be a time when swords will finally be turned into plowshares, but in the interim, the demands of divine justice and love of the neighbor sometimes require the use of force in the legitimate defense of innocent human life.

THE JUST-WAR TRADITION

As the name implies, the just-war tradition in the history of the Christian church holds that under some circumstances the Christian may participate in war for the sake of the preservation of justice. This tradition holds that some but not all wars are morally justifiable. The just-war position represents the dominant majority within Christianity, including the Roman Catholic, Eastern Orthodox, and Protestant expressions of the faith.

Augustine (354-430) was the first major figure in a long line of Christian thinkers who attempted to develop criteria for distinguishing justifiable and unjustifiable wars.[21] In his great work *The City of God*, written after the barbarians had sacked Rome in A.D. 410, Augustine responded to the pagan charges that the Christians, by their indifference to civic affairs and the military virtues of the Roman tradition, were helping to undermine the state and the values of civilization.[22] In this and other writings Augustine defended the legitimacy of Christian participation in just wars.

In the *Summa Theologica* Thomas Aquinas reiterated the teachings of Augustine. Aquinas concluded that it is not always sinful to wage war. For a war to be just, three criteria had to be met: the war must be declared by a legitimate authority, and not private individuals; second, "a just cause is required, namely that those who are attacked, should be attacked because they deserve it on account of some fault"; and third, "it is necessary that the belligerents should have a rightful intention, so that they intend the advancement of the good, or the avoidance of evil."[23] As Augustine had stated earlier, the aim of just war is the restoration of peace and a more just social order. In the subsequent Roman Catholic tradition, the teachings of Aquinas were refined and elaborated by the casuists Vitoria (1487?-1546) and Suarez (1548-1617).[24]

The mainstream Protestant Reformers did not break with the Catholic tradition of just-war teaching. Luther stated that "without armaments peace cannot be kept; wars are waged not only to repel injustice but also to establish a firm peace."[25] Violent means must sometimes be used to preserve the life and health of the body politic, just as a physician must at times amputate an arm or leg in order that the whole body not perish—and this can be a work of Christian love.[26] In the *Institutes of the Christian Religion* Calvin taught the legitimacy of a just war, stating that "both natural equity and the nature of the office dictate that princes must be armed not only to restrain the misdeeds of private individuals by judicial punishment, but also to defend by war the domin-ions entrusted to their safekeeping, if at any time they are under enemy attack."[27]

Modern discussions of just-war criteria are largely refinements upon and expansions of the teachings of Augustine and Aquinas. Such dis-cussions commonly distinguish between *jus ad bellum* criteria, i.e., those governing the decision whether or not a given war is justified, and *jus in bello* criteria, those used to evaluate given lines of conduct once war has commenced. The *jus ad bellum* criteria include competent author-ity, just cause, proportionality of proposed means and the probable costs in the light of the probability of success, exhaustion of peaceful means of resolution, and right intent. The principle of proportion of means in light of the probability of success holds that the costs of going to war to secure justice should not be greater than the costs of allowing an un-just state of affairs to persist. Put another way, the latter principle states that "the cure (war) should not be worse than the disease (injustice)." A right intention implies that the "just belligerent confine military op-erations to pursuit of the just cause, that charity rather than hatred and desire for vengeance motivate his policies toward the enemies, and that a just and lasting peace be the ultimate aim of the war."[28]

Once war has been entered into, the *jus in bello* criteria include a principle of proportionality, i.e., the use of force and violence must be limited in terms of legitimate military necessity and the principle of dis-crimination: direct, intentional attacks on noncombatants are prohib-ited.[29] These criteria, like the *jus ad bellum* ones, are all attempts to limit the level of violence and destruction that inevitably are a feature of every war.

The biblical arguments for the just-war position begin with the ob-servation that the Old Testament clearly presupposes that warfare can be a legitimate activity for a believer. Abraham, set forth as an exam-ple of faith by the New Testament writers (Rom. 4:11, 12; Heb. 11:8-10), led a military expedition to rescue his nephew Lot (Gen. 14:13-16). Joshua, the judges, and David all engaged in wars that were clearly approved or even commanded by God. It is quite notable that a New Testament writer, the author of Hebrews, explicitly referred to the mil-itary exploits of the judges and David and saw their actions not as ex-pressions of "hardness of heart," but rather as demonstrations of living *faith* in God. These men of God "through faith conquered kingdoms, enforced justice . . . became mighty in war, put foreign armies to flight" (Heb. 11:33, 34). They are set before the New Testament church as *pos-*

itive examples of faith, and their faith in this case was exhibited in their military valor. God clearly approved their "putting foreign armies to flight" and their use of arms in the enforcement of justice. This Hebrews text clearly shows that from a New Testament perspective the use of armed force is not inconsistent with true faith in God, and that in the divine scale of values, the enforcement of justice has higher priority than nonviolence when these two values conflict.

When soldiers came to John the Baptist and asked him what type of behavior is consistent with life in the kingdom of God, John told them, "Rob no one by violence or false accusation, and be content with your wages" (Luke 3:14). The soldiers were not to abuse their authority for personal gain, but John made no suggestion that entering the kingdom requires leaving the army, or that the profession of soldier is inherently incompatible with true repentance and faith in God.

Jesus' encounters with Roman centurions are also notable in this regard. In one case he gave the Roman officer high commendation for his faith, saying, "Not even in Israel have I found such faith" (Luke 7:9). Again, as with John the Baptist, there is no suggestion that a soldier must leave the army to demonstrate the sincerity of his faith. This inference, drawn by the pacifist tradition, was not taught by Jesus or the writers of the New Testament.

The apostle Peter's attitude in this regard was the same as that of Jesus and John the Baptist. Peter was sent to preach the gospel to Cornelius, a devout man who feared God (Acts 10:2) and who had a good reputation among the Jews (10:22), even though he represented the authority of the occupying Roman power. Peter realized that God shows no partiality, and that in every nation "any one who fears him and does what is right is acceptable to him" (10:22). Peter never suggested, either before or after Cornelius' conversion, that "doing what is right" required resigning his commission in the Roman legions.

In his discussion of the proper role of civil government, the apostle Paul stated that the magistrate does "not bear the sword in vain; he is the servant of God to execute his wrath on the wrongdoer" (Rom. 13:4). The sword in question (*machaira*) is not merely a ceremonial instrument; in the Septuagint, the Greek translation of the Old Testament, the same word is used of a deadly weapon (Gen. 34:26; Judges 3:16). Like the power to tax (vv. 6, 7), the magistrate's power to use the sword can be a proper expression of authority delegated from God himself.

In relation to the New Testament's witness to the teachings and actions of Christ, we have already observed his interactions with the

Roman centurion. In the cleansing of the temple (John 2:13-22), Christ himself drove out the moneychangers with a whip of cords. This incident alone shows the insuperable difficulties that surround an insistence on a literalistic understanding of the saying, "Do not resist one who is evil." Christ did not remain passive in the face of evil; he acted forcibly to remove evil from his presence.

In the Book of Revelation, John sees a heavenly vision of the risen Christ, who is mounted upon a horse, and who "in righteousness judges and makes war" (19:11). John saw nothing morally offensive about portraying the activities of the risen Christ in martial terms. In the mind of the inspired writer, there was nothing inherently wrong with warfare. While the warfare in question is spiritual, nevertheless the suitability of the war metaphor implies that the activity itself is not a violation of the purposes of God. By way of contrast, God is never described as a "harlot" or in terms of other occupations that are by their very nature immoral.[30]

The foregoing observations support the contention of W. P. Paterson, who in a discussion of just war and pacifism stated that Christian thinkers need to "take their orders from the whole Christ and not a fragmentary Christ—from the Christ who is the expression of the complete moral purpose of God, the revelation of justice and love as well as meekness."[31] In such a light the cross of Christ, for example, is a demonstration not only of patient suffering of an innocent victim, but preeminently a vindication of the righteousness and justice of God (Rom. 3:25, 26)—even at the price of violence directed against his own Son.

An objection that naturally arises from the pacifist perspective concerns Christ's admonition to love one's enemy. How can the command to love one's enemy be reconciled with the use of deadly force against him? Does that not preclude the possibility that the enemy soldier will later repent and believe the gospel? These are significant questions that advocates of the just-war position need to address.

In the first place, the paradox of love and wrath is found in the character of God himself. The same God who inspired John 3:16 ("For God so loved the world that he gave his only Son . . .") also inspired II Thessalonians 1:5-10, where it is said that the same Jesus Christ, when he comes to judge the world, will inflict vengeance and everlasting judgment upon those who reject the gospel. God's love and God's justice cohere in the divine nature in a way that does not always seem understandable to human reason, but those of an evangelical persuasion must be faithful to the full witness of Scripture concerning the revealed character of God. An emphasis on love to the exclusion of the sterner dimensions of God's wrath and justice soon leads to a concept of love that is sentimental and humanistic, quite different from that revealed in Scripture.

At the last judgment each one will give an account of the deeds done in the body (II Cor. 5:10). By restraining an evil aggressor, even through deadly force, one can act in love, because in so doing one can reduce the eternal weight of guilt for which the aggressor will have to answer. Love acts with the enemy's eternal welfare in view, and it is in no one's interest to compound an eternal weight of guilt.

It is true, of course, that anyone who enters the field of battle cannot reckon on leaving the battlefield alive. Since now is the acceptable time, and today the day of salvation (cf. II Cor. 6:2), anyone who is called to military combat should consider well the state of his soul and his eternal relationship to his Creator; in an uncertain world, God does not guarantee anyone unlimited time to repent (cf. Luke 13:1-5).

The just-war tradition, then, attempts to place the emphasis where Scripture itself does: when the values of justice and nonviolence conflict in a fallen world, the vindication of divine standards of justice takes precedence. The cross of Jesus Christ is the demonstration of God's own vindication of justice (Rom. 3:25, 26), even at the terrible cost of violence directed against his own Son.

Those who truly desire peace must be willing to defend life against those who would destroy it unjustly. As Pope John Paul II has stated, "However paradoxical it may appear, the person who deeply desires peace rejects any kind of pacifism which is cowardice or the simple preservation of tranquillity. In fact those who are tempted to impose their domination will always encounter the resistance of intelligent and courageous men and women, prepared to defend freedom in order to promote justice."[32]

WAR AND PEACE IN A NUCLEAR AGE

"The policy debate about deterrence is not a debate between those in favor of nuclear war and those against it," David Hollenbach has observed. "It is a debate between persons with differing perspectives and convictions on how to prevent nuclear violence."[33] This is a good reminder in the modern debate about the morality of nuclear weapons. Various parties within the Christian community agree that nuclear weapons have raised a new set of issues regarding war and peace, and they agree that all-out nuclear war would represent an unparalleled tragedy for the human race; but they have legitimate differences concerning the policies and strategies that, in the present world, are most likely to prevent such an event.

At the outset of the discussion, it should be noted that the Christian's hope in a dangerous and uncertain world rests in the confidence that God in his sovereignty is in control of the world situation and is working out his plans for mankind. There seem to be clear indications in Scripture that it is not God's purpose to allow the human race to annihilate itself prior to the return of Christ, which marks the close of human history as we now know it. After sending the catastrophic judgment upon the generation of the flood, God made the following promise to Noah and to his descendants: ". . . neither will I ever again destroy every living creature as I have done. While the earth remains, seedtime and harvest, cold and heat, summer and winter, day and night, shall not cease" (Gen. 8:21, 22). God promised that the normal processes of nature, which make human life and agriculture possible, will not cease while history goes on.

In the Great Commission (Matt. 28:18-20) we are reminded that it is Jesus Christ who has all power in heaven *and on earth*. The decisions of kings, presidents, and prime ministers are in his hands; not a sparrow falls to the ground apart from the Father's will (Matt. 10:29). It is the will of the Father that all people groups have an opportunity to hear the gospel before the end comes (Matt. 24:14). The heavenly vision of Revelation 7:9 transports us to a time when a great multitude from every tongue and tribe and nation have not only heard the gospel, but actually responded to it. It is not the Father's purpose to destroy the human race prior to the return of Christ, but to have the gospel universally proclaimed and a church established among every people.

It is sometimes suggested that II Peter 3:10, 12, which speaks of the "elements being dissolved with fire," refers to the destruction and heat of nuclear weapons. It may be that this imagery is a very vivid and intense way of expressing the universal judgment of God upon an unbelieving world (for examples of such cosmic language in connection with acts of judgment, cf. Joel 2:28-32, quoted in Acts 2:19, 20; Ezek. 32:6-8). Even if the language is taken literally, the destruction occurs *at* the return of Christ, and not before—in which case, believers have no cause to fear for their safety, Christ being present.[34]

None of the above precludes, of course, possibility of the limited use of nuclear weapons. The point is, however, that there is no reason for the believer to live in constant dread and despair, as if nuclear weapons were entirely beyond the sovereign control of God. God has his own purposes for history, and those purposes will surely be fulfilled.

THE U.S.-SOVIET NUCLEAR BALANCE: RECENT TRENDS

Any discussion of the moral issues surrounding nuclear weapons must take into account the historical trends in arms acquisition by the world's two major nuclear powers. In 1967, Secretary of Defense Robert Mc-Namara froze the number of U.S. ICBMs at 1000 Minutemen plus 54 of the older Titans. The number of nuclear missiles carried by U.S. submarines was also voluntarily frozen at 656.[35] Since 1968 the United States has not deployed new land-based intercontinental ballistic missiles.

The hope that the Soviet Union would voluntarily reciprocate in this restraint was not, however, realized. During the 15 years from 1968 to 1983 the Soviets were adding two new nuclear missile launchers each week—100 per year—so that by 1983 the strategic balance, once massively in favor of NATO and the West, now stands heavily in favor of the Soviet Union.[36]

Since 1970 the Soviet Union has been spending approximately $40 billion per year in the area of strategic forces, while U.S. expenditures in this critical area of defense have averaged about $12 billion per year.[37] This difference in budget priorities has produced a Soviet advantage in the number of strategic launchers of 1.63 to 1. In the area of missile throwweight—the weight of the warhead and warhead compartment on a missile—the ratio stands at 3.68 to 1 in favor of the Soviet Union. In the area of number of warheads, the United States has a slight advantage of 1.2 to 1 in the ratios. In the area of equivalent megatonnage—a measure of the destructive power of warheads—the Soviet Union has an advantage of 4 to 1.[38] Defense analyst Jeffrey Barlow concludes that with the exception of a few measurements, such as the number of warheads, "the Soviet Union has a discernible advantage across-the-board in strategic forces."[39]

More than half the Soviet ICBMs—the SS-17, SS-18, and SS-19 missiles—have been deployed since the last U.S. ICBMs were deployed.

Over 600 of these recently deployed missiles, the SS-18s and SS-19s, have payloads as large as or larger than the proposed U.S. MX missile and are accurate enough to land within 250 yards of a hardened U.S. missile silo and destroy it. According to General John W. Vessey, Jr., chairman of the Joint Chiefs of Staff, the Soviet Union may now have the capacity to destroy 70 to 75 percent of the United States' land-based missiles in a preemptive strike.[40] The U.S. ICBM force is not capable of inflicting equivalent damage on Soviet missile silos. The ability of aging B-52 bombers to penetrate extensive Soviet air defenses is problematic, and the missiles on our relatively invulnerable nuclear submarines at sea are not powerful enough and accurate enough to threaten hardened Soviet military targets. A successful Soviet preemptive strike could leave a U.S. president with the unsatisfactory alternatives of "suicide or surrender," because a strike by U.S. submarine-launched missiles against Soviet cities could be answered by a devastating Soviet second strike against U.S. cities. The growing vulnerability of the land-based component of the U.S. strategic triad was thus a matter of the most serious concern. Even with the introduction of the MX and improvements in submarine-launched missile accuracy, this vulnerability and imbalance seemed likely to persist.

Proposals for arms limitation talks must be based on hard and realistic appraisals of the historical trends in U.S.-Soviet arms acquisition, which since 1968 tended to tilt the balance in favor of the Soviet Union, a government not known for its consistent honoring of its treaty obligations.

NUCLEAR PACIFISM

"We do not perceive any situation in which the deliberate initiation of nuclear warfare, on however restricted a scale, can be morally justified."[41] This statement, from the American Catholic bishops' pastoral letter of May 1983, "The Challenge of Peace," expresses a position that has come to be termed "nuclear pacifism." While not disavowing the just-war tradition or opposing possession of or every conceivable use of nuclear weapons, the bishops concluded that the dangers of escalation were so great that the actual use of such weapons would be catastrophic.

Other scholars have reached similar conclusions. According to the Jesuit scholar David Hollenbach, "The use of nuclear weapons can never be morally justified."[42] Hollenbach is not a pacifist across the board, but adopts a pacifist position with respect to nuclear weapons.

Those who are drawn to this position frequently raise the issue of "overkill." We live in a world where each of the major nuclear powers possesses enough weaponry to "destroy the world x times over." The American nuclear arsenal is equivalent to half a ton of TNT for every person alive in the world. The Soviet nuclear arsenal is the equivalent of two tons of TNT for every man, woman, and child alive today.[43]

Considerations of "overkill" are linked with the dangers of escalation. Given so much explosive power, it is argued, it seems almost certain that a limited nuclear exchange would lead to an all-out war that could devastate the planet. On such grounds, surrender to the most vicious of tyrannies would be preferable to the suicide of the race.

Advocates of nuclear pacifism are also skeptical about the possibilities of preserving the just-war distinction between civilians and combatants in a nuclear war. Does not in fact the policy of "Mutual Assured Destruction" deliberately hold the civilian population of the Soviet Union hostage to the U.S. nuclear arsenal? Such a policy, it is argued, is blatantly immoral on the basis of traditional just-war criteria. According to Gordon Zahn, "Because nuclear war involves the near-certainty of mutual destruction and passes far beyond all limits of human decency, any statement of the pacifist position must begin with a negative—the outright repudiation of nuclear war as a conceivable option."[44]

Nuclear pacifists and other religious leaders tend to condemn increases in spending for nuclear (and even conventional) weapons because, in their view, such funds should be directed toward meeting the needs of the poor. Roman Catholic bishop Thomas Gumbleton of Detroit has stated that the arms race "is to be condemned unreservedly because it is an injustice, even if those arms are never used. The arms race itself is an act of aggression against the poor."[45]

Nuclear pacifists claim that while the immediate effects of nuclear war would be catastrophic enough, the long-range side effects would be even worse. Radiation would produce mutations in bacteria that would make them more virulent and lethal to humans. Radiation would also impair the strength of white blood cells and hence make human beings more susceptible to the ravages of disease and epidemics.[46] As few as 100 megatons exploded over major urban centers could, it is claimed, throw enough dust and smoke into the upper atmosphere to block sunlight and induce a "nuclear winter" that could devastate agriculture around the world, or at least in the Northern Hemisphere.[47] Given the dangers of escalation, it is argued, such considerations should lead one to adopt the pacifist position on the use of nuclear weapons.

A RESPONSE TO NUCLEAR PACIFISM

Advocates of nuclear pacifism tend to overlook the actual trends in strategic armaments when discussing the arms race. As was noted earlier, the United States essentially stopped "racing" in 1967 when it voluntarily and unilaterally froze the number of its land-based and submarine-launched nuclear missiles. The Soviet Union did not reciprocate, but continued its massive build-up. The United States' budget for defense went down 19 percent in constant 1983 dollars from $223 billion in 1970 to $182 billion in 1983.[48] The number of U.S. strategic bombers has fallen by attrition from 1,364 in 1964 to 316 in 1983, and the total throwweight of U.S. nuclear warheads has been reduced by more than half.[49]

Since 1967 the United States has unilaterally reduced 8,000 nuclear weapons. During this same period the Soviet Union has not reciprocated, but has continued to build its nuclear arsenal.[50]

The average destructive power of U.S. nuclear weapons started declining in 1957, when it was *ten* times as great as it is now.[51] The total destructive power of the U.S. nuclear arsenal, measured in equivalent megatons, was *four* times as great in 1960 as it is today.[52] In the meantime yields of Soviet warheads have tended to remain high. Warheads on the heavy SS-18 Soviet missiles are estimated to be in the 20-24 megaton range. The SS-17 and SS-19 missiles are estimated to carry 3.6 and 4.3 megaton warheads. The U.S. Minuteman II missiles, on the other hand, carry warheads with yields of 1.2 megatons.[53] These figures are rarely if ever mentioned in discussions of the arms race, and critics of U.S. policy rarely acknowledge these documented examples of unilateral American restraint.

These reductions in the total megatonnage of the U.S. arsenal, as well as of the average destructive power of a given missile warhead, have been made possible by dramatic advances in computer and radar technology, which have led to startling improvements in missile accuracy. The early ICBMs were relatively inaccurate, generally landing about a mile from the target, and thus required a very large warhead to be militarily effective. The new Pershing II, however, has an on-board radar that can "see" the terrain as it makes its final approach and can make course adjustments based on a map stored in its computer memory, consequently delivering its warhead within 30 yards of the target.[54] It is thus possible to achieve a legitimate military objective with a much smaller warhead, producing much less collateral damage. The dramatic improvements in guidance technology thus make it more feasible than before to observe the just-war criteria of proportionality and discrimination between civilians and combatants. As Professor Robert Jastrow has pointed out, the greater accuracies being produced by computerized guidance systems mean that "nearly every task allotted to nuclear weapons today can be accomplished in the future by missiles armed with nonnuclear, smart warheads."[55]

Albert Wohlstetter, a leading analyst in the area of nuclear strategy, has pointed out that recent improvements in midcourse guidance on cruise missiles have produced accuracies in the range of 200 feet, compared with the 12,000-30,000 feet misses expected for ballistic missiles in the late 1950s.[56] Furthermore, he points out, improved terminal guidance techniques feasible during the next few years "could enable a cruise missile with a suitable *non*-nuclear warhead to destroy a military target and reduce the area of fatal collateral damage to about one-thousandth of a square mile—an enormous contrast with World War II."[57] Technological progress in missile guidance systems, far from making just-war criteria such as proportionality and discrimination obsolete, has made such distinctions more relevant and attainable than in previous periods of modern warfare.

Another misconception often reinforced by nuclear pacifists is the idea that "Mutual Assured Destruction" (MAD) is still the official targeting policy of the United States. In actual fact, as early as the 1970s the United States began moving away from a targeting policy that focused on civilian population and shifted this focus to military targets. This new policy direction was embodied in National Security Decision Memorandum 242, which remained in effect during the Ford administration and was extended by President Carter in Presidential Directive 59, issued in 1980.[58] Today the primary targets of U.S. nuclear weapons are Soviet strategic and theater nuclear forces, conventional forces, political and military command and control centers, and war supporting industries.[59] These priorities are in line with traditional just-war criteria, which direct military weapons against military targets.

Nuclear pacifists tend to argue that even the most limited use of nuclear weapons leads to unlimited exchanges and the ultimate holocaust. Such arguments, while deserving serious consideration, must be recognized for what they are: projections and prudential judgments, not established facts. The fact is that total nuclear war is an eventuality that human societies have never experienced, and all projections about such eventualities and how human leaders would react under such circumstances are hypothetical, not subject to experimental verification before the fact. Such projections run the risk of falling into "technological determinism," which assumes that human beings cannot rationally control the technical means at their disposal.

As Edward Luttwak has written, the outlook of "technological determinism" would suggest that "the instinct for survival would have been utterly extinguished in political leaders, and also that the armies in the field and their commanders . . . would behave as robots throughout."[60]

When the United States had a nuclear monopoly vis-à-vis the Soviet Union immediately after the conclusion of the Second World War, it did not use these weapons against the Soviets, nor did the United States use nuclear weapons against the Chinese communists or North Koreans during the Korean War. These historical examples show that restraint in the use of nuclear weapons is a genuine possibility.

This is not to say, of course, that the dangers of escalation are not serious. Such dangers make it imperative, for instance, to make every possible improvement in command and control centers so that, should war actually occur, the legitimate civilian authorities would be in a position to exert rational control over our strategic nuclear forces. Such improvements and modernizations are now actually under way as an essential part of U.S. strategic policy.[61]

The argument that "defense spending is an injustice committed against the poor" does not stand up well in light of the actual trends in the U.S. budget. In 1955, transfer payments to individuals represented only about 20 percent of the federal budget, while defense accounted for more than half of the budget. During the next three decades social spending increased steadily, reaching 49 percent of the federal budget in 1982, while defense spending had fallen to 23 percent of the budget by 1980.[62] Since 1976, Americans have spent more money on alcohol each year than they have spent to fund all the operations of the Air Force.[63] In 1982 Americans spent $9 billion on coin-operated electronic games and $3 billion going to the movies—a total greater than the Air Force spent on new planes and missiles.[64] The share of the U.S. defense budget allocated to nuclear weapons-related expenditures is now under 10 percent.[65] To cut this figure and still maintain necessary security needs would mean greater reliance on conventional weapons, a more costly alternative that would increase the competition for dollars spent on social programs. The fact of the matter is that since the 1950s, rather than "defense beggaring welfare," the reality has been quite the opposite. The policies proposed by the

Reagan administration sought to restore balance to the budgetary priorities of the previous several decades.

As noted earlier, predictions of a "nuclear winter," a global climatic catastrophe produced by the dust and smoke thrown up into the upper atmosphere, have been a prominent feature in recent debate. It has been pointed out, however, that a different set of assumptions factored into the computer models produces a much different result: not a nuclear winter, but a "nuclear summer"—a temporary warming trend analogous to the "greenhouse effect."[66] Smoke and dust in the upper atmosphere not only make it more difficult for sunlight to penetrate to the earth's surface, but also make it more difficult for heat at the earth's surface to escape into space. It is also assumed in these calculations that the smoke and dust would be spread uniformly over the globe, an assumption open to question. The calculations of Carl Sagan and others also tend to ignore the far from negligible amount of heat that would be released into the atmosphere by the burning produced by nuclear explosions. By the very nature of the case, such predictions based on computer simulations have not been subjected to experimental verification, and hence are hypothetical in nature.

Suppose for the sake of argument, however, that the Sagan calculations are essentially correct. Sagan himself has noted some of the possible policy implications of this line of reasoning: e.g., a transition toward the development and deployment of low-yield, high-accuracy weapons.[67] Technology is already emerging that will permit the delivery of a nuclear warhead within 35 meters of its target over intercontinental ranges. Burrowing technology is on the way that will permit the warhead to penetrate the ground upon impact and explode even closer to a hardened military target. Sagan notes that "high-accuracy penetrating warheads in the one-to-ten kiloton range would be able, with high reliability, to destroy even very hardened silos and underground command posts."[68] Such highly accurate, low-yield weapons would produce much less unintended collateral damage than the larger weapons of today, would throw far less dust and smoke into the upper atmosphere, and as a result would be very unlikely to trigger the "nuclear winter."

Sagan, however, does not favor this policy direction, inasmuch as he believes that such weapons would be "destabilizing," tempting the nation that possessed them to launch a preemptive first strike. *Mobile* weapons, however, would be invulnerable to such a first strike and as a result would not be destabilizing, but on the contrary would provide a very stable form of deterrence. The Pershing II represents exactly such a mobile, highly accurate missile, and such weapons with intercontinental range are without question technologically possible.

The basic principle of nuclear deterrence, which has preserved the peace between the great powers and protected the NATO alliance since the end of the Second World War, is still a morally valid one. The strategy of a "nuclear bluff" suggested by some nuclear pacifists—that nuclear weapons may be possessed but not used, in the hope that mere possession will deter—is a fundamentally incoherent idea. As Charles Krauthammer has pointed out, deterrence is not inherent in the weapons themselves; it results from a combination of the possession of the weapons and the willingness to use them if necessary. "If one side renounces, for moral or other reasons, the intent of ever actually using nuclear weapons, deterrence ceases to exist," he notes.[69] A strategy of "bluff deterrence" is self-defeating.

In a fallen world deterrence is necessary to protect the innocent from the unjust depredations of unprincipled aggressors. In their statement on the morality of nuclear deterrence, "Winning the Peace," the Roman Catholic bishops of France stated that "peace at any price leads a nation to all sorts of capitulations. Unilateral disarmament can even provoke the aggressiveness of neighbors by feeding their temptation to seize too easy a prey."[70] Furthermore, "In a world where man is still a wolf to man, turning into a lamb can provoke the wolf."[71]

According to the Bible, "peace" is not merely the absence of war; more fundamentally it is a condition that obtains when such basic human freedoms as freedom of speech and worship are possible. The "peace" of the concentration camp or a Gulag Archipelago is not the peace of which the Bible speaks. A nation such as the Soviet Union, which does not allow believers the freedom to teach their own children the Christian faith, is not a society marked by the internal peace mandated by Scripture.

The fundamental justice of deterrence appears when it is recognized that the United States and the other nations of the free world are attempting to defend themselves and other innocent peoples from the aggressive desires of a Soviet regime that, since 1923, has put 65 million of its own citizens to death for political reasons and has subjugated some 31 nations.[72] This regime has deliberately murdered 269 innocent civilian passengers in a Korean airliner and in Afghanistan has deliberately used, for purposes of terrorism, booby-trapped toys designed to blow off the hands and arms of Afghan children.[73] Critics of the strategy of deterrence today at times seem to be as naive about the reality of evil as Neville Chamberlain was in the 1930s concerning the real nature of Hitler's intentions.

Ronald Sider and Richard Taylor, prominent nuclear pacifists in the evangelical world, have proposed a strategy of "nonmilitary defense," in which the United States would announce its intention to disarm unilaterally and begin training its citizens to accept death rather than cooperate with an invading enemy.[74]

Against a vicious foe, this strategy invites genocide. "Nonmilitary resistance" would not have helped the Jews against the Nazis. Such genocidal prescriptions are a travesty of both biblical peace and biblical justice.

During the Second World War, the Nazis were apparently provoked to greater brutality by the "pacifism" of their victims. As Jan Narveson has noted, "Some of the S.S. men apparently became curious to see just how much torture the victim would put up with before he began to resist."[75] And Gary Gammon has observed, "Noncooperation did not liberate Dachau; General Patton did."[76]

Recent events in the former Soviet Union have, of course, caused the threat of global nuclear war to recede dramatically. Nevertheless, Christian prudence and the lessons of history continue to indicate that a strong defense and a credible deterrent are still necessary to secure a just and lasting peace.

Notes

CHAPTER 1: DIMENSIONS OF DECISION MAKING

1. On virtues and dispositions in ethics, see Carl F. H. Henry, *Christian Personal Ethics* (Grand Rapids: Eerdmans, 1957), chaps. 16-25, especially 21-23; George F. Thomas, *Christian Ethics and Moral Philosophy* (New York: Charles Scribner's Sons, 1955), chaps. 21, 22; Paul Ramsey, *Basic Christian Ethics* (New York: Charles Scribner's Sons, 1954), chap. 6; William K. Frankena, *Ethics* (Englewood Cliffs, N.J.: Prentice-Hall, 1963), chaps. 4, 5. On New Testament ethics, see C. H. Dodd, *Gospel and Law: the Relation of Faith and Ethics in Early Christianity* (New York: Columbia University Press, 1951).

2. On the history of ethics, see Raziel Abelson and Kai Nielsen, "Ethics, History of," *Encyclopedia of Philosophy*, ed. Paul Edwards (New York: Macmillan, 1967), 3:81-117, and George Wolfgang Forell, *History of Christian Ethics* (Minneapolis: Augsburg, 1979).

3. Geoffrey W. Bromiley, "Casuistry," in Carl F. H. Henry, ed., *Baker's Dictionary of Christian Ethics* (Grand Rapids: Baker, 1973), p. 86.

4. Calvin, *Institutes* II. vii. 12.

5. From F. Sieffert, "Casuistry," *The New Schaff-Herzog Encyclopedia of Religious Knowledge*, ed. Samuel Macauley Jackson (New York: Funk and Wagnalls, 1908), 2:438-39.

6. For recent evangelical expositions of biblical authority, see Carl F. H. Henry, *God, Revelation and Authority* (Waco: Word Books, 1979), vol. 4; Millard J. Erickson, *Christian Theology* (Grand Rapids: Baker, 1983), vol. 1; John Jefferson Davis, *Foundations of Evangelical Theology* (Grand Rapids: Baker, 1984).

7. On biblical interpretation in an evangelical context, see Davis, *Founda-*

tions of Evangelical Theology, chap. 8, and A. Berkeley Mickelsen, *Interpreting the Bible* (Grand Rapids: Eerdmans, 1963). The hermeneutical understanding presupposed in the present work is best demonstrated in the interaction with specific issues.

8. On the importance of a world view controlled by Scripture, see Harry Blamires, *The Christian Mind* (Ann Arbor: Servant Books, 1963, 1978); Cornelius Van Til, *The Defense of the Faith* (Philadelphia: Presbyterian and Reformed, 1955); Gary North, ed., *Foundations of Christian Scholarship* (Vallecito, Calif: Ross House, 1976).

9. For a discussion of the deontological motif in Christian ethics, see Edward LeRoy Long, Jr., *A Survey of Christian Ethics* (New York: Oxford University Press, 1967), pp. 73ff., and Norman L. Geisler, *Ethics: Alternatives and Issues* (Grand Rapids: Zondervan, 1971), pp. 20ff.

10. Rudolf Schnackenburg, *The Moral Teaching of the New Testament* (New York: Herder and Herder, 1965), p. 83; Dodd, *Gospel and Law,* p. 14.

11. W. D. Davies, "Ethics in the New Testament," *Interpreter's Dictionary of the Bible,* ed. George Arthur Buttrick (New York: Abingdon, 1962), 4:175.

12. Ibid.

13. Harmon L. Smith and Louis W. Hodges, *The Christian and His Decisions* (Nashville: Abingdon, 1969), p. 31.

14. John H. Leith, ed., *Creeds of the Churches* (Richmond: John Knox, 1973), p. 195.

15. Cf. Paul Ramsey, *The Patient as Person* (New Haven: Yale University Press, 1970), p. 35.

16. Abraham Kuyper, *Encyclopedia of Sacred Theology* (New York: Charles Scribner's Sons, 1898), pp. 106-76.

17. J. Robertson McQuilkin, "The Behavioral Sciences Under the Authority of Scripture," *Journal of the Evangelical Theological Society* 20, 1 (1977): 42.

18. See especially Van Til, *Defense of the Faith,* on the crucial connection of fact and the framework of interpretation.

19. Stephen Charles Mott, *Biblical Ethics and Social Change* (New York: Oxford University Press, 1982), pp. 154-60.

20. Ibid., p. 155. See also Norman L. Geisler, *Options in Contemporary Christian Ethics* (Grand Rapids: Baker, 1981).

21. Joseph Fletcher, *Situation Ethics: The New Morality* (Philadelphia: Westminster, 1966), p. 69.

22. Ibid., p. 78.

23. Emil Brunner, *The Divine Imperative* (Philadelphia: Westminster Press, 1947), p. 134.

24. Harmon L. Smith, *Storm Over Ethics* (Philadelphia: United Church Press, 1967), p. 100.

25. Paul L. Lehmann, *Ethics in a Christian Context* (New York: Harper and Row, 1963), p. 138.
26. James M. Gustafson, *Protestant and Roman Catholic Ethics* (Chicago: University of Chicago Press, 1978), p. 44.
27. The approach here is similar to the "graded absolutism" of Geisler, *Options in Contemporary Christian Ethics*, pp. 81-101.
28. Many evangelical scholars would hold that the fourth commandment, concerning Sabbath observance, is not an absolute in the same sense as the other stipulations of the Decalogue, being given with Old Testament theocratic Israel in view. On the matter of the Sabbath, see D. A. Carson, *From Sabbath to Lord's Day* (Grand Rapids: Zondervan, 1981).
29. Charles Hodge, *Systematic Theology* (Grand Rapids: Eerdmans, 1975), 3:442.
30. Ibid., p. 443.
31. For an alternative view that every lie is inherently sinful, see Thomas Aquinas, *Summa Theologica* 2.2.110, and James Strong, "Lie," *Cyclopedia of Biblical, Theological, and Ecclesiastical Literature*, ed. John M'Clintock and James Strong, 1878, pp. 423-24.
32. See Harold J. Berman, "Religious Foundations of Law in the West: an Historical Perspective," *Journal of Law and Religion* 1, 1 (1983): 3-43 for a helpful survey of the data.
33. For recent constitutional interpretation in this area, see Ronald B. Flowers, "The Supreme Court's Three Tests of the Establishment Clause," *Religion in Life* 45 (1976): 41-52, and "The Supreme Court's Interpretation of the Free Exercise Clause," *Religion in Life* 49 (1980): 322-35.
34. For a careful study of First Amendment issues and historical interpretation, see Robert L. Cord, *Separation of Church and State* (New York: Lambeth Press, 1982).
35. Jack R. Van Der Slik, "Respecting an Establishment of Religion in America," *Christian Scholars Review* 13, 3 (1984): 226.
36. Ibid., p. 227.
37. The Supreme Court citations are from Leo Pfeffer, "The Deity in American Constitutional History," *Journal of Church and State* 23, 2 (1981): 215-39.
38. On the concept of general revelation, see Bruce A. Demarest, *General Revelation* (Grand Rapids: Zondervan, 1982); S. Lewis Johnson, "Paul and the Knowledge of God," *Bibliotheca Sacra* 129 (1972): 61-74; H. P. Owen, "The Scope of Natural Revelation in Romans 1 and Acts 17," *New Testament Studies* 5, 2 (1959): 133-43.
39. J. D. Unwin, "Monogamy as a Condition of Social Energy," *Hibbert Journal* 25 (1927): 663-77.
40. For a discussion of the view known as "theonomy," which holds that Christians, given the opportunity, should seek to have the civil penalties

of the Mosaic law (e.g., capital punishment for homosexuality) reflected in American criminal statutes, see Davis, *Foundations of Evangelical Theology*, pp. 266-70. The view adopted in the text is not that of the "theonomic" position.

41. See Chapters 5 and 6 of the present volume for a discussion of abortion and homosexuality, including the political and legal dimensions of these problems.
42. For a discussion of the problems connected with the Prohibition experiment, see Paul Johnson, *Modern Times* (New York: Harper and Row, 1983), pp. 209-12.
43. Lynn Buzzard, "There Oughta Be a Law," *Eternity* (October 1978), p. 22.

CHAPTER 2: CONTRACEPTION

1. Cited by Kenneth Kantzer, "Planned Parenthood Attacks a Parent's Right to Know," *Christianity Today* (May 20, 1983), p. 12.
2. This and the following information on the history of contraceptive practices is derived from John T. Noonan, Jr., "Contraception," in Warren T. Reich, ed., *Encyclopedia of Bioethics* (New York: Macmillan, 1978), 1:204-16, and Noonan, *Contraception* (Cambridge: Harvard University Press, 1966), pp. 9-29.
3. The most comprehensive discussion of contraception in the Jewish legal tradition is found in David M. Feldman, *Marital Relations, Birth Control and Abortion in Jewish Law* (New York: New York University Press, 1968).
4. F. Kett, review of James Reed, *From Private Vice to Public Virtue: The Birth Control Movement and American Society Since 1830* (New York: Basic Books, 1978), in *Science* (May 12, 1978), pp. 645-46.
5. Loretta McLaughlin, "The Pill Receives Good Health Report," *Boston Globe*, July 11, 1982.
6. Sandra R. Gregg, "Tailoring Contraception to Patients," *Medical World News* (February 16, 1981), p. 48.
7. Ibid.
8. Barbara Ehrenreich, "Bitter Pill," *New York Times Book Review* (March 6, 1983).
9. Ibid.
10. Irwin R. Fisch and Jess Frank, "Oral Contraceptives and Blood Pressure," *Journal of the American Medical Association* 237, 3 (June 6, 1977): 2499, 2503.
11. "New Risks Linked to Birth Pill Use," *New York Times*, August 20, 1981.
12. McLaughlin, "The Pill," p. 64. See also Barbara S. Hulka, "Oral Contraceptives: The Good News," *Journal of the American Medical Association* 249, 12 (March 25, 1983): 1624-25.

13. McLaughlin, "The Pill," p. 64.

14. "Oral Contraceptive Is Most Effective, New Study Shows," *American Medical News* (July 25, 1980), p. 16.

15. J. C. Willke, "The Physiologic Function of Certain Birth Control Measures," *National Right to Life News* (March 9, 1981), p. 3.

16. Sandra R. Gregg, "Tailoring Contraception to Patients," *Medical World News* (February 6, 1981), p. 53.

17. Ibid.

18. Ramaa P. Rao and Antonio Scommegna, "Intrauterine Contraception," *American Family Physician* (November 1977), p. 177.

19. Ibid., p. 178.

20. Ibid., p. 179.

21. Gregg, "Tailoring Contraception," p. 53.

22. Ibid.

23. Thomas W. Hilgers, "The Intrauterine Device: Contraceptive or Abortifacient," *Marriage and Family Newsletter* (January-March 1974), p. 14.

24. Robert A. Hatcher, "IUD-PID link: Data Needed on Long-term Fertility Effects," *Contraceptive Technology Update* (April 1980), p. 15.

25. Ibid.

26. Gerald Bernstein et al., "When Avoiding Pregnancy Is the Issue," *Patient Care* (September 15, 1978), p. 258.

27. Ibid.

28. Ramaa and Scommegna, "Intrauterine Contraception," p. 185.

29. Gregg, "Tailoring Contraception," p. 47.

30. William J. Bremner and David M. De Kretser, "The Prospects for New, Reversible Male Contraceptives," New England Journal of Medicine 295, 20 (November 11, 1976): 1114.

31. Ibid.

32. "A Survey of Current Contraception Methods," *Harvard Medical School Health Letter* 2, 7 (May 1977): 1.

33. Gregg, "Tailoring Contraception," p. 55.

34. Ibid.

35. Jen Seligmann, "Warning on Spermicides," *Newsweek* (April 13, 1981), p. 84. Other researchers have discounted Jick's results. See, for example, James L. Mills et al., "Are Spermicides Teratogenic?" *Journal of the American Medical Association* 248, 17 (November 5, 1982): 2148-51. According to Mills, the data indicate that "accidental exposure to spermicides after conception is probably not teratogenic" (p. 2151).

36. Seligmann, "Warning on Spermicides."

37. Robert Pear, "F.D.A. Approves New Sponge Contraceptive," *New York Times*, April 7, 1983.

38. "UN Surveys Global Sex, Fertility Trends, " *Boston Globe*, June 25, 1992, p. 85.

39. "Surgical Sterilization: Now More Popular than the Pill," *The Futurist* (December 1981), p. 75.
40. Ibid.
41. "Report Calls Sterilization Top Birth Control Method," *Boston Globe*, April 29, 1981.
42. "Surgical Sterilization," p. 75.
43. "Sterilization Passed the Pill," *Our Sunday Visitor* (August 28, 1977).
44. Stephen D. Mumford et al., "Laparoscopic and Minilaparotomy Female Sterilization Compared in 15,167 Cases," *The Lancet* (November 1, 1980), p. 1066.
45. Elizabeth B. Connell, "Your Questions Answered on Female Sterilization Referrals," *Practical Psychology for Physicians* (September 1976), p. 46.
46. Ibid., p. 47.
47. Ibid.
48. Ibid.; see also Jane E. Brody, "Gynecologist Describes Quick Method of Sterilization," *New York Times*, April 7, 1972.
49. Connell, "Female Sterilization Referrals," p. 51.
50. "Deaths Following Female Sterilization with Unipolar Electrocoagulating Devices," *Morbidity and Mortality Weekly Report* (April 10, 1981), pp. 149, 150.
51. "Sterilization Side-effects Can Include Some Menstrual Disturbances," *Journal of the American Medical Association* 237, 23 (June 6, 1977): 2457, 2459.
52. Ibid.
53. Connell, "Female Sterilization Referrals," p. 51.
54. Nancy Day, "New Hope for Untying the Tubes," *Boston Herald American*, November 14, 1982.
55. "How to Counsel Vasectomy Patients and Their Partners," *Sexual Medicine Today* (July 1981), p. 20.
56. Sylvia Porter, "The 'Boom' Growing," *Boston Herald American*, May 10, 1973.
57. "Last State Drops Sterilization Ban," *American Medical News* (June 19, 1972), p. 12.
58. *American Medical News* (April 3, 1972).
59. Joseph E. Davis, "The Significance and Challenges of the Vasectomy Revolution," *Medical Counterpoint* (December 1971), p. 16.
60. Ibid.
61. Idid.
62. H. J. Roberts, "Is Vasectomy Safe?" *Sexual Medicine Today* (June 1979), p. 38.
63. Ibid.
64. "Cell Antibodies Demonstrated in Vasectomy," *Medical Tribune* (September 27, 1972).

65. "Vasectomy, Prostate Cancer: Unexplained Link," *Science News* 139:2 (January 12, 1991), p. 29.
66. Edward Giovannucci et al., "A Long-Term Study of Mortality in Men Who Have Undergone Vasectomy," *New England Journal of Medicine* 326:21(May 21, 1992): 1392.
67. Ibid., p. 1397.
68. Ibid.
69. Harold M. Schmeck, Jr., "Cancer Institute Chief Cautions on the Use of Birth Control Pill," *New York Times*, February 28, 1975.
70. Harold Lear, "Vasectomy—a Note of Concern," *Journal of the American Medical Association* 219, 9 (February 28, 1972): 1207.
71. Ibid.
72. Shirley Southwiek, "The Psychological Side Effeets of Vasectomy," *New York Times*, January 14, 1972.
73. Joan Rattner Heilman, "What Vasectomy Means to a Man and His Marriage," *Reader's Digest* (April 1980), p. 38.
74. Ibid.
75. Charles Austin, "Catholics Try Natural Family Planning," *New York Times*, June 4, 1981.
76. Nona Aguilar, "Natural Family Planning," *Family Circle* (March 1, 1978), p. 196; see also Phyllis Avedon, "Natural Family Planning: 'Rhythm' Redefined," *Intercom* 7, 10 (October 1979): 1, 4-8.
77. Aguilar, "Natural Family Planning," p. 196.
78. "New, Green Light for Contraception," *New York Times*, February 8, 1981.
79. Mary Kenny, "The Birth Control Debate," *The Tablet* (January 22, 1983), p. 50.
80. Ibid.
81. For the patristic and classical citations in the following section, see Noonan's 1966 book, *Contraception*, and his article "Contraception" (1978), both cited above.
82. Noonan (1978), p. 207.
83. Ibid., p. 208.
84. Ibid.
85. Ibid.
86. Noonan (1966), p. 424.
87. Ibid., p. 427.
88. Quoted in Charles J. McFadden, *Medical Ethics* (Philadelphia: F. A. Davis, 1967), p. 111.
89. Noonan (1966), p. 446.
90. Cited in Walter O. Spitzer and Carlyle L. Saylor, eds., *Birth Control and the Christian* (Wheaton: Tyndale House, 1969), p. 483.
91. Richard A. McCormick, "Notes on Moral Theology," *Theological Studies* 40 (1979): 80.

92. McFadden, *Medical Ethics*, p. 77.
93. "Birth Control Ban," *Christian Century* (December 30, 1981), p. 1361.
94. Cited by Robert M. Cooper, "Vasectomy and the Good of the Whole," *Anglican Theological Review* 54 (April 1972): 102.
95. Ibid.
96. "Vatican Paper Publishes a 1975 Condemnation of Direct Sterilization," *New York Times*, December 12, 1976.
97. See Richard M. Fagley, "Protestant Thought on Population Problems," *Engage/Social Action* 2 (1974): 51-61, and Lloyd A. Kalland, "Views and Positions of the Christian Church—an Historical Review," in Spitzer and Saylor, *Birth Control*, pp. 417-64, for the history of the development of the Protestant position.
98. Noonan (1966), p. 409.
99. Ibid.
100. Fagley, "Population Problems," pp. 52, 53.
101. Spitzer and Saylor, *Birth Control*, pp. xxiii-xxxi.
102. Barth, *Church Dogmatics* III/4 (Edinburgh: T. & T. Clark, 1961), p. 269.
103. Ibid., p. 270.
104. Helmut Thielicke, *The Ethics of Sex* (Grand Rapids: Baker, 1964), p. 209.
105. Spitzer and Saylor, *Birth Control*, p. xxv.
106. See the various articles on the biblical material in Spitzer and Saylor, and also C. E. Cerling, Jr., "Abortion and Contraception in Scripture," *Christian Scholar's Review* 2 (1971): 42-58.
107. Peter C. Craigie, *The Book of Deuteronomy* (Grand Rapids: Eerdmans, 1976), pp. 296-97.
108. F. W. Beare, *The Gospel According to Matthew* (San Francisco: Harper and Row, 1981), p. 391.
109. Leon Morris, *The Revelation of St. John* (Grand Rapids: Eerdmans, 1969), pp. 176-77.
110. John T. Noonan, Jr., ed., *The Morality of Abortion* (Cambridge: Harvard University Press, 1970), pp. 8, 9. Noonan cites the philological study by Clyde Pharr, "The Interdiction of Magic in Roman Law," *Transactions and Proceedings of the American Philological Association* 272, 3 (1932), p. 63. Noonan also notes that in the early Christian document *Didache* 2.2, the practice of "medicine" is mentioned in the immediate context of a prohibition of slaying the child in the womb by abortion.
111. Henry George Liddell and Robert Scott, eds., *A Greek-English Lexicon*, 9th ed. (Oxford: Oxford University Press, 1940, repr. 1977), p. 1917.
112. Richard P. Frisbie, *Who Shall Be Born?* (Chicago: Claretian, 1968), p. 11.
113. Ibid.
114. Allan Chase, "Passing the Word on Sterilization," *Medical Tribune* (September 21, 1977).
115. Ibid.

116. William J. Curran, "Sterilizing the Poor: Judge Gesell's Roadblock," *New England Journal of Medicine* 291, 1 (July 4, 1974): 25.

117. Tom Littlewood, "Doctors Sterilize Welfare Mothers," *Boston Globe*, September 4, 1975.

118. Cited by Lloyd Shearer, *Parade* (January 16, 1983), p. 12.

119. "Statistics Discourage Sex at an Early Age," *Boston Globe*, April 14, 1983.

120. Hauck and Schulz, *"porne,"* *Theological Dictionary of the New Testament* (Grand Rapids: Eerdmans, 1968), 4:590.

121. O. J. Baab, "Fornication," *Interpreter's Dictionary of the Bible* (New York: Abingdon, 1962), 2:321.

122. *Boston Globe*, January 24, 1983.

123. *Atlanta Journal* (February 2, 1982), p. 3b.

124. *Family Practice News* (December 15, 1977).

125. Ibid.

126. Ibid.

127. *New York Times*, February 10, 1983.

128. *Monthly AIDS Update*, July 14, 1989, p. 4.

129. Ibid.

130. J. D. Unwin, "Monogamy as a Condition of Social Energy," *The Hibbert Journal* 25 (July 1927): 663-77.

131. Cited in Onalee McGraw, *The Family, Feminism, and the Therapeutic State* (Washington, D.C.: Heritage Foundation, 1980), p. 57.

132. Ibid., p. 59.

133. Jacqueline Kasun, "Turning Children into Sex Experts," *Public Interest* 55 (Spring 1979): 8.

134. *USA Today*, April 14, 1992, p. 11a.

135. Ibid.

136. Ibid.

137. Cited in the *Family Protection Report* 3, 4 (April 1981): 5.

138. Paul R. Ehrlich et al., *Human Ecology: Problems and Solutions* (San Francisco: W. H. Freeman, 1973), p. 278.

139. "Survey Reports Fertility Levels Plummet in Developing Nations," *New York Times*, August 10, 1979.

140. "Where Population Bomb Has Stopped Ticking," *U.S. News and World Report* (November 26, 1979), p. 94.

141. William P. Butz et al., *Demographic Challenges in America's Future* (Santa Monica: Rand Corp., 1982), p. 3.

142. The replacement rate is 2.2 rather than 2.0, because some women do not marry, are infertile as a result of medical problems, or choose to have no children.

143. Andrew Hacker, "Farewell to the Family?" *New York Review of Books* (March 18, 1982), p. 41.

144. Cited in *U.S. News and World Report* (June 15, 1981), p. 52.
145. *Statistical Abstract of the United States* (Washington, D.C.: U.S. Bureau of the Census, 1992), p. 19.
146. "This Is Reform?" *Wall Street Journal*, October 7, 1982.
147. Peter F. Drucker, "Are Unions Becoming Irrelevant?" *Wall Street Journal*, September 22, 1982.
148. Warren Brookes, "Coming, A Labor Shortage in 1980," *Boston Herald American*, January 16, 1979. The effects of the demographic trends noted by Brookes were delayed by the recession that followed; but in the longer run, these effects are likely to show up in the general economy.
149. "Demographic Challenges in America's Future," *The Futurist* (December 1982), p. 74.
150. These and the following figures on population densities are taken from the *World Almanac* (1983), pp. 497ff.
151. Julian Simon, "Resources, Population, Environment: An Oversupply of False Bad News," *Science* 208, 4451 (June 27, 1980): 1434.
152. Ibid.
153. See Edward Feigenbaum and Pamela McCorduck, *The Fifth Generation: Artificial Intelligence and Japan's Computer Challenge to the World* (Reading, Mass.: Addison-Wesley, 1983).
154. Julian Simon, "World Population Growth," *Atlantic Monthly* (August 1981), p. 73. Simon's thesis concerning the long-range benefits is presented more comprehensively in the major study, *The Ultimate Resource* (Princeton: Princeton University Press, 1981).

CHAPTER 3: REPRODUCTIVE TECHNOLOGIES

1. Robert Cooke, "Sperm Bank Established for Nobel Science Winners," *Boston Globe*, March 1, 1980.
2. Ibid.
3. "Theologian Raps High I.Q. Sperm Bank," *National Catholic Register* (August 15, 1982).
4. George J. Annas, "Artificial Insemination: Beyond the Best Interest of the Donor," *Hastings Center Report* (August 1979), p. 14.
5. Diane Swanbrow, "Immaculate Conceptions," *New West* (August 25, 1980), p. 28.
6. Ibid.
7. Annas, "Artificial Insemination."
8. Swanbrow, "Immaculate Conceptions."
9. Ibid.
10. Ibid.
11. Michael Dorgan, "Feminists Open a Sperm Bank," *Boston Globe*, October 10, 1982.

12. Anne Taylor Fleming, "Feminists Start Own Sperm Bank Business," *Boston Herald American,* October 30, 1982.
13. Dorgan, "Feminists Open Sperm Bank."
14. "Artificial Insemination by Donor: Survey Reveals Surprising Facts," *Journal of the American Medical Association* 241, 12 (March 23, 1979): 1219.
15. Georgia Dullea, "Artificial Insemination of Single Women Poses Difficult Questions," *New York Times,* March 9, 1979.
16. "Single Mom Defends Her Insemination Decision," *Boston Herald American,* April 18, 1982.
17. Dullea, "Difficult Questions."
18. Jeffrey M. Shaman, "Legal Aspects of Artificial Insemination," *Journal of Family Law* 18 (1979-80): 331.
19. Robert T. Francoeur, "We Can—We Must: Reflections on the Technological Imperative," *Theological Studies* 33, 3 (September 1972): 431.
20. Ibid.
21. Shaman, "Legal Aspects."
22. Ibid.
23. Ivar K. Johansson, "Animal Breeding," *The New Encyclopedia Britannica,* 15th ed. (Chicago: Encyclopedia Britannica, 1977), 1:906-7.
24. Wayne King, "Microscopic Techniques Have a Gigantic Effect on Cattle Breeding Industry," *New York Times,* December 6, 1982.
25. Ibid.
26. Thomas Katzorke et al., "Results of Donor Artificial Insemination (AID) in 415 Couples," *International Journal of Fertility* 26, 4 (1981): 263.
27. Shaman, "Legal Aspects," p. 332.
28. Francoeur, "We Can—We Must," p. 432.
29. "Frozen Sperm Increasingly Used for Artificial Insemination," Reporter on Human Reproduction and the Law (October 1979), p. II-A-4.
30. Thomas O'Toole, "Frozen Sperm Seen Conception Aid," *Washington Post,* January 7, 1979.
31. Ibid.
32. Alan F. Guttmacher, "Value of Sperm Banks," *Human Sexuality* (February 1974), p. 163.
33. D. Mortimer and D. W. Richardson, "Sex Ratio of Births Resulting from Artificial Insemination," *British Journal of Obstetrics and Gynaecology* 89 (February 1982): 132.
34. Ronald C. Strickler et al., "Artificial Insemination with Fresh Donor Semen," *New England Journal of Medicine* 293, 17 (October 23, 1975): 852.
35. Herbert W. Horne, Jr., "Artificial Insemination, Donor: An Issue of Ethical and Moral Values," *New England Journal of Medicine* 293, 17 (October 23, 1975): 874.
36. Ibid.
37. Ibid., p. 873.

38. *Journal of the American Medical Association* (March 23, 1979), p. 1220.
39. Theresa M. Mady, "Surrogate Mothers: The Legal Issues," *American Journal of Law and Medicine* 7, 3 (Fall 1981): 343.
40. Richard L. Trammell, "Religion and Artificial Insemination," *Christianity and Crisis* 28 (December 23, 1968), p. 317.
41. Shaman, "Legal Aspects," pp. 337, 338.
42. Joan Beck, "Who Is My Father?" Chicago Tribune, August 22, 1982.
43. Ibid., p. 10.
44. Cited in Charles J. McFadden, *Medical Ethics* (Philadelphia: F. A. Davis, 1967), p. 60.
45. Ibid.
46. Roger Van Allen, "Artificial Insemination (AIH): A Contemporary Re-analysis," *Homiletic and Pastoral Review* 70 (1970): 371.
47. Trammell, "Religion and Artificial Insemination," p. 317.
48. G. Aiken Taylor, "Thoughts on Artificial Insemination," *Christianity Today* (January 21, 1957), p. 25.
49. "Artificial Insemination," *The Modern Churchman*, n.s., 2:4 (June 1959), p. 211.
50. Trammell, "Religion and Artificial Insemination," p. 319.
51. Joseph Fletcher, *Morals and Medicine* (Princeton: Princeton University Press, 1954), p. 139. In more recent works, such as *The Ethics of Genetic Control* (1974), Fletcher writes from a humanistic rather than from a liberal Protestant point of view.
52. Fletcher, *Morals and Medicine*.
53. Norman L. Geisler, *Ethics: Alternatives and Issues* (Grand Rapids: Zondervan, 1971), pp. 229, 230.
54. Ibid., p. 230.
55. Helmut Thielicke, *The Ethics of Sex* (New York: Harper and Row, 1964; repr. Baker, 1975), pp. 256, 257.
56. Ibid., p. 258.
57. Ibid., p. 259.
58. Ibid., p. 262.
59. P. C. Craigie, *The Book of Deuteronomy* (Grand Rapids: Eerdmans, 1976), pp. 312, 313.
60. "Guidelines Issued on Surrogate Motherhood," *American Medical News* (June 10, 1983).
61. "Motherhood for Sale," *Boston Globe*, February 1, 1983.
62. "ACOG Concern on Surrogate Mothers," *Medical World News* (June 13, 1983), p. 6.
63. "Physician Sees No Problems in Surrogate Mother Business," *American Medical News* (June 20, 1980), p. 3.
64. Ibid.
65. Ibid., p. 17.

66. Elizabeth Bibb, "Infant Needs Three Birth Certificates," *Boston Globe*, February 9, 1981.
67. Elizabeth Bibb, "The Emotional Impact of the Surrogate Parents," *Boston Globe*, February 13, 1981.
68. Elizabeth Bibb, "The Women Who Choose to Be Surrogates," *Boston Globe*, February 10, 1981.
69. "Woman Advertises as Surrogate Mother," *Evening Gazette* (Worcester, Mass.), September 21, 1981.
70. Ibid.
71. Dava Sobel, "Surrogate Mothers: Why Women Volunteer," *New York Times*, June 29, 1981.
72. "Surrogate Moms' Motivation Complex, But Money Figures," *Medical Tribune*, August 26, 1981.
73. Bernard D. Hirsh, "Parenthood by Proxy," *Journal of the American Medical Association* 249, 16 (April 22/29, 1983): 2251.
74. George Annas, "Surrogate Mothering: Baby Selling?" *Boston Globe*, February 27, 1981.
75. "Study Ordered of Surrogate Mother Issue," *American Medical News* (December 17, 1982).
76. Iver Peterson "Legal Snarl Developing Around Case of a Baby Born to Surrogate Mother," *New York Times*, February 7, 1983.
77. "Surrogate Mother-to-Be Fights to Keep Unborn Child," *New York Times*, March 25, 1981.
78. Roger Rosenblatt, "The Baby in the Factory," *Time* (February 14, 1983), p. 90.
79. Douglas Colligan, "Making Baby's Sex a Parental Option," *Parade* (November 25, 1979).
80. Ibid.
81. Lawrence Galton, "Decisions, Decisions, Decisions," *New York Times Magazine* (June 30, 1974), pp. 22ff.
82. Ibid.
83. I. Stolkowski and J. Choukroun, "Preselection of Sex in Man," *Israel Journal of Medical Sciences* 17 (1981): 1061-67. In addition to the special diets, these researchers also prescribed certain drugs to assist in achieving the desired mineral balance. This method should be tried only after consultation with a knowledgeable physician, who, on the basis of a thorough physical examination, can be aware of the many physiological factors that affect fertility and conception. According to Stolkowski and Choukroun, the evidence for a clear connection between the time of conception relative to ovulation and sex determination is somewhat equivocal—a 65 percent correlation at best (p. 1061). For an earlier work describing a diet method, see David M. Rorvik and Landrum B. Shettles, *Choose Your Baby's Sex* (New York: Dodd, 1977).

84. Colligan, "Baby's Sex a Parental Option."
85. Robert Cooke, "Sex Selection in Animals," *Boston Globe*, May 23, 1983.
86. Ibid.
87. "Progress Is Reported on Sex Selection Study," *Boston Globe*, May 12, 1983.
88. "Studies Show Pre-Selection of Sex Could Mean a Minority of Women," *Evening Gazette* (Worcester, Mass.), January 7, 1980.
89. Galton, "Decisions."
90. Ibid.
91. Anne Hollister, "Test-Tube Baby Boom," *Life* (November 1982), p. 46.
92. Richard A. Knox, "New Hope for Infertile Couples," *Boston Globe*, April 4, 1983.
93. Annetta Miller, "Baby Makers Inc.," *Newsweek* (June 29, 1992), 38-39.
94. Walter Sullivan, "Doctor in Laboratory Conception Says First 100 Attempts Failed," *New York Times*, December 1, 1978.
95. Clifford Grobstein, "External Human Fertilization," *Scientific American* (June 1979), p. 57.
96. John D. Biggers, "In Vitro Fertilization and Embryo Transfer in Human Beings," *New England Journal of Medicine* 304, 6 (February 5, 1981): 337.
97. Lori B. Andrews, "Embryo Technology," *Psychology Today* (May 1981), pp. 63, 64.
98. Ibid., p. 64.
99. Harold M. Schmeck, Jr., "Prenatal Adoption Is the Objective of New Technique," *New York Times*, June 14, 1983.
100. John Leeton et al., "The Technique for Human Embryo Transfer," *Fertility and Sterility* 38, 2 (August 1982): 157.
101. Howard W. Jones et al., "The Program for In Vitro Fertilization at Norfolk," *Fertility and Sterility* 38, 1 (July 1982): 20.
102. John F. Leeton et al., in William Walters and Peter Singer, eds., *Test-Tube Babies* (Melbourne: Oxford University Press, 1982), pp. 4ff.
103. Gary D. Hodgen, "In Vitro Fertilization and Alternatives," *Journal of the American Medical Association* 246, 6 (August 7, 1981): 593.
104. Ibid., p. 594.
105. Ibid., p. 596.
106. "In Vitro Pregnancy Rate Rivals Nature," *Medical World News* (July 11, 1983), p. 40
107. "Two Teams Attempt Implantation of 'Donor Embryos,'" *Medical World News* (May 9, 1983), p. 9.
108. "Ending Infertility with 'Ovum Transfer,'" *Newsweek* (August 1, 1983).
109. Debra Braun, "Frozen Embryos Create Controversy," *National Right to Life News* (May 26, 1983), p. 8.
110. Ibid.
111. William J. Sweeney and Lee S. Goldsmith, "Will Test Tube Babies Spawn Legal Problems?" *Legal Aspects of Medical Practice* (October 1979), pp. 30-32.

112. Cited in *Reporter on Human Reproduction and the Law* (July 1979), II-B-5.
113. Mark I. Evans and Alan O. Dixler, "Human In Vitro Fertilization: Some Legal Issues," *Journal of the American Medical Association* 245, 22 (June 12, 1981): 2325.
114. Ibid., p. 2326.
115. "Pope Blasts Experiments on Embryos," *American Medical News* (November 12, 1982).
116. Joseph Duerr, "Test-tube Baby Morality Debate Continues in Church," *Our Sunday Visitor* (April 24, 1983).
117. Ibid.
118. Donald DeMarco, "In Vitro Fertilization and Implantation" (unpublished manuscript, April 1983), p. 15.
119. Albert S. Moraczewski, "Selected Ethical and Theological Issues Regarding In Vitro Fertilization," testimony of December 4, 1978, published in *Issues in Ethical Decision Making* (St. Louis: Pope John XXIII Medical-Moral Research Center), p. 7.
120. Joan Densberger and Sharon Schwartz, "In Vitro Fertilization Isn't Free of Risks," *Boston Globe*, May 13, 1983.
121. "Report of the H.E.W. Ethics Advisory Board," *Reporter on Human Reproduction and the Law* (July 1979), II-B-6.
122. Ibid.
123. John D. Biggers, "In Vitro Fertilization and Embryo Transfer in Human Beings," *New England Journal of Medicine* 304, 6 (February 5, 1981): 341.
124. Ibid., p. 340.
125. V. Beral et al., "Outcome of Pregnancies Resulting from Assisted Conception," *British Medical Bulletin* 46:3 (1990): 753-67.
126. Paul Ramsey, *On In Vitro Fertilization* (Chicago: Americans United for Life, n.d.), p. 10.

CHAPTER 4: DIVORCE AND REMARRIAGE

1. Aric Press et al., "Divorce American Style," *Newsweek* (January 10, 1983), p. 42.
2. Ibid.
3. Ibid.
4. *Intercom* 11(3/4), p. 4.
5. "Breaking the Divorce Cycle," *Newsweek* (January 13, 1992), p. 48.
6. "Sick Children," *The Family in America* (May 1992), p. 5.
7. Norval D. Glenn and Michael Supancic, "The Social and Demographic Correlates of Divorce and Separation in the United States," *Journal of Marriage and the Family* 46, 3 (1984): 566.
8. Ibid.
9. Ibid., p. 568.

10. W. F. Kenkel, "Divorce," *The New Catholic Encyclopedia* (New York: Mc-Graw-Hill, 1967), 4:928.
11. Ibid., p. 929.
12. Ibid.
13. Ibid.
14. FAC-Sheet No. 38, "Love, Marriage and the Family" (Marlborough, N.H.: Plymouth Rock Foundation), p. 2, citing National Center for Health Statistics, Public Health Service.
15. George Elliot Howard, "Divorce," *New Schaff-Herzog Religious Encyclopedia,* ed. S. M. Case (New York: Funk and Wagnalls, 1909), 3:453.
16. Ibid.
17. Ibid.
18. Aug. Lehmkuhl, "Divorce," *The Catholic Encyclopedia,* ed. Charles G. Herbermann (New York: Encyclopedia Press, 1909), 5:58.
19. Howard, "Divorce," p. 453.
20. G. W. Bromiley, "Divorce," *The International Standard Bible Encyclopedia,* rev. ed., ed. Geoffrey W. Bromiley (Grand Rapids: Eerdmans, 1979), 1:979.
21. Howard, "Divorce," p. 454.
22. "How to Get an Annulment," *Parade* (September 16, 1984), p. 21.
23. Ibid.
24. G. J. Wenham, "Gospel Definitions of Adultery and Women's Rights," *Expository Times* 95, 11 (1984): 330.
25. Abel Isaksson, *Marriage and Ministry in the New Temple* (Lund: C.W.K. Gleerup, 1965), p. 44 n. 2.
26. Joachim Jeremias, *Jerusalem in the Time of Jesus* (Philadelphia: Fortress, 1969, 1975), p. 370.
27. P. C. Craigie, *The Book of Deuteronomy* (Grand Rapids: Eerdmans, 1976), p. 305.
28. John Murray, *Divorce* (Philadelphia: Presbyterian and Reformed, 1961), p. 12.
29. Isaksson, *Marriage and Ministry,* p. 26.
30. Ibid., p. 45 n. 1.
31. See also S. R. Driver, *A Critical and Exegetical Commentary on Deuteronomy* (Edinburgh: T. & T. Clark, 1902), p. 271.
32. Isaksson, *Marriage and Ministry,* pp. 27-34.
33. Ralph L. Smith, *Micah-Malachi* (Waco: Word, 1984), p. 325. For a thorough discussion of the entire passage, see pp. 318-25.
34. See, for example, Alfred Plummer, *The Gospel according to Saint Matthew* (London: Elliot Stock, 1909), pp. 81, 82; Robert H. Gundry, *Matthew: A Commentary on His Literary and Theological Art* (Grand Rapids: Eerdmans, 1982), p. 90.
35. A. W. Argyle, *The Gospel according to Matthew* (Cambridge: Cambridge University Press, 1963), p. 52.

36. K. Stendahl, "Matthew," in *Peake's Commentary on the Bible*, ed. Matthew Black and H. H. Rowley (London: Thomas Nelson, 1962), p. 777.

37. R. C. H. Lenski, *The Interpretation of St. Matthew's Gospel* (Columbus, Ohio: Wartburg Press, 1943), pp. 230-35. For modern Roman Catholic interpretation of the Gospel texts, see Bruce Vawter, "The Divorce Clauses in Matt. 5:32 and 19:9," *Catholic Biblical Quarterly* 16 (1954): 155-67; Bruce Vawter, "Divorce and the New Testament," *Catholic Biblical Quarterly* 39 (1977): 528-42; Thomas V. Fleming, "Christ and Divorce," *Theological Studies* 24 (1963): 106-20.

38. Leopold Sabourin, *The Gospel according to Saint Matthew* (Bandra, India: St. Paul's Press, 1982), p. 372; Augustine Stock, "Matthean Divorce Texts," *Biblical Theology Bulletin* 8, 1 (1978): p. 28.

39. Mark Geldard, "Jesus' Teaching on Divorce," *Churchman* 92 (1978): 140.

40. Donald W. Shaner, *A Christian View of Divorce* (Leiden: E. J. Brill, 1969), p. 107.

41. Walter Bauer, *A Greek-English Lexicon of the New Testament*, 4th ed., trans. William F. Arndt and F. Wilbur Gingrich (Chicago: University of Chicago Press, 1957), p. 699; J. R. W. Stott, "The Biblical Teaching on Divorce," *Churchman* 85 (1971): 170; H. G. Coiner, "Those 'Divorce and Remarriage' Passages," *Concordia Theological Monthly* 39, 6 (1968): 378.

42. Stott, "The Biblical Teaching on Divorce," p. 170.

43. Carroll D. Osburn, "The Present Indicative in Matthew 19:9," *Restoration Quarterly* 24, 4 (1981): 193-203.

44. Ibid., p. 202.

45. William L. Lane, *The Gospel according to Mark* (Grand Rapids: Eerdmans, 1974), p. 358.

46. Ibid., pp. 352 n. 5, 358.

47. Ibid., p. 358.

48. I. Howard Marshall, *The Gospel of Luke* (Grand Rapids: Eerdmans, 1978), p. 631.

49. M. J. Down, "The Sayings of Jesus About Marriage and Divorce," *Expository Times* 95, 11 (1984): 333.

50. Ibid.

51. A. D. Verhy, "Divorce," *International Standard Bible Encyclopedia*, ed. Geoffrey W. Bromiley (Grand Rapids: Eerdmans, 1979), 1:977.

52. As J. A. Fitzmyer has pointed out, *choristhenai* in v. 10 is an aorist passive infinitive, and should be translated "the wife should not be separated from her husband": cited in Jerome Murphy-O'Connor, "The Divorced Woman in I Cor. 7:10-11," *Journal of Biblical Literature* 100 (1981): 601.

53. Archibald Robertson and Alfred Plummer, *The First Epistle of Saint Paul to the Corinthians* (Edinburgh: T. & T. Clark, 1914), p. 140; Murphy-O'Connor, "Divorced Woman in I Cor. 7:10-11," p. 605.

54. C. K. Barrett, *The First Epistle to the Corinthians* (New York: Harper and Row, 1968), p. 162.

55. Robertson and Plummer, *First Epistle to the Corinthians*, p. 143

56. Walter Bauer, *Greek-English Lexicon*, p. 796. The six occurrences are found in Luke 11:48; Acts 8:1; 22:20; Rom. 1:32; I Cor. 7:12 and 7:13.

57. John Stott, "The Biblical Teaching on Divorce," p. 173; John Murray, *Divorce*, p. 98. Murray goes on to argue (pp. 98-103) that there is no clear biblical warrant for declaring the remarriage of the guilty party to be a further act of adultery. On such a construction the sense of Matt. 19:9, spoken in the context of a Jewish culture that took divorce lightly, is that "whoever divorces his wife, except for unchastity, and marries another, [without genuine repentance and necessary restitution for the prior act of divorce] commits adultery."

58. It should be recognized, of course, that, in most cases leading to divorce, both parties will have contributed in some degree to the dissolution of the marriage relationship. Both will likely stand in need of repentance, even though one party may bear a relatively greater degree of guilt than the other.

59. Jay E. Adams, *Marriage, Divorce and Remarriage* (Phillipsburg, N.J.: Presbyterian and Reformed, 1980), p. 94.

60. Cf. Matt. 18:17, where a professing Christian who refuses to respond to corrective discipline is to be treated as an unbeliever: "If he refuses to listen even to the church, let him be to you as a Gentile and a tax collector."

61. Jay E. Adams, *Marriage, Divorce and Remarriage*, p. 81; cf. Ed Glasscock, "The Husband of One Wife Requirement in I Tim. 3:2," *Bibliotheca Sacra* 140, 559 (1983): 254.

62. Glasscock, "Husband of One Wife," p. 251.

63. Ibid., pp. 249, 253. For similar conclusions, see Robert L. Saucy, "The Husband of One Wife," *Bibliotheca Sacra* 131 (1974): 229-40, esp. 237, 240.

CHAPTER 5: HOMOSEXUALITY

1. Rep. Gerry Studds, quoted in the *Boston Globe*, July 15, 1983.

2. Judd Marmor, ed., *Homosexual Behavior: A Modern Reappraisal* (New York: Basic Books, 1980), p. 5.

3. Ibid., p. 6.

4. Arno Karlen, "Homosexuality in History," in Marmor, *Homosexual Behavior*, p. 76.

5. Ibid., p. 79.

6. Ibid., p. 80.

7. Ibid.

8. Ibid., p. 81.
9. Ibid., p. 84.
10. Ibid., p. 93.
11. Robert L. Spitzer, "The Diagnostic Status of Homosexuality in DSM-III: A Reformulation of the Issues," *American Journal of Psychiatry* 138, 2 (1981): 210.
12. Cited by Fred Barshaw, "The Truth about Homosexuality, Part I," *Grace to You* (Jan-Feb 1984), p. 2.
13. J. M. Carrier, "Homosexual Behavior in Cross-Cultural Perspective," in Marmor, *Homosexual Behavior*, p. 118.
14. Karlen, "Homosexuality in History," p. 76.
15. Warren J. Gadpaille, "Cross-Species and Cross-Cultural Contributions to Understanding Homosexual Activity," *Archives of General Psychiatry* 37 (1980): 354.
16. Ibid., p. 355.
17. Ibid.
18. Ibid.
19. J. D. Unwin, "Monogamy as a Condition of Social Energy," *Hibbert Journal* 25 (1927): 663.
20. Ibid.
21. Paul Cameron, "A Case Against Homosexuality," *Human Life Review* 4 (1978): 20. Marmor, *Homosexual Behavior*, p. 7 cites figures of 5-10 percent for men and 3-5 percent for women, which in the light of Cameron's information seem somewhat high.
22. Cameron, "Against Homosexuality," p. 18.
23. Ibid., p. 20.
24. Karlen, "Homosexuality in History," pp. 81, 82.
25. John Money, "Genetic and Chromosomal Aspects of Homosexual Etiology," in Marmor, p. 66.
26. Garfield Tourney, "Hormones and Homosexuality," in Marmor, *Homosexual Behavior*, p. 42.
27. Ibid. According to Masters and Johnson, in some cases hormonal factors may interact with environmental factors to lead to a homosexual orientation, but in most cases this does not appear to be so. *Homosexuality in Perspective* (Boston: Little, Brown, and Co., 1979), p. 411. See also Verle E. Headings, "Etiology of Homosexuality," *Southern Medical Journal* 73 (1980): 1024-27, 1030, and Warren J. Gadpaille, "Research into the Physiology of Maleness and Femaleness," *Archives of General Psychiatry* 26 (1972): 193-206. Gadpaille sees early childhood rearing, not hormones, as the major determinant of later sexual adaptation.
28. Tourney, "Hormones and Homosexuality," p. 55.
29. Money, "Genetic and Chromosomal Aspects," p. 70.
30. Evelyn Hooker, "Sexual Behavior: Homosexuality," *International Encyclo-*

pedia of the Social Sciences, ed. David L. Sills (New York: Macmillan, 1968), 14:224.

31. Ibid., p. 225.
32. David H. Barlow, "Homosexuality: Changing Sexual Preference Not Particularly Difficult—For Those Who Make the Choice," *The Pilot* (May 2, 1980), p. 5.
33. Ibid.
34. Armand M. Nicholi, cited in the *Presbyterian Layman* (June/July 1978), p. 6.
35. Ibid.
36. William H. Masters and Virginia E. Johnson, *Homosexuality in Perspective* (Boston: Little, Brown, and Co., 1979), p. 407.
37. Edward J. Artnak and James J. Cerda, "The Gay Bowel Syndrome," *Current Concepts in Gastroenterology* (July/August 1983), p. 6.
38. Ibid.
39. Ibid., p. 7.
40. William F. Owen, Jr., "Sexually Transmitted Diseases and Traumatic Problems in Homosexual Men," *Annals of Internal Medicine* 92 (1980): 807.
41. Bruce Voeller, "Anorectal Cancer and Homosexuality," *Journal of the American Medical Association* 249 (1983): 2459.
42. *AIDS: Issues and Answers*, 6, 2 (April 1992): 3. For medical and biblical analysis of the AIDS epidemic from a conservative Christian perspective, see Franklin E. Payne, Jr., M.D., *What Every Christian Should Know About the AIDS Epidemic* (Augusta, Ga.: Covenant Books, 1991). On the question of AIDS and divine judgment, see Andrew A. White, M.D., "AIDS as Divine Judgment," *Journal of Biblical Ethics in Medicine* 2, 3 (July 1988): 60-67. For current statistical information on the AIDS epidemic and editorial comment from a Christian perspective, see *AIDS: Issues and Answers*, a bimonthly newsletter (P.O. Box 14488, Augusta, GA 30919).
43. Artnak and Cerda, "Gay Bowel Syndrome," p. 7.
44. Ibid.
45. William W. Darrow et al., "The Gay Report on Sexually Transmitted Diseases," *American Journal of Public Health* 71 (1981): 1009.
46. P. Michael Ukleja, "Homosexuality and the Old Testament," *Bibliotheca Sacra* 140 (1983): 259-68.
47. D. Sherwin Bailey, *Homosexuality and the Western Christian Tradition* (London: Longmans, Green and Co., 1955); John J. McNeill, *The Church and the Homosexual* (Kansas City: Sheed Andrews and McNeill, 1976).
48. Don Williams, *The Bond That Breaks: Will Homosexuality Split the Church?* (Los Angeles: BIM, 1978), p. 53.
49. Bailey, *Homosexuality and the Western Christian Tradition*, pp. 3-5.
50. Ukleja, "Homosexuality and the Old Testament," p. 261.
51. . . . *ekporneusasai kai apelthousai opiso sarkos heteras*, lit., "committing for-

nication and going away after different flesh." The words "different flesh" (*sarkos heteras*) evidently refer to the angels.

52. *Midrash Rabbah: Genesis 1*, trans. and ed. H. Freedman and Maurice Simon (London: Soncino Press, 1939), 1:438.

53. "On Abraham," xxvi, in Nahum N. Glatzer, ed., *The Essential Philo* (New York: Schocken, 1971).

54. *Ant. I*, 200-2, *Jewish Antiquities*, Books l-IV, trans. H. Thackeray (London: William Heinemann, 1930).

55. *First Apol.*, 53, *Saint Justin Martyr*, ed. Thomas B. Falls (New York: Christian Heritage, 1948).

56. Origen, *Homilies on Genesis and Exodus*, trans. Ronald E. Hein (Washington, D.C.: Catholic University of America Press, 1982), pp. 110, 111.

57. *The Banquet of the Ten Virgins* 5.5.

58. Abraham Ben Isaiah and Benjamin Sharfman, *The Pentateuch and Rashi's Commentary: Genesis* (Brooklyn, N.Y.: S.S. and R. Publishing Co., 1949), p. 167.

59. Gordon J. Wenham, *The Book of Leviticus* (Grand Rapids: Eerdmans, 1979), p. 259. See also Stephen F. Bigger, "The Family Laws of Leviticus 18 in their setting, *Journal of Biblical Literature* 98, 2 (1979): 203: Homosexuality was seen by the Hebrews as an unnatural variant of heterosexuality.

60. J. Alberto Soggin, *Judges* (Philadelphia: Westminster, 1981), p. 288.

61. Boling, 1975, cited in ibid.

62. C. F. Keil and F. Delitsch, *Biblical Commentary on the Old Testament: Joshua, Judges, Ruth*, trans. James Martin (Grand Rapids: Eerdmans, repr. 1950), p. 445. Cf. also George F. Moore: The word is "frequently used of offenses against the laws governing the relations of the sexes (Gen. 34:7, Deut. 22:21)." *A Critical and Exegetical Commentary on Judges* (Edinburgh: T. & T. Clark, 1895), p. 418.

63. William Orbach, "Homosexuality and Jewish Law," *Journal of Family Law* 14, 3 (1975-76): 359. References to tractates of the Talmud are as cited by Orbach.

64. Kiddushin 82a.

65. Pesachim 51a.

66. Sanhedrin 6:3.

67. Avodah Zarah 2b.

68. Gittin 38a.

69. Ernst Kasemann, *Commentary on Romans*, trans. Geoffrey W. Bromiley (Grand Rapids: Eerdmans, 1980), p. 49. The connection in Wisdom 14:22-31 between idolatry and sexual perversion among the Gentiles has been noted by various commentators.

70. See S. Lewis Johnson, Jr., "God Gave Them Up: A Study in Divine Retribution," *Bibliotheca Sacra* (1972): 124-33, for a study of this theme.

71. C. K. Barrett, *A Commentary on the First Epistle to the Corinthians* (New

York: Harper and Row, 1968), p. 140; Hans Conzelmann, *First Corinthians*, trans. James W. Leitch (Philadelphia: Fortress Press, 1975), p. 106.

72. John Boswell, *Christianity, Social Intolerance, and Homosexuality* (Chicago: University of Chicago Press, 1980), p. 353.

73. Ibid., pp. 340, 344.

74. Ibid., pp. 345, 346.

75. Adolf Deissmann, *Light from the Ancient East*, rev. ed. (Grand Rapids: Baker, 1965), p. 164 n. 4. See also Dionysius of Halicarnassus [1st cent. B.C.], *Roman Antiquities* 7.2 for an occurrence of *malakos* which can clearly bear the meaning "effeminate" in a homosexual sense.

76. Donald Guthrie, *The Pastoral Epistles* (Grand Rapids: Eerdmans, 1957), pp. 61, 62. Cf. the similar comment by H. R. Reynolds, "The First Epistle to Timothy," *Expositor*, 1st series, 2 (1875): 135: "In *menstealers* the worst kind of theft is referred to; and in *sodomites* the foulest transgression of the seventh commandment." Martin Dibelius and Hans Conzelmann, *The Pastoral Epistles*, trans. P. Buttolph and Adela Yarbro (Philadelphia: Fortress Press, 1972) translate v. 10 as "fornicators, pederasts." See also Otto E. Sohn, "Study on I Tim. 1:3-11," *Concordia Theological Monthly* 21 (1950): 419-28, esp. 427.

77. P. Michael Ukleja, "Homosexuality in the New Testament," *Bibliotheca Sacra* 140 (1983): 356.

78. McNeill, *Church and the Homosexual*, p. 66.

79. Greg L. Bahnsen, *Homosexuality: A Biblical View* (Grand Rapids: Baker, 1978), p. 67.

80. John M. Batteau, "Sexual Differences: A Cultural Convention?" *Christianity Today* (July 8, 1977), 10.

81. Charles Curran, for example, proposes a "mediating position" that "recognizes that homosexual acts are wrong but also acknowledges that homosexual behavior for some people might not fall under the total condemnation proposed in the first opinion." *Catholic Moral Theology in Dialogue* (Notre Dame: University of Notre Dame Press, 1976), p. 209. That seems to be a fundamentally inconsistent and unstable position. Should the church also recognize certain exceptions to the prohibitions against adultery and other forms of heterosexual lust if the person in question has a "constitutional" bent in that direction? Such an approach may reinforce the person in his old untransformed behaviors; that is the heresy of "powerless grace." For an outlook similar to Curran's, and having some of the same problems, see Helmut Thielicke, *The Ethics of Sex*, trans. John W. Doberstein (Grand Rapids: Baker, 1964), pp. 284-87.

82. Ellen M. Barrett, "Legal Homophobia and the Christian Church," *Hastings Law Journal* 30, 2 (1979): 1021.

83. Ibid.

84. Ibid.

85. David F. Greenberg and Marcia H. Bystryn, "Christian Intolerance of Homosexuality," *American Journal of Sociology* 88, 3 (1982): 531.
86. Barrett, "Legal Homophobia," p. 1023.
87. Ibid., p. 1025.
88. Ibid.
89. Ibid., p. 1026.
90. Rhonda R. Rivera, "Recent Developments in Sexual Preference Law," *Drake Law Review* 30 (1980-81): 315. The case was *Gay Law Students Association v. Pacific Telephone and Telegraph Co.*
91. Ibid., p. 319.
92. Ibid., p. 346. See also Rhonda R. Rivera, "Our Straight-Laced Judges: The Legal Position of the Homosexual Person in the United States," *Hastings Law Journal* 30, 4 (1979): 950, 951.
93. Enrique T. Rueda, *The Homosexual Network* (Old Greenwich, Conn.: Devin-Adair, 1983), cited in Allan Browfield, "The Homosexual Network—a New Political Force," *Presbyterian Layman* (September/October 1983), p. 8.
94. Bahnsen, *Homosexuality*, p. 103. For example, a Christian employer (or church) could be compelled to hire avowed and practicing homosexuals.
95. Ibid.
96. George F. Will, "How Far Out of the Closet," *Newsweek* (May 30, 1977), p. 92.
97. Bahnsen, *Homosexuality*, p. 133.

CHAPTER 6: ABORTION

1. Ann Rodgers, personal communication, August 18, 1979.
2. Alan Guttmacher Institute, "Facts in Brief," cited in *Presbyterian Pro-Life News*, Spring 1992, p. 4.
3. Matthew J. Bulfin, letter to the editor, *New York Times*, July 1, 1983.
4. Ibid.
5. Gary Bergel, "Abortion: A Biblical Issue That Must Be Resolved," *Intercessors for America* (February 1, 1983), p. 1.
6. "Complications of Abortion in Developing Countries," *Population Reports* (July 1980), p. F-107.
7. John A. Rasmussen, "Abortion: Historical and Biblical Perspectives," *Concordia Theological Quarterly* 43 (1979): 19.
8. Ibid.
9. Ibid.
10. Thomas W. Hilgers and Dennis J. Horan, eds., *Abortion and Social Justice* (New York: Sheed and Ward, 1972), p. 122.
11. Ibid.
12. Rasmussen, "Abortion," p. 19.

13. Cited from the translation of Kirsopp Lake, *The Apostolic Fathers*, vol. I (Cambridge, Mass.: Harvard, 1912).

14. John T. Noonan, Jr., ed., *The Morality of Abortion* (Cambridge, Mass.: Harvard, 1970), p. 11. On early Christian attitudes toward abortion, see also Michael J. Gorman, *Abortion and the Early Church* (Downers Grove, Ill.: Inter-Varsity, 1982).

15. Noonan, *Morality of Abortion*, p. 12.

16. Ibid., p. 14.

17. Ibid., p. 16.

18. Hilgers and Horan, *Abortion and Social Justice*, p. 122.

19. Louis M. Hellman and Jack A. Pritchard, *Williams Obstetrics*, 14th ed. (New York: Appleton Century Crofts, 1971), pp. 1085, 1086.

20. James C. Mohr, *Abortion in America* (New York: Oxford, 1978) traces the developments in American law. It is quite ironic that the American Medical Association, which led the efforts in the nineteenth century to protect the unborn, is now decidedly pro-abortion.

21. Hellman and Pritchard, *Williams Obstetrics*, p. 1086.

22. Roe v. Wade 410 U.S., pp. 113-78.

23. For the text of *Harris v. McRae*, see the *Journal of Church and State* 22, 3 (1980): 575-95.

24. "Point of View," *Action Line*, July/August 1992, p. 4.

25. On the techniques of abortion, see Robert A. Hatcher et al., *Contraceptive Technology 1982-1983* (New York: Irvington, 1982), pp. 170-74, and C. Everett Koop, *The Right to Live: The Right to Die* (Wheaton, Ill.: Tyndale, 1976), pp. 30-32.

26. Hatcher, *Contraceptive Technology*, p. 171.

27. Dr. and Mrs. J. C. Willke, *Handbook on Abortion* (Cincinnati: Hayes, 1975), p. 31.

28. Hellman and Pritchard, *Williams Obstetrics*, p. 1089.

29. Koop, *Right to Live*, pp. 29, 30.

30. *California Medicine* 113, 3 (September 1970).

31. Susan K. Golant, "The World in the Womb," *Boston Globe*, March 18, 1983.

32. Reprinted in *National Right to Life News* (May 26, 1983), p. 5.

33. Anne Fadiman, "The Unborn Patient," *Life* (April 1983), pp. 38-44.

34. Scott A. Lebolt et al., "Mortality from Abortion and Childbirth: Are the Populations Comparable?" *Journal of the American Medical Association* 248, 2 (July 9, 1982): 188-91.

35. Thomas W. Hilgers, "Is Abortion Safer than Childbirth?" *National Right to Life News* (February 3, 1983), p. 7.

36. Thomas W. Hilgers, Dennis J. Horan, and David Mall, eds., *New Perspectives on Human Abortion* (Frederick, Md.: University Publications of America, 1981), p. 90.

37. Cf. Hatcher, *Contraceptive Technology*, p. 178.

38. "Risky Abortions," *Time* (November 27, 1978), p. 52.

39. Jeff Lyon, "Aftermath of Abortions Gone Wrong," *Boston Globe*, September 9, 1982.

40. Ibid.

41. Olav Meirik et al., "Outcome of Delivery Subsequent to Induced Vacuum-Aspiration Abortion in Parous Women," *American Journal of Epidemiology* 116, 3 (1982): 415.

42. Chin S. Chung et al., "Induced Abortion and Ectoptic Pregnancy in Subsequent Pregnancies," *American Journal of Epidemiology* 115 (1982): 886; and Chin S. Chung et al., "Induced Abortion and Spontaneous Fetal Loss in Subsequent Pregnancies," *American Journal of Public Health* 72, 6 (June 1982): 548-54.

43. Susan Harlap et al., "A Prospective Study of Spontaneous Fetal Losses After Induced Abortions," *New England Journal of Medicine* 301, 13 (September 27, 1979): 680.

44. Carol Madore et al., "A Study of the Effects of Induced Abortion on Subsequent Pregnancy Outcome," *American Journal of Obstetrics and Gynecology* 139 (1981): 516.

45. Erik L. Obel, "Pregnancy Complications Following Legally Induced Abortion," *Acta Obstetrica et Gynecologica Scandinavica* 58 (1979): 485.

46. Knut Dalaker et al., "Delayed Reproductive Complications after Induced Abortion," *Acta Obstetrica et Gynecologica Scandinavica* 58 (1979): 491.

47. D. Trichopoulos et al., "Induced Abortion and Secondary Infertility," *British Journal of Obstetrics and Gynecology* 83 (August 1976): 645.

48. Stefanos N. Pantelakis et al., "Influence of Induced and Spontaneous Abortions on the Outcome of Subsequent Pregnancies," *American Journal of Obstetrics and Gynecology* 116, 6 (July 1973): 799.

49. Susan Harlap and A. Michael Davies, "Late Sequelae of Induced Abortion: Complications and Outcome of Pregnancy and Labor," *American Journal of Epidemiology* 102, 3 (1975): 217.

50. Ann A. Levin et al., "Association of Induced Abortion with Subsequent Pregnancy Loss," *Journal of the American Medical Association* 243 (June 27, 1980): 2495.

51. Jeffrey M. Barrett et al., "Induced Abortion: A Risk Factor for Placenta Previa," *American Journal of Obstetrics and Gynecology* 141 (1981): 772.

52. M. C. Pike et al., "Oral Contraceptive Use and Early Abortion as Risk Factors for Breast Cancer in Young Women," *British Journal of Cancer* 43 (1981): 72.

53. Cited by Richard C. Maddock and Ray O. Sexton, "The Rising Cost of Abortion," *Medical Hypnoanalysis* (Spring 1980), p. 62.

54. Ibid.

55. Ibid., p. 63.

56. David Mall and Walter F. Watts, eds., The *Psychological Aspects of Abortion* (Washington, D.C.: University Publications of America, 1979), pp. 128, 131.
57. Bob Greene, "Abortion: As Males Recall," *Evening Gazette* (Worcester, Mass.), June 21, 1983.
58. Charles and Bonnie Remsberg, "Second Thoughts on Abortion from the Doctor Who Led the Crusade for It," *Good Housekeeping* (March 1976), p. 130.
59. Joseph Fletcher, *The Ethics of Genetic Control* (Garden City, N.Y.: Anchor Press, 1974), p. 135.
60. Ibid., p. 137.
61. Ibid., p. 142. For similar conclusions, cf. Garrett Hardin, *Mandatory Motherhood* (Boston: Beacon Press, 1974).
62. D. Gareth Jones, *Brave New People: Ethical Issues at the Commencement of Life* (Downers Grove, Ill.: Inter-Varsity Press, 1984). Other writers who hold the "Indications" position include Daniel Callahan, *Abortion: Law, Choice, and Morality* (New York: Macmillan, 1970); R. F. R. Gardner, *Abortion: The Personal Dilemma* (Old Tappan, N.J.: Fleming H. Revell, 1974); Harmon L. Smith, *Ethics and the New Medicine* (Nashville: Abingdon, 1970).
63. Jones, *Brave New People*, p. 158.
64. Ibid., p. 162.
65. Ibid., p. 163.
66. Ibid., p. 166.
67. Ibid., pp. 171, 172.
68. Ibid., pp. 178, 179.
69. Ibid., pp. 173, 181.
70. Harold O. J. Brown, *Death Before Birth* (Nashville: Thomas Nelson, 1977), p. 119. Other evangelical writers defending this general position include Clifford E. Bajema, *Abortion and the Meaning of Personhood* (Grand Rapids: Baker, 1974); C. Everett Koop, *The Right to Live: The Right to Die* (Wheaton: Tyndale House, 1976); C. C. Ryrie, *You Mean the Bible Teaches That* (Chicago: Moody Press, 1974); Richard L. Ganz, ed., *Thou Shalt Not Kill* (New Rochelle, N.Y.: Arlington House, 1978); Francis A. Schaeffer and C. Everett Koop, *Whatever Happened to the Human Race?* (Old Tappan, N.J.: Fleming H. Revell, 1979).

On the development of the Roman Catholic position, see John Connery, *Abortion: The Development of the Roman Catholic Perspective* (Chicago: Loyola University Press, 1977).

Also representative of this position are Baruch Brody, *Abortion and the Sanctity of Life* (Cambridge: MIT Press, 1975); Thomas W. Hilgers and Dennis J. Horan, eds., *Abortion and Social Justice* (New York: Sheed and Ward, 1972); Dr. and Mrs. J. C. Willke, *Handbook on Abortion* (Cincinnati: Hayes, 1975); Thomas W. Hilgers, Dennis J. Horan, and David Mall, eds., *New Perspectives on Human Abortion* (Frederick, Md.: University Publications of America, 1981).

71. Brown, *Death Before Birth*, p. 119.
72. Ibid., p. 120.
73. Ibid., p. 122.
74. Ibid., p. 127. It is sometimes argued that the references in Ps. 139:13-16 to God's involvement in David's life during its embryonic stages prove little, since this is a poetic passage. That argument, however, confuses the literary form of a biblical teaching with its ethical and doctrinal content. The truth of God's omnipresence is no less true because it happens to be expressed in poetic form in Ps. 139:7-12. The fatherly care of God is no less real because it is expressed poetically through the figure of sheep and the shepherd in Ps. 23. Likewise, the reality of God's personal relationship with David even in his embryonic state is not to be denied merely because it is found in a poetic text.
75. Ibid., p. 135.
76. John R. W. Stott, "Does Life Begin Before Birth?" *Christianity Today* (September 5, 1980), p. 50.
77. See Graham A. D. Scott, "Abortion and the Incarnation," *Journal of the Evangelical Theological Society* 17, 1 (1974): 29-44.
78. Noonan, *Morality of Abortion*, p. 9. The term is also used three times in the book of Revelation, in 9:21, 21:8, and 22:15, each time with a pejorative sense.
79. Liddell and Scott, *A Greek-English Lexicon* (Oxford: Oxford University Press, 1940), p. 1917.
80. See, for example, Bruce M. Waltke, "Old Testament Texts Bearing on the Issues," *Birth Control and the Christian*, Walter O. Spitzer and Carlyle L. Saylor, eds. (Wheaton: Tyndale House, 1969), pp. 10-11. The "miscarriage" translation was adopted by the editors of the Revised Standard Version.
81. For exegetical discussion from this perspective, see Jack W. Cottrell, "Abortion and the Mosaic Law," *Christianity Today* (March 16, 1973), pp. 6-9; H. Wayne House, "Miscarriage or Premature Birth: Additional Thoughts on Exodus 21:22-25," *Westminster Theological Journal* 41 (1978): 108-23; and Meredith G. Kline, "Lex Talionis and the Human Fetus," *Journal of the Evangelical Theological Society* 20, 3 (1977): 193-201. The "premature live birth" interpretation of the passage is followed by the translators of the King James Version and the New International Version.
82. Stephen Mott, "SE 361 Biblical Social Ethics," Minutes of April 15, 1980, Gordon-Conwell Theological Seminary.
83. For a detailed philosophical analysis of the concept of personhood in relation to the abortion debate, see Gabriel Pastrana, "Personhood and the Beginning of Human Life," *Thomist* 41, 2 (1977): 247-94.

84. This argument is not merely hypothetical, but has been published in a leading medical journal: Peter Singer, "Sanctity of Life or Quality of Life?" *Pediatrics* 72, 1 (July 1983): 128, 129. Singer argues that infanticide would be acceptable for profoundly retarded newborns, since they lack the intelligence of normal human beings. According to Singer, "We can no longer base our ethics on the idea that human beings are a special form of creation, made in the image of God, singled out from all other animals, and alone possessing an immortal soul" (p. 129).

85. Sandra K. Mahkorn and William V. Dolan, "Sexual Assault and Pregnancy," in Hilgers, Horan, and Mall, *New Perspectives*, p. 187.

86. Ibid., p. 188.

87. Ibid., pp. 188, 189.

88. Cited in Koop, *Right to Live*, pp. 51, 52.

CHAPTER 7: INFANTICIDE AND EUTHANASIA

1. "Baby's Death Brings End to Court Battle," *The Evansville Courier*, April 16, 1982.

2. Ibid.

3. George F. Will, "Being Unwanted Baby: Capital Offense," *Baltimore Sun-Times*, April 23, 1982.

4. Eugene F. Diamond, "The Deformed Child's Right to Life," in Dennis J. Horan and David Mall, eds., *Death, Dying, and Euthanasia* (Frederick, Md.: University Publications of America, 1980), p. 127.

5. John A. Robertson, "Involuntary Euthanasia of Defective Newborns: A Legal Analysis," in Horan and Mall, *Death, Dying, and Euthanasia*, p. 140, citing Duff and Campbell, "Moral and Ethical Dilemmas in the Special-Care Nursery," *New England Journal of Medicine* 289 (1973): 890.

6. Joseph R. Stanton, *Infanticide* (Chicago: Americans United for Life, n.d.), p. 1.

7. Peter Singer, "Sanctity of Life or Quality of Life?" *Pediatrics* 72, 1 (July 1983): 129.

8. C. Everett Koop, "Ethical and Surgical Considerations in the Care of the Newborn with Congenital Abnormalities," in Dennis J. Horan and Melinda Delahoyde, eds., *Infanticide and the Handicapped Newborn* (Provo, Utah: Brigham Young University Press, 1982), p. 90.

9. Plato *Republic* v. 460f.

10. Aristotle *Politics* vii. 16.

11. Mary Batten, "Slaughter of the Innocents: The Evolution of Infanticide," *Science Digest* (January 1983), p. 108.

12. Ibid.

13. William E. H. Lecky, *History of European Morals from Augustus to Charlemagne* (London: Longmans, Green, and Co., 1911), 2:34.

14. A. M. Hocart, "Infanticide," *Encyclopedia of the Social Sciences,* ed. Edwin R. A. Seligman (New York: Macmillan, 1937), 7:28.

15. James H. Worman, "Infanticide," *Cyclopedia of Biblical, Theological and Ecclesiastical Literature,* ed. John M'Clintock and James Strong (New York: Harper and Bros., 1880), 4:577.

16. John A. Robertson, "Involuntary Euthanasia," reprinted in Dennis J. Horan and David Mall, p. 143.

17. Ibid., p. 144.

18. Ibid., p. 150.

19. Ibid., p. 160. In law, a conspiracy is an agreement or combination to achieve an unlawful objective.

20. William Bradford Reynolds, "Handicapped Newborns Protected by Law," letter to the editor, *New York Times,* August 8, 1983.

21. John A. Robertson, "Dilemma in Danville," *Hastings Center Report* (October, 1981), p. 7.

22. Ibid., p. 5.

23. Ibid.

24. Edward W. Keyserlingk, "The Unborn Child's Right to Prenatal Care (Part 1)," *Health Law in Canada* 3 (1982): 13.

25. Ibid., p. 14.

26. Ibid.

27. "Neonatal Progress," *American Medical News* (February 19, 1982).

28. "The Smallest Patients," *Medical World News* (September 14, 1981), p. 28.

29. Ibid., p. 30.

30. Ibid., p. 33.

31. Anne Gilmore, "Ethics: Is the Fetus a Patient?" *Canadian Medical Association Journal* 128 (June 15, 1983): 1472.

32. Robertson, "Dilemma in Danville," p. 139 n. 6.

33. Claire Leonard and John Freeman, "Spina Bifida: A New Disease," *Pediatrics* 88, 1 (July 1981): 136.

34. Howard Burrell, letter to the editor, *Pittsburgh Press,* July 6, 1981.

35. Leonard and Freeman, "Spina Bifida," p. 136.

36. Ibid.

37. Ibid., p. 137.

38. Burrell, letter.

39. Laura White, "Down's Syndrome Kids Bring a Special Love to Family Life," *Boston Herald American,* July 2, 1981.

40. Robertson, "Involuntary Euthanasia," p. 139 n. 5.

41. Laurence E. Karp, *Genetic Engineering* (Chicago: Nelson-Hall, 1976), p. 17.

42. Eugene F. Diamond, "The Deformed Child's Right to Life," in Horan and Mall, Death, Dying, and Euthanasia, p. 129.

43. Ibid.

44. Laura White, "Down's Syndrome Kids."

45. Elizabeth Villani, letter to the editor, *New York Times*, May 7, 1982.
46. Robertson, "Involuntary Euthanasia," p. 183.
47. Ibid.
48. Robertson, "Dilemma in Danville," p. 6.
49. Ibid.
50. Ibid.
51. Rosalyn Benjamin Darling, "Deck Often Stacked Against Defective Newborns," *American Medical News* (January 14, 1983).
52. Ibid.
53. Robertson, "Involuntary Euthanasia," p. 194.
54. Testimony of Dr. C. Everett Koop, Surgeon General of the United States, before the Select Committee on Education and Welfare, U.S. House of Representatives, September 16, 1982.
55. Ibid.
56. Stephen P. Coburn, letter to the editor, *The Lancet* (January 12, 1980), p. 102.
57. Testimony of Dr. C. Everett Koop.
58. Peter Singer, "Sanctity of Life or Quality of Life?" *Pediatrics* 72, 1 (July 1983): 129.
59. Ibid.
60. Ibid.
61. Michael Tooley, "A Defense of Abortion and Infanticide," in Joel Feinberg, ed., *The Problem of Abortion* (Belmont, Ca.: Wadsworth, 1973), p. 91.
62. Ibid.
63. "The Smallest Patients," *Medical World News* (September 14, 1981), p. 32.
64. John Robertson, in *Death, Dying, and Euthanasia*, p. 187.
65. Eugene Diamond, in *Death, Dying, and Euthanasia*, p. 129.
66. James Gustafson, in *Death, Dying, and Euthanasia*, 275.
67. "Heroin and Crime: Rx for a Solution," *Reason* (April 1983), p. 20.
68. Roe v. Wade, 410 U.S. 113, 163 (1973). The Court also held that abortion is permissible after viability if it is necessary to preserve the "life or health of the mother" (164). The very broad definition of "health" adopted by the Court actually permitted abortion at any stage of pregnancy, right up to the time of birth.
69. Paul Ramsey, "Reference Points in Deciding About Abortion," in John T. Noonan, Jr., ed., *The Morality of Abortion* (Cambridge: Harvard University Press, 1970), p. 81.
70. Tooley, "Defense of Abortion and Infanticide."
71. Eugene F. Diamond, "Treatment versus Nontreatment for the Handicapped Newborn," in Dennis J. Horan and Melinda Delahoyde, eds., *Infanticide and the Handicapped Newborn* (Provo, Utah: Brigham Young University Press, 1982), p. 63.

72. Ibid.
73. Testimony of Dr. C. Everett Koop.
74. Horan, in Death, *Dying, and Euthanasia*, p. 212.
75. Ibid., p. 215.
76. Testimony of Dr. C. Everett Koop.
77. Patrick B. Friel, "Death and Dying," *Annals of Internal Medicine* 97 (1982): 767.
78. George D. Lundberg, "Rationing Human Life," *Journal of the American Medical Association* 249, 16 (April 22/29, 1983): 2223.
79. Stanley Joel Reiser, "The Dilemma of Euthanasia in Modern Medical History: The English and American Experience," in Stanley Joel Reiser, Arthur J. Dyck, and William J. Curran, eds., *Ethics in Medicine* (Cambridge, Mass.: MIT Press, 1977), p. 489.
80. Ibid.
81. Willard Gaylin, "Modern Medicine and the Price of Success," *Bulletin of the American College of Surgeons* (June 1983), p. 5.
82. Ibid.
83. Alexander Morgan Capron and Leon R. Kass, "A Statutory Definition of the Standards for Determining Human Death: An Appraisal and a Proposal," in Horan and Mall, eds., *Death, Dying, and Euthanasia*, p. 42.
84. Anne Wyman, "Life or Death: Who Decides?" *Boston Globe*, April 25, 1983.
85. Lisa Nelson, "Doctors Debate Right to Stop 'Heroic' Effort to Keep Elderly Alive," *Wall Street Journal*, September 7, 1982.
86. Ibid.
87. Ibid.
88. Gaylin, "Modern Medicine," p. 6.
89. Daniel G. Suber and William J. Tabor, "Withholding of Life-Sustaining Treatment from the Terminally Ill, Incompetent Patient: Who Decides?" *Journal of the American Medical Association* 248, 18 (November 12, 1982): 2250.
90. Ibid., p. 2251.
91. Ibid.
92. Ibid.
93. George R. Dunlop, "President's Commission Offers Guidelines on Life-Supporting Therapy," *Bulletin of the American College of Surgeons* (June 1983), p. 11.
94. "Court Vacates Murder Charges Against Two MDs," *American Medical News* (October 28, 1983), pp. 1, 34.
95. Pius XII, "The Prolongation of Life," in *Death, Dying, and Euthanasia*, p. 284.
96. Gerald Kelly, "The Duty to Preserve Life," *Theological Studies* 12 (1951): 550.

97. Thomas J. O'Donnell, "A Catholic Historical Perspective on Prolonging Life Decisions," in *The New Technologies of Birth and Death* (St. Louis: Pope John Center, 1980), pp. 163-65.

   In recent years the question of "ordinary" versus "extraordinary" means has been raised with respect to the question of whether it could ever be morally permissible to discontinue the intravenous feeding and hydration of a terminally ill patient. For cautious affirmative answers, in particular with respect to irreversibly comatose, dying patients, see Charles J. Mc-Fadden, *Medical Ethics* (Philadelphia: F. A. Davis, 1967), pp. 243-46, and Joanne Lynn and James F. Childress, "Must Patients Always Be Given Food and Water?" *Hastings Center Report* (October 1983), pp. 17-21; for a contrary view, see Daniel Callahan, "On Feeding the Dying," *Hastings Center Report* (October 1983), p. 22. Callahan wisely notes that while plausible arguments can be made for discontinuing intravenous feeding under some circumstances, the instinctive sentiment in favor of feeding the hungry is a crucial human value that should not be undermined by preoccupation with exceptional cases.

98. McFadden, *Medical Ethics*, p. 28.

99. Ibid., p. 442.

100. James Rachels, "Active and Passive Euthanasia," *New England Journal of Medicine* 292 (January 9, 1975): 78-80.

101. Ibid.

102. Robert M. Veatch, *Death, Dying and the Biological Revolution* (New Haven: Yale University Press, 1976), pp. 77-93.

103. Ibid., p. 93.

104. Paul Ramsey, *The Patient as Person* (New Haven: Yale University Press, 1970), p. 118.

105. Thomas J. O'Donnell, "Guidelines for Limiting Therapy," *Medical-Moral Newsletter* 20, 6 (June 1983): 22.

106. Ibid., p. 24.

107. O'Donnell, "Prolonging Life Decisions," p. 168.

108. "The Health Care Proxy and the Living Will," *New England Journal of Medicine* (April 25, 1991), p. 1210.

109. Nelson, "Doctors Debate," p. 20.

110. Thomas J. O'Donnell, "The Living Will," in *The New Technologies of Birth and Death*, p. 177.

111. Cited in Kenneth Vaux, *Will to Live, Will to Die* (Minneapolis: Augsburg, 1978), p. 86.

112. Ibid.

113. Wyman, "Life or Death," p. 40.

114. See Paul Ramsey, *Ethics at the Edges of Life* (New Haven: Yale University Press, 1978), pp. 145-46 for a discussion of the semantic ambiguities in this area.

115. Reiser, "Dilemma of Euthanasia," p. 488.

116. Fundraising letter from Hemlock (P.O. Box 66218, Los Angeles, CA 90066), dated October 20, 1982. Humphry writes that "when we judge the time to be ripe, we shall push for legislative change."

117. James Dempsey, "Hemlock's Way: Choosing to Die," *Evening Gazette* (Worcester, Mass.), January 26, 1983.

118. Joseph Fletcher, *Morals and Medicine* (Princeton: Princeton University Press, 1954), p. 191. See also the important work by Glanville Williams, *The Sanctity of Life and the Criminal Law* (New York: Knopf, 1957), in which the author argues a case for euthanasia.

119. Fletcher, "Morals and Medicine," pp. 183-206.

120. Joseph Fletcher, *Humanhood: Essays in Biomedical Ethics* (Buffalo, N.Y.: Prometheus Books, 1979), p. 152.

121. Ibid., p. 155.

122. John Warwick Montgomery, "Do We Have the Right to Die?" *Christianity Today*, (January 21, 1977), p. 50.

123. Eric J. Cassell, "The Relief of Suffering." *Archives of Internal Medicine* 413 (March 1983): 523.

124. Robert G. Twycross, "Euthanasia," in A. S. Duncan, G. R. Duncan, and R. B. Welbourn, eds., *Dictionary of Medical Ethics* (New York: Crossroad Publishing Co., 1981), p. 165.

125. Vincent J. Collins, "Managing Pain and Prolonging Life," in *The New Technologies of Birth and Death*, pp. 147-49.

126. Yale Kamisar, "Some Non-Religious Views Against Proposed 'Mercy-Killing' Legislation," in *Death, Dying, and Euthanasia*, p. 423.

127. Ibid., p. 427.

128. Ibid., p. 434.

129. Ibid., p. 453.

130. Ibid., pp. 468, 469.

131. Germain Grisez, "Suicide and Euthanasia," in *Death, Dying, and Euthanasia*, p. 810. The precedent of abortion is worth noting here: the proponents of legalized abortion, who first began arguing for abortion as a *private* right, later argued that the public had an *obligation* to pay for abortions with tax money in many cases.

132. Ibid., p. 807.

133. For the connections between the concepts of *spirit* and *image* in Scripture and extrabiblical literature in the ancient Near East, see D. J. A. Clines, "The Image of God in Man," *Tyndale Bulletin* 19 (1968): 53-127, and M. G. Kline, "Creation in the Image of the Glory-Spirit," *Westminster Theological Journal* 39, 2 (1977): 250-72. The concept of the image of God as the "dwelling place of God's Spirit" makes the important point that the sacredness of man's life is not limited exclusively to his conscious mental functions. If the crucial aspect of the divine image is constituted by the

presence of the divine Spirit, then it is clear that the Spirit is not limited to the conscious aspects of man's life. This latter identification has been the dominant tendency in the Cartesian and humanistic understandings of human nature. But God's Spirit can be just as much a reality in the body of an unborn child or a comatose, dying patient as in the body of a healthy, fully conscious adult. In the biblical view, the value of a person's life is not limited to conscious mental functions.

CHAPTER 8: CAPITAL PUNISHMENT

1. Sam Meddis, "States May See Execution Increases," *USA Today*, July 9, 1984.
2. Christy Hoppe, "Life in Jail, or Death?" *Charlotte Observer*, March 22, 1992, p. 12a.
3. William H. Baker, *Worthy of Death* (Chicago: Moody Press, 1973), p. 9.
4. Ibid.
5. The following historical data is drawn from Baker, *Worthy of Death*, Francis A. Allen, "Capital Punishment," in David Sills, ed., *International Encyclopedia of the Social Sciences* (New York: Macmillan, 1968), 2:290-94, and Norman Krivosha, Robert Copple, and Michael McDonough, "A Historical and Philosophical Look at the Death Penalty—Does It Serve Society's Needs?" *Creighton Law Review* 16 (1982-83): 1-46.
6. Baker, *Worthy of Death*, p. 16.
7. Ibid., p. 17.
8. Ibid., p. 21.
9. Aquinas, *Summa Theologica*, pt. II-II, q. 64, art. 2, 3.
10. Martin Luther, "Against the Murdering and Robbing Peasants," in *The Works of Martin Luther* (Philadelphia: Muhlenberg, 1931), 4:251.
11. Calvin, *Institutes*, IV. xx. 10.
12. Krivosha, Copple, and McDonough, "Death Penalty," p. 12.
13. Ibid., p. 14.
14. Baker, Worthy of Death, p. 24.
15. Krivosha, Copple, and McDonough, "Death Penalty," p. 22.
16. Ibid.
17. Ibid., p. 24.
18. Ibid., p. 27.
19. Ibid., p. 28.
20. Ibid., p. 29.
21. Sam Meddis, "Death Row Inmates Run Out of Pleas," *USA Today*, July 9, 1984.
22. Krivosha, Copple, and McDonough, "Death Penalty," p. 30.
23. Baker, *Worthy of Death*, p. 27.
24. Krivosha, Copple, and McDonough, "Death Penalty," pp. 33-35.

25. Charles C. Ryrie, "The Doctrine of Capital Punishment," *Bibliotheca Sacra* 129 (1972): 213.

26. H. C. Leupold, *Exposition of Genesis* (Grand Rapids: Baker, 1965), p. 334.

27. U. Cassuto, *A Commentary on the Book of Genesis, Part II* (Jerusalem: Magnes Press, 1949, 1964), p. 127.

28. John Murray, *Principles of Conduct* (Grand Rapids: Eerdmans, 1957), p. 110 n. 3. The verb in question (*yishaphek*) could be the Jussive, as well as the Niphal of *shaphak*.

29. Ibid., p. 111.

30. Dave Llewellyn, "Restoring the Death Penalty: Proceed With Caution." *Christianity Today* 19 (1975): 11; Ryrie, "Capital Punishment," pp. 213, 214.

31. Llewellyn, "Restoring the Death Penalty," p. 10.

32. Eric E. Hobbs and Walter C. Hobbs, "Contemporary Capital Punishment: Biblical Difficulties with the Biblically Permissible," *Christian Scholar's Review* 11 (1981-82): 260.

33. Gordon H. Clark, "Capital Punishment," *Faith and Thought* 93 (1963): 16.

34. Ryrie, "Capital Punishment," p. 213.

35. Baker, *Worthy of Death*, p. 39.

36. Murray, *Principles of Conduct*, p. 112.

37. Bruce Metzger, *A Textual Commentary on the Greek New Testament* (United Bible Societies, 1971), pp. 219-22. The pericope is absent from such important early manuscripts as p[66], p[75], Sinaiticus, and B. No Greek church father prior to the twelfth century comments on it. The style and vocabulary of the passage are noticeably different from the rest of John's gospel, and it appears to interrupt the natural sequence of 7:52 and 8:11ff.

38. *Theological Dictionary of the New Testament*, 1:334.

39. Stephen A. James, "The Adulteress and the Death Penalty," *Journal of the Evangelical Theological Society* 22 (1979): 45-53; see also J. D. M. Derrett, "Law in the New Testament: The Story of the Woman Taken in Adultery," *New Testament Studies* 10 (1963-64): 1-26, for the legal background of the passage.

40. In texts such as Matt. 19:9, however, it seems to be clearly assumed that in the New Testament era, *divorce* rather than stoning is to be penalty of last resort in cases of adultery.

41. F. Godet, *Commentary on St. Paul's Epistle to the Romans*, trans. A. Cusin (New York: Funk and Wagnalls, 1883), p. 443.

42. Baker, *Worthy of Death*, p. 72.

43. A. R. Vidler, cited in F. F. Bruce, *The Epistle of Paul to the Romans* (Grand Rapids: Eerdmans, 1963), p. 238.

44. F. F. Bruce, *Commentary on the Book of the Acts* (Grand Rapids: Eerdmans, 1954), p. 478.

45. L. Harold DeWolf, "The Death Penalty: Cruel, Unusual, Unethical, and Futile," *Religion in Life* 42(1973): 39.
46. Baker, *Worthy of Death*, p. 83.
47. Chana Kasachkoff Poupko, "The Religious Basis of the Retributive Approach to Punishment," *Thomist* 39, 3 (1975): 541.
48. Robert S. Gerstein, "Capital Punishment—'Cruel and Unusual'?: A Retributivist Response," *Ethics* 85 (1974-75): 77.
49. Norman Geisler, *Ethics: Alternatives and Issues* (Grand Rapids: Zondervan, 1971), p. 247.
50. Baker, *Worthy of Death*, p. 146.
51. Cesare Beccaria, *On Crimes and Punishments*, trans. Henry Paolucci (Indianapolis: Bobbs-Merrill, 1963, 1964), pp. 47, 48.
52. Ibid., p. 45.
53. Ibid., p. 48.
54. C. S. Lewis, *God in the Dock* (Grand Rapids: Eerdmans, 1970), p. 291.
55. DeWolf, "Death Penalty," p. 40.
56. Cited by Ernest Van Den Haag, "The Collapse of the Case Against Capital Punishment," *National Review* (March 31, 1978), p. 402.
57. Stephen J. Knorr, "Deterrence and the Death Penalty: A Temporal Cross-Sectional Approach," *Journal of Criminal Law and Criminology* 70 (1979): 253.
58. William J. Bowers, with Glenn L. Pierce and John F. McDevitt, *Legal Homicide* (Evanston: Northwestern University Press, 1983), review by Jay S. Goodman, *Boston Globe*, June 24, 1984.
59. Ibid.
60. Walter Berns, *For Capital Punishment* (New York: Basic Books, 1979), p. 186.
61. Ibid.
62. Joseph W. Bishop, Jr., "On Capital Punishment," *Commentary* (February 1984), p. 72.
63. Berns, *For Capital Punishment*, p. 186.
64. Jerry and Laura Gladson, "Should We Restore the Death Penalty?" *Presbyterian Journal* (April 5, 1979), p. 8.
65. Cited by Frank Carrington, *Crime and Punishment* (Washington, D.C.: Heritage Foundation, 1983), p. 34.
66. Ibid.
67. Stanley A. Ellisen, "The Bible and the Death Penalty," *Moody Monthly* (June 1972), p. 102.

CHAPTER 9: CIVIL DISOBEDIENCE AND REVOLUTION

1. *Omaha World-Herald*, April 25, 1984.
2. *Omaha World-Herald*, April 27, 1984.
3. John Rawls, "The Justification of Civil Disobedience," in James Rachels, ed., *Moral Problems* (New York: Harper and Row, 1971), p. 186.

4. In Christian Bay, "Civil Disobedience," *International Encyclopedia of the Social Sciences,* ed. David L. Sills (New York: Macmillan, 1968), 2:478.

5. William G. McLaughlin, "Civil Disobedience and Evangelism among the Missionaries to the Cherokees, 1829-1839," *Journal of Presbyterian History* 51 (1973): 116-39.

6. In F. F. Bruce, *The Book of the Acts* (Grand Rapids: Eerdmans, 1954), p. 104.

7. Bay, "Civil Disobedience," p. 479.

8. Ibid., p. 480.

9. Martin Luther King, Jr., *Stride Toward Freedom* (New York: Harper and Row, 1958), p. 85.

10. In Paul Ramsey, *Christian Ethics and the Sit-In* (New York: Association Press, 1961), p. 85.

11. For a sympathetic analysis of the ethical issues raised for the Christian community by the tactics of Operation Rescue, see Randy C. Alcorn, *Is Rescuing Right? Breaking the Law to Save the Unborn* (Downers Grove, Ill.: Inter-Varsity Press, 1990).

12. Norman L. Geisler, *Ethics: Alternatives and Issues* (Grand Rapids: Zondervan, 1971), p. 188.

13. Ibid.

14. Bruce, *Book of the Acts,* p. 121.

15. In J. Stevenson, ed., *A New Eusebius* (London: S.P.C.K., 1957), p. 30.

16. Calvin, *Institutes* IV. xx. 32.

17. Gunther Bornkamm, *Jesus of Nazareth* (New York: Harper and Row, 1960), p. 122.

18. Ibid., p. 123.

19. Archie P. Jones, "Natural Law and Christian Resistance to Tyranny," in Gary North, ed., *The Theology of Christian Resistance* (Tyler, Texas: Geneva Divinity School, 1983), p. 104.

20. Aquinas, *Summa Theologica,* pt. I-II, p. 96, art. 4.

21. Calvin, *Institutes* IV. xx. 32.

22. "Civil Obedience and Disobedience," *Concordia Theological Monthly* 38, 6 (1967): 378; statement of Lutheran Church, Missouri Synod.

23. James Luther Adams, "Civil Disobedience: Its Occasions and Limits," in J. Roland Pennock and John W. Chapman, eds., *Political and Legal Obligations* (New York: Atherton Press, 1970), p. 301.

24. In James F. Childress, *Civil Disobedience and Political Obligation* (New Haven: Yale, 1971), p. 233.

25. Rawls, "Justification of Civil Disobedience," p. 194.

26. John Howard Yoder, *The Politics of Jesus* (Grand Rapids: Eerdmans, 1972), p. 208.

27. Ernst Kasemann, *New Testament Questions of Today* (Philadelphia: Fortress, 1969), p. 213.

28. Stephen Charles Mott, *Biblical Ethics and Social Change* (New York: Oxford, 1982), p. 150.
29. Yoder, *Politics of Jesus*, p. 212.
30. Charles C. Ryrie, "The Christian and Civil Disobedience," *Bibliotheca Sacra* 127 (1970): 162.
31. Mott, *Biblical Ethics*, p. 152.
32. Ibid., pp. 161-65.
33. Ibid., p. 163.
34. Jacques Ellul, *Autopsy of Revolution* (New York: Knopf, 1971), p. vii.
35. Walter Laqueur, "Revolution," *International Encyclopedia of the Social Sciences*, ed. David L. Sills (New York: Macmillan, 1968), 13:501.
36. M. Campbell Smith, "Rebellion, Revolution," *Encyclopedia of Religion and Ethics*, ed. James Hastings, (New York: Charles Scribner's Sons, 1919), 10:598.
37. Locke, *Second Treatise*, xix. 229.
38. For an incisive analysis of the development of the ideology of revolution from the eighteenth to the twentieth centuries, see James H. Billington, *Fire in the Minds of Men: Origins of the Revolutionary Faith* (New York: Basic Books, 1980).
39. Loyd D. Easton and Kurt H. Guddat, eds., *Writings of the Young Marx on Philosophy and Society* (New York: Doubleday, 1967), p. 402.
40. J. G. Davies, *Christians, Politics, and Violent Revolution* (London: S.C.M. Press, 1976), p. 108.
41. Gustavo Gutierrez, *A Theology of Liberation* (Maryknoll, N.Y.: Orbis Books, 1973), p. 159.
42. Laqueur, "Revolution," p. 505.
43. Ibid.
44. Cited in Vernon C. Grounds, *Revolution and the Christian Faith* (Philadelphia: J. B. Lippincott, 1971), p. 153.
45. F. F. Bruce, *The Epistle of Paul to the Romans* (Grand Rapids: Eerdmans, 1963), p. 233.
46. J. N. D. Kelly, *The Epistles of Peter and Jude* (New York: Harper and Row, 1969), pp. 108, 109.
47. Calvin, *Institutes* IV. xx. 31.
48. John T. McNeill, ed., Calvin, *Institutes of the Christian Religion* (Philadelphia: Westminster Press, 1960), 2:1519 n. 54
49. John T. McNeill, "John Calvin on Civil Government," *Journal of Presbyterian History* 42, 2 (1964): 86.
51. Locke, *Second Treatise*, xix. 229.
52. In the following discussion I am indebted to Mott, *Biblical Ethics*, pp. 188-91. The criteria proposed are quite parallel to those for a just war: see pp. 234, 235 for related discussion.
53. Ibid., p. 188.

54. Ibid., p. 190.

55. Martin H. Scharlemann, *The Ethics of Revolution* (St. Louis: Concordia, 1971), p. 44.

56. Brian Griffiths, ed., *Is Revolution Change?* (Downers Grove: Inter-Varsity, 1972), p. 107.

CHAPTER 10: WAR AND PEACE

1. Cited by Jeffrey Barlow, "The Hard Facts the Nuclear Freeze Ignores," *Backgrounder* (Washington, D.C.: Heritage Foundation, 1982), p. 7.

2. Quincy Wright, "War: the Study of War," *International Encyclopedia of the Social Sciences*, ed. David P. Sills (New York: Macmillan, 1968), 16:455.

3. F. J. Montalbano, "War (In the Bible)," *New Catholic Encyclopedia* (New York: McGraw-Hill, 1967), 14:802.

4. Wright, "War," p. 456.

5. Ibid.

6. W. V. O'Brien, "War," *New Catholic Encyclopedia* (New York: McGraw-Hill, 1967), 14:796.

7. Ibid.

8. Ibid.

9. Ibid., p. 797.

10. Ibid., p. 798.

11. Wright, "War," p. 458.

12. Ibid.

13. Ibid., p. 459.

14. L. L. McReavy, "Pacifism," *New Catholic Encyclopedia* (New York: Mc-Graw-Hill, 1967), 10:855.

15. Ibid. For an excellent analysis of pacifism in the early church, see Edward A. Ryan, "The Rejection of Military Service by the Early Christians," *Theological Studies* 13 (1952): 1-32. The author shows that pacifism was never the dominant position in the early church, even prior to the conversion of Constantine, and that pacifist sentiment during this period generally was related to concern over idolatrous practices in the Roman legions rather than objection to armed combat itself.

16. McReavy, "Pacifism," p. 856.

17. For a statement of Swiss Brethren pacifist sentiment, see John C. Wenger, "The Schleitheim Confession of Faith," *Mennonite Quarterly Review* 19, 4 (1945): 243-53. The confession was adopted in 1527.

18. Wright, "War," p. 453.

19. Ronald J. Sider and Richard K. Taylor, *Nuclear Holocaust and Christian Hope* (Downers Grove: Inter-Varsity, 1982), p. 124. For pacifist biblical interpretation, see also Jean Lasserre, *War and the Gospel* (Scottsdale, Pa.:

Herald Press, 1962); Robert G. Clouse, ed., *War: Four Christian Views* (Downers Grove: Inter-Varsity, 1981), pp. 27-97.

20. David Hollenbach, "Nuclear Weapons and Nuclear War: The Shape of the Catholic Debate," *Theological Studies* 43 (1982): 586.

21. For the views of Augustine, see Henry Paolucci, ed., *The Political Writings of St. Augustine* (South Bend: Henry Regnery, 1962), pp. 162-83.

22. Ralph B. Potter, Jr., "The Moral Logic of War," *McCormick Quarterly* 23, 4 (1970): 209.

23. *Summa Theologica*, pt. II-II, q. 40, art. 1, trans. Fathers of the English Dominican Province (New York: Benziger Brothers, 1947).

24. R. A. McCormick, "War, Morality of," *New Catholic Encyclopedia* (New York: McGraw-Hill, 1987), p. 803.

25. Cited in Ewald M. Plass, compiler, *What Luther Says* (St. Louis: Concordia, 1959), 3:1428.

26. Ibid., p. 1429.

27. *Institutes* IV. xx. 11, "On the Right of the Government to Wage War," trans. Ford Lewis Battles (Philadelphia: Westminster, 1960).

28. William V. O'Brien, "Just War Doctrine in a Nuclear Context," *Theological Studies* 44, 2 (June 1983): 208, 197. See also James F. Childress, "Just-War Theories: the Bases, Interrelations, Priorities, and Functions of Their Criteria," *Theological Studies* 39 (1978): 427-45.

29. O'Brien, "Just War Doctrine," p. 197.

30. Paul's saying in II Tim. 2:3 is also pertinent in this regard: "Share in suffering as a good soldier of Jesus Christ." For Paul, the occupation of soldier could provide an appropriate illustration of features of the Christian life. As in Rev. 19:11 and elsewhere, it is difficult to see how the inspired writers would draw positive illustrations for the Christian life from these activities if they were in themselves inappropriate and immoral.

31. W. P. Paterson, "War," *Encyclopedia of Religion and Ethics*, ed. James Hastings (New York: Charles Scribner's Sons, 1922), 12:680.

32. Pope John Paul II, "Peace Must Be Won," *The Pilot*, (January 6, 1984), p. 7.

33. Hollenbach, "Nuclear Weapons," p. 598.

34. For exegetical discussions of this difficult text, see J. N. D. Kelly, *The Epistles of Peter and Jude* (New York: Harper and Row, 1969), pp. 363-68, and R. Larry Overstreet, "A Study of 2 Peter 3:10-13," *Bibliotheca Sacra* 137 (1980): 354-71.

35. Robert Jastrow, "Why Strategic Superiority Matters," *Commentary* (March 1983), p. 29.

36. Winston S. Churchill II, "The Only Way to Peace," *Imprimis* 11 (December 1982): 4.

37. Jastrow, "Strategic Superiority," p. 29.

38. Jeffrey G. Barlow, "Hard Facts," p. 13.

39. Ibid.

40. Robert Jastrow, "Reagan vs. the Scientists: Why the President Is Right about Missile Defense," *Commentary* (January 1984), p. 25; *Report of the President's Commission on Strategic Forces*, the Scowcroft Commission (Washington, D.C.: Library of Congress, Congressional Research Service, April 1983), p. 4. Matthew Bunn and Kosta Tsipis, "The Uncertainties of a Preemptive Nuclear Attack," *Scientific American* (November 1983), pp. 38-47, argue that only 50 percent of U.S. ICBMs could be destroyed in a Soviet surprise attack. They admitted, however, that by the 1990s, Soviet missiles could be twice as accurate, dramatically altering their calculations.

41. Thomas J. Reese, "The Bishops' 'Challenge of Peace,'" *America* (May 23, 1983), p. 393.

42. Hollenbach, "Nuclear Weapons," p. 596.

43. Jastrow, "Strategic Superiority," p. 30.

44. Cited by Joseph C. Kunkel, "Just-War Doctrine and Pacifism," *Thomist* 47, 4 (October 1983): pp. 510, 511.

45. Cited by Michael Novak, "Arms and the Poor," *National Review* (September 3, 1982), p. 1086.

46. Helen Caldicott, "Medical Consequences of Nuclear War," *New Catholic World* (November/December 1983), p. 279.

47. R. P. Turco et al., "Nuclear Winter: Global Consequences of Multiple Nuclear Explosions," *Science* 222, 4630 (December 23, 1983): 1283-92; Paul R. Ehrlich et al., "Long-Term Biological Consequences of Nuclear War," *Science* 222, 4630 (December 23, 1983): 1293-1300; Carl Sagan, "Nuclear War and Climatic Catastrophe: Some Policy Implications," *Foreign Affairs* 62, 2 (Winter 1983/84): 257-92.

48. Michael Novak, "The Bishops and Soviet Reality," *New Catholic World*, (November/December 1983), p. 260.

49. Ibid.

50. Churchill, "Only Way to Peace," p. 2.

51. Albert Wohlstetter, letter to the editor, *Commentary* (December 1983), p. 20.

52. Ibid.

53. Harlow, "Hard Facts," p. 10.

54. Jastrow, "Reagan vs. the Scientist," p. 29.

55. Ibid., p. 32.

56. Albert Wohlstetter, "Bishops, Statesmen, and Other Strategists on the Bombing of Innocents," *Commentary* (June 1983), p. 22.

57. Ibid.

58. Seymour Weiss, "Why We Must Think About Protracted Nuclear War," *Wall Street Journal*, August 30, 1982.

59. Robert Foelber, "Strategic Defense: Avoiding Annihilation," *Backgrounder* (Washington, D.C.: Heritage Foundation, 1983), p. 7.

60. Edward N. Luttwak, "How to Think About Nuclear War," *Commentary* (August 1982), p. 26.
61. Cf. the recommendations of the Scowcroft Commission, p. 10: "Our first defense priority should be to ensure that there is continuing, constitutionally legitimate, and full control of our strategic forces under conditions of stress or actual attack."
62. Donald L. Gilleland, "The Perils of a Nuclear Freeze," *Vital Speeches of the Day* (June 15, 1983), p. 516.
63. Ibid.
64. Ibid., p. 517.
65. W. Bruce Weinrod, "The Nuclear Freeze: Myths and Realities," *Backgrounder* (Washington, D.C.: Heritage Foundation, 1983), p. 7.
66. S. Fred Singer, "The Big Chill? Challenging a Nuclear Scenario," *Wall Street Journal*, February 3, 1984.
67. Sagan, "Nuclear War," pp. 279, 280.
68. Ibid., p. 279.
69. Charles Krauthammer, "On Nuclear Morality," *Commentary* (October 1983), p. 49.
70. "The French Bishops' Statement: Winning the Peace," *Origins* 13, 26 (December 8, 1983): 442.
71. Ibid.
72. Novak, "Bishops and Soviet Reality," p. 261.
73. Claude Malhuret, "Report from Afghanistan," *Foreign Affairs* (Winter 1983/84), p. 430.
74. Sider and Taylor, *Nuclear Holocaust*, pp. 229-92.
75. Jan Narveson, "Pacifism: a Philosophical Analysis," in Richard A. Wasserstrom, ed., *War and Morality* (Belmont, Ca.: Wadsworth, 1970), pp. 68, 69.
76. Gary E. Gammon, review of *Nuclear Holocaust and Christian Hope*, in *Eternity* (May 1983), p. 42.

Index of Scripture

271

Index of Persons

Abednego, 192
Abelson, Raziel, 229 n. 2
Abraham, 67-68, 215
Aeschylus, 96
Alcorn, Randy C., 265 n. 11
Alexander the Great, 208
Althusius, Johannes, 202
Ames, William, 3
Amos, 11
Anacreon, 96
Andrews, Lori B., 63
Annas, George J., 65
Anselm of Canterbury, 113
Antipas, 88
Aquinas, Thomas, 32, 176, 193, 214, 215, 231 n. 31
Argyle, A. W., 86
Aristophanes, 96
Aristotle, 16, 96, 120, 145
Artnak, Edward J., 101
Athenagoras, 119
Augustine of Hippo, 31-32, 33, 82, 119-20, 176, 208, 214, 215, 268 n. 21
Avedon, Phyllis, 235 n. 76
Avicenna, 17

Baab, O. J., 43
Bahnsen, Greg L., 110, 115
Bailey, D. Sherwin, 102, 103, 105
Bajema, Clifford E., 254 n. 70
Baker, William H., 180, 183, 184
Barak, 203
Barber, Neil, 162
Barlow, David H., 100
Barlow, Jeffrey G., 220
Barrett, C. K., 108
Barrett, Jeffrey M., 128
Barth, Karl, 36
Batteau, John M., 111
Bavister, 72
Baxter, Richard, 3
Beach, 97, 98, 111
Beccaria, Cesare, 177, 185
Beernink, Ferdinand, 68
Bell, 102
Benendo, Franciszek, 69
Bennett, Paul, 125
Bentham, Jeremy, 177
Beral, V., 79
Bergler, 100
Bermon, Harold J., 231 n. 32
Bernstein, Charles, 187
Bickner, 100

277

Index of Subjects